Un/Settled Multiculturalisms

Recent Zed Books of Related Interest

Un/Settled Multiculturalisms: Diasporas, Entanglements, 'Transruptions'

Edited by Barnor Hesse

Zed Books

LONDON · NEW YORK

IN MEMORY OF BARBARA CHRISTIAN

Un/Settled Multiculturalisms: Diasporas, Entanglements, 'Transruptions' was first published by Zed Books Ltd, 7 Cynthia Street, London N1 9JF, UK and Room 400, 175 Fifth Avenue, New York, NY 10010, USA in 2000.

Distributed in the USA exclusively by St Martin's Press, Inc., 175 Fifth Avenue, New York, NY 10010, USA.

Cover designed by Andrew Corbett
Set in Monotype Ehrhardt and Franklin Gothic by Ewan Smith
Printed and bound in the United Kingdom by Biddles Ltd, Guildford and King's Lynn

A catalogue record for this book is available from the British Library

Library of Congress Cataloging-in-Publication Data

Un/settled multiculturalisms: diasporas, entanglements, transruptions / edited by Barnor Hesse.
    p. cm.
    Includes bibliographical references and index
    ISBN 1-85649-559-0 (cased) – ISBN 1-85649-560-4 (limp)
     1. Great Britain–Ethnic relations. 2. Multiculturalism–Great Britain. 3. Great Britain–Race relations. 4. Immigrants–Great Britain. 5. Minorities–Great Britain. I. Hesse, Barnor.

DA125.A1U57 2000
305.8'00941–dc21

                        00-032071

ISBN 1 85649 559 0 cased
ISBN 1 85649 560 4 limp

Contents

Preface and Acknowledgements

The background to *Un/Settled Multiculturalisms* lies in a project loosely conceived to generate a rethinking of the conceptual meaning and impact of western multiculturalism in Britain. What interested me then, as now, was how to develop the sorts of concepts and distinctive theoretical and empirical interventions that took seriously the recurrent and transformative qualities of social processes associated with the contestation of particular cultural differences. This means that questions of inequality and power in Britain and beyond are constitutive of the western formations in which cultural differences, particularly structured around race, ethnicity and gender, are *recurrently politicized*. Those of us engaged in this project were intrigued as to how this might be conceptualized as well as documented. Unfortunately, British social sciences in the late 1990s lacked anything resembling a movement of critical thinking informed by even a notional multiculturalism. Consequently, this project was also inspired by a critical engagement with conceptual developments in the disparate politics and discourses of multiculturalism taking place in the United States and its academy.

If *Un/Settled Multiculturalisms* bears traces of an uneven British/American dialogue, it is worth recalling some of the circular contours of that dialogue. During the 1980s the theoretical impetus of cultural studies in the US was directly informed by the importation of so-called British cultural studies with its open indebtedness to western Marxism and post-structuralism in *European* critiques of empiricism, capitalism and liberalism. An ancillary development, of course, was the impact of its rarely acknowledged progeny, *Black British Cultural Studies*. This innovated sophisticated accounts of racisms, nationalism, imperialism and cultural identity, drawing upon critical analyses of the colonial formations of Africa and the Asian sub-continent, as well as the diaspora histories of the Caribbean and Black America. In the transformative hands of its US practitioners, however, what becomes available as a cultural studies export to Britain from the mid-1990s onwards is what might be described as American Multi-cultural

Studies. This linked together transatlantic and trans-pacific American identities, internal American migratory cultures, political ethnicities, contested genders and the Eurocentric universalism of American democracy. Although much of this hardly pointed to the singular coherence of a political project, it nevertheless raised an important conceptual problem: the difficulty of trying to *settle* the meaning of western multiculturalism within a national vortex of *unsettled* and *unsettling* diverse accounts of its implications, values and trajectories. Conceptualizing the meaning of these implications defines the various points of departure for the contributions collected in *Un/Settled Multiculturalisms*.

During the finalization of this book a number of conversations and contacts with people on both sides of the Atlantic were important in stimulating and energizing the praxis which enabled me to bring the project to fruition. In the United States I should like to thank: Jade Banks, Cheryl Roberts, Stephan Small, David Goldberg, Gia White, Lynnea Steven, Byron Spicer, Donald Moore, Percy Hintzen, Peter McClaren, Haldane Chase, Carla Palmer, Elisa Joy White, Maggie Moorehouse, Lea Redmond, Shanette Slaughter, Barbara Christian, Tina Campt, Jackie Brown, Inderpal Grewal, Caren Kaplan. In Britain I should like to thank: Avtar Brah, Cheryl Gore, Ben Carrington, Tracey Reynolds, Debbie Weekes, Ernesto Laclau, Ashwani Sharma, Paula Williams, Farish Noor, David Okefuna, Kwamla Hesse, Diane Ball, Barbara Harrison, Louise Murray, Robert Molteno. Finally, I am especially grateful to all the contributors to this book who gave their time, thinking and application to something they actually believed in.

Barnor Hesse
London, February 2000

Notes on Contributors

CLAIRE ALEXANDER is a senior lecturer in sociology at South Bank University. She is author of *The Art of Being Black* (1996) and *The Asian Gang* (2000).

ZIMITRI ERASMUS is a lecturer in sociology at the University of Cape Town, South Africa. She teaches in the fields of race and gender. Her specific field of research is Creole identities in South Africa

STUART HALL is Emeritus Professor of Sociology at the Open University.

BARNOR HESSE is a senior lecturer in sociology at the University of East London. He is co-author of *Beneath the Surface: Racial Harassment* (1992).

DENISE NOBLE was a senior lecturer in social work and sociology at the University of East London from 1985–97. She currently divides her time between being a freelance trainer/consultant and undertaking research into Black women's perspectives on the Black diaspora through an exploration of the Black body in historical and cultural modernity.

DAVID PARKER is a lecturer in sociology at the University of Birmingham. He is author of *Through Different Eyes: Young Chinese People in Britain* (1995).

ROIYAH SALTUS-BLACKWOOD is a Bermudian who has studied and worked in England for the last decade. She is a senior data-processing officer in the Department of Sociology, University of Essex. Her doctoral work examined relations of power, 'race' and gender at pivotal periods in Bermudian history.

S. SAYYID is a lecturer in sociology at the University of Salford. He is author of *A Fundamental Fear: Eurocentrism and Islamism* (1997).

BRETT ST. LOUIS is a lecturer in sociology at the University of Bristol. He received his PhD from the University of Southampton and is currently completing a book on the cultural politics of race, revolution and modernity in the work of C. L. R. James.

1

Introduction: Un/Settled Multiculturalisms

Barnor Hesse

> Multiculturalism – a portmanteau term for anything from minority discourse to postcolonial critique, from gay and lesbian studies to chicano/a fiction – has become the most charged sign for describing the scattered social contingencies that characterise contemporary *Kulturkritik*. The multicultural has itself become a 'floating signifier' whose enigma lies less in itself than in the discursive uses of it to mark social processes where differentiation and condensation seem to happen almost synchronically. (Homi Bhabha 1998)

Throughout the 1990s the concept of 'multiculturalism' entered the American and British lexicons of western cultural studies in various portentous guises. Previously it had simply been a vaguely western political ideal. Between the 1960s and 1980s the dominant vauge sense of multiculturalism had been one which valorized the incidence of harmonious cultural differences in the social, particularly where this meant the decontestation of 'race' and ethnicity and their conflation with the individualist ethos of nationalist liberal-democracies. From the mid-1980s onwards this distinctive transatlantic configuration became increasingly and diversely unsettled by ethnically marked and cross-culturally mobilized interrogations of the nation's imagined communities. Whether inflected in celebratory or condemnatory idioms, the undulating, urban vernaculars of multiculturalism were gradually transformed into a critical concept. Multiculturalism had become a contested frame of reference for thinking about the quotidian cohesion of western civil societies uncertain about their national and ethnic futures.

Although the political meanings of western multiculturalism now have a transatlantic resonance, it would be misleading to suggest that there have been parallel intellectual developments. It is rare for serious critical thought to be given to the challenges multiculturalism represents to the social sciences or humanities in Britain. By contrast the theoretical discourse in the United States, expansively rich and creatively varied, is currently disturbing the conventional polarity between mainstream and margins in

the American academy.[1] Sustained reflections on the idea of multiculturalism have had a chequered history in Britain, while attempts to
conceptualize its critical dimensions beyond the confines of school curricula
have been extremely underdeveloped. The aim of *Un/Settled Multiculturalisms*, then, is to kick-start critical thought into taking seriously the issues
posed by western multiculturalism in Britian at both the theoretical and
the empirical levels. It also attempts to provide an alternative range of
perspectives to the dominant parochial currents of the American debates,
by expanding the transnational lineaments of the transatlantic dialogue. In
this sense, although British-related themes are a significant consideration,
the remit of the arguments deployed here is much wider.

The premise underlining the contributions is that, at the end of the
twentieth century, late western modern societies lived in the broadly
uncharted relational terrain between the *multicultural* and *multiculturalism*
(cf. Hesse 1999a). Multiculturalism refers to particular discourses or social
forms which incoporate marked cultural differences and diverse ethnicities.
In this 'substantive' sense, multicuturalism can be named, valued, celebrated
and repudiated from many different political perspectives (see Hall in his
conclusion to this volume). However, constitutive of that political configuration is the colonial formation of the *multicultural* as a signifying
relation. The multicultural is a signifier of the unsettled meanings of
cultural differences in relation to multiculturalism as the signified of
attempts to fix their meaning in national imaginaries. The multicultural
always refers contextually to the 'western' and 'non-western' cross-cultural
processes involved in establishing the meanings invested in the racially
marked incidence of contested cultural differences. In this book we explore
the multicultural in a number of ways. First, through considering the
meaning of different *diaspora formations* which as transnational processes
deeply unsettle the idea of self-contained, culturally inward-looking
nationalist identities. Second, through the analysis of *cultural entanglements*
which, as commonplace forms of *creolization*, *hybridity*, *syncretism*, represent
a profound challenge to the idea that national and social forms are logically
coherent, unitary or tidy. Third, this book introduces a conceptual
neologism, *transruptions*, in an attempt to provide an account of why the
dynamic of the multicultural (e.g. diaspora formations and cultural entanglements) is a recurrent unsettling feature of modern western societies.
And how only ·in this context does multiculturalism become a specifically
contested political focus. This suggests that discourses of multiculturalism
comprise various uneven interventions to understand and find a national
resolution of the unsettled relation between marked cultural differences.
Within western liberal-democracies these interventions either question or
accept racialized forms of *governmentality*.[2] When cast against this back-

ground, even the well-rehearsed British narrative of multiculturalism can yield significant conceptual insights. This is the task in the following sections.

No Multiculturalism, Please – We're British

I begin in October 1997. This was the occasion of a rare opportunity to see the British Conservative Party holding its annual party conference in a crestfallen state. It was the first time the Conservatives had met since their overwhelming general election defeat by the Labour Party in May. Of central concern to the Tory faithful was the future of the party and the public standing of the newly elected leader. The Conservative sky had fallen in. Nothing appeared to be certain any longer. Their politics of conviction was suspect, at least electorally, and almost everywhere advice was being proffered that the Conservatives had to change their image, ideas and instincts. New political designs and rebranding were the seductive panaceas vying for their spin-doctors' attention. Up against the national background of New Labour (the Conservatives' nemesis), and their in-auguration of a new Britain (subsequently, albeit vaguely, 'Cool Britannia'), the Conservatives felt compelled to come up with their own accentuations of something prospectively new. Additionally, they were under pressure to embrace an undefined British cultural diversity. Within this scenario, quite unexpectedly, former conservative MP Lord Tebbit chose to make some publicity-seeking remarks about the compatibility of Britain with what he termed multiculturalism:

> Multi-culturalism is a divisive force. One cannot uphold two sets of ethics or be loyal to two nations, any more than a man can have two masters. It perpetuates ethnic divisions because nationality is in the long term more about culture than ethnics [sic]. Youngsters of all races born here should be taught that British history is their history, or they will forever be foreigners holding British passports and this kingdom will become a Yugoslavia.[3]

Although Tebbit was widely reported, roundly condemned and just as quickly forgotten, there were some aspects of his remarks that deserved scrutiny outside the usual knee-jerk response of liberal abhorence. Retro-spectively, the significance of this moment lay in the simple fact that multiculturalism had long since ceased to feature in the semantics of British political discourse, whether of the *Left* or the *Right*. Multiculturalism had not been credited with winning Labour the election or indeed losing it for the Conservatives: there was in other words no contemporary debate. Although throughout the 1990s the incidence of racist attacks in Britain had soared exponentially (Human Rights Watch 1997), contested issues of 'race', racism and ethnicity, particularly in their socially dislocating and dehumanizing consequences, had been cut adrift from the mainstream political agenda. It was as if the 1980s, characterized by local political projects of anti-racism, high-profile Black and Asian community struggles, prominent ethnic identifications and popular valorizations of cultural diversity, had never happened (cf. Mercer 1994: 1–31). Yet into this climate of repressions stepped the former Rt Hon. member for Chingford, Norman Tebbit. As if sensing a Pandora's box of social change was about to be opened (by of all people the Conservative Party), Tebbit apparently felt duty-bound to warn the great British public that the shifting political agenda was haunted by the spectre of multiculturalism. For this reason alone it is worth examining Tebbit's pre-emptive strike. It took the form of indicting anything perceived as putting into question the possibility, if not actuality, of a tidy, codified representation of an autochthonous British nation. That multiculturalism could be construed in this way, as a threat to society as we know it, the implacable return of 'the enemy within', all within the context of a protracted non-discussion, is quite remarkable. Its significance however does not stop there.

Let us consider Tebbit's diagnosis of multiculturalism as a threat. First, he placed it in a relation of exteriority to the nation, like an alien visitation or an undesirable close encounter. Second, he suggested that cultural differences cannot be translated into dialogues and interactions between ethnic identities, but can be represented only as a uniformity through some formal allegiance to the history of the British nation. Third, Tebbit argued that a nation is defined by its history and national identity and is culturally accountable to that history. Finally, he concluded: 'You can't have a whole load of different cultures in one society, you have one culture for one society and if you get different societies mixed up, living close cheek-by-jowl, you will splinter our society in the way that devolution is splintering the United Kingdom.'[4]

Tebbit's specific diagnosis is striking because in stating that indivisibility and particularity in the British nation needs to be preserved, it cannot avoid recognizing the difficulty of disentangling the nation from the formation of its own cultural diversities. After all, the analogy with the United Kingdom conveniently seems to forget that its construction as Great Britain (England, Wales and Scotland) and Northern Ireland (i.e. forming the United Kingdom) between the sixteenth and twentieth centuries symbolizes part of the multicultural articulation he is inveighing against. Equally distortingly, Tebbit attributes to the phenomenon of multiculturalism anti- or transnational qualities which appear to be disproportionate to its social influence in Britain as anything resembling an article of faith. In Tebbit's world-view, multiculturalism is other-worldly. Although it is presented as a minor, peripheral or artificial term with regard to the apparent organic 'monoculturalism' (Goldberg 1994) of nationalism, somehow it wields tremendous signifying power in the threat its other-worldliness poses. There is, however, an interesting, unacknowledged, alternative conceptual gloss on multiculturalism stalking Tebbit's fulminations which points to something quite insightful. In short it might be transliterated as follows: *'Multiculturalism cannot be eliminated but it can be repressed. Hence it cannot be ignored because it refuses to go away. But it must be feared because it can re-emerge at any time; and consequently it must be condemned because it has the capacity to unsettle what has been and needs to be settled.'*

Whatever credence we give to Tebbit's apocalyptic understanding of national cultural formations, once we ignore the histrionics, we can see in adumbration the logic of what I describe much later in this Introduction as a multicultural *transruption*. Before that, however, we need to remind of ourselves of the reasons why the politics of multiculturalism had become a non-debate in Britain by the middle of 1990s.

The Demise of the Multiculturalist Discourse

The strange death of multicultural Britain after the early 1980s has its antecedents in the failure of multiculturalism as a *particularized* discourse to overcome the specific critiques from anti-racist politics that came to dominate radical thinking throughout the 1980s. In its initial formulation, the idea of multiculturalism in Britain emerges as one of successive political horizons within which equivocal post-colonial reformulations of the governance of Britain were being conceptualized and practised directly in relation to the prominence of post-1945 'non-white' immigration from the so-called Commonwealth. The racialized reconstruction of Britain as an imagined community in the initial post-war period (1945–62) is partly characterized by developments in public culture which attempt to turn the common sense of Britain away from an imperial cosmopolitanism towards a nationalist parochialism. This turn in common sense was profoundly racialized throughout the twentieth century by the gradual and then accelerated collapse of the imperial juxtaposition between Britain's racial hierarchy and the social exteriority of 'non-whites' (i.e. the geographical segregation at the level of the social of the European metropolis and the 'non-European' colonies). With the post-war transformation of the contested imperial relation (pro-active overseas developments) into a contested relation of migration (reactive inner-city developments), Britain experienced the cultural shock of racial hierarchy inscribed by the social interiority of the 'non-whites', the dissolution of rigid colonial segregation.

During the 1950s and 1960s an uneven transition in British public culture from the politics of 'race' as empire to the politics of 'race' as nation (Hesse 1997) produced a new nationalist parochialism. A reinvented white national identity in British common sense was forced to contend with the explicit marking of 'race' and the ancillary profusion of cultural differences, antagonisms and solidarities. This reinvention had both conservative and liberal orientations fluctuating like quantum particles at expected and unexpected points of the trans-party political spectrum. The conservative orientation at its extreme, where it mostly resided, was emphatically anti-'non-white' immigration and hostile to the generational presence and equal social treatment of 'coloured' immigrants. Without qualification, it reconceptualized the landscape and populace of Britain in a racially exclusive injunction: *Keep Britain White*. In contrast to the conservative orientation, although not always, the liberal take on the white reinvention of British nationalism was less inflexible, more tolerant, no less thrown, but more open to accommodation of cultural differences. The post-war genealogy of British multiculturalism is located in successive governmental, liberal responses to 'non-white' immigration and its relation to a public reconfiguration of British national identity. In this sense, *assimilationist* policies and the passage of tighter immigration controls defined the national horizon up to the early 1960s (Anthias and Yuval-Davis 1992). In contrast to the expulsionist framework of the conservative orientation, assimilation sought to address the racialized injection of cultural differences into British society by promoting their diversification across rather than concentration in particular geographical areas. It assumed that any difficulties caused by the 'coloured' presence were 'temporary, related to culture shock and lack of knowledge of the language' (Anthias and Yuval-Davis 1992: 159). Assimilationism utopianized the prospect of a British national identity preserved through the eventual cultural acceptance of the migrants into the putative British way of life, in exchange for the generational dissipation of ethnically marked cultural differences. However, the 1958 anti-Black race-riots in Nottingham and Notting Hill, London (Solomos 1993), punctured the fantasy that a rapprochement between the 'indigenous' and the 'immigrant' populations in civil society would develop this cultural contract organically.

Coaxed into existence from the early 1960s onwards was a second liberal response to the racialized profusion of cultural differences in Britain's major cities, *integrationism* (Anthias and Yuval-Davis 1992). It was expressed in policy interventions designed to support and encourage the ideal of the 'non-white immigrant' disappearing into the norms and habits of (white) British culture. As an extension of assimilationism, it was a publicly sponsored cultural one-way ticket from the 'coloured immigrant's' veil of ignorance to participation in the good society. However, in assuming the passivity, malleability and inferiority of Black and Asian cultures, state-sponsored integrationism had illiberally posited the 'common sense' of the 'good' (white) British society over the rights of the migrants to their own cultural orientations and decisions. By the early 1970s a self-proclaimed multiculturalism had emerged as a third liberal response to cultural differences and their impact on the curricula within primary and secondary school education. Although it did so against the background of the legalislatively inflected evolution of 'race-relations'[5] as a framework for the national accommodation of 'non-white' immigration. This established a social equation in 'British' common sense between draconian, racialized immigration controls and good or harmonious 'race-relations'. Consequently, successive Conservative and Labour governments attempted to depoliticize the so-called 'race card'[6] by brokering this as a compromise (unacknowledged, of course) between the conservative/expulsionist and liberal/integrationist orientations to 'non-white' cultural differences. It was an attempt to prevent the chimera of racial harmony being blown apart by the moment of *Powellism*[7] in 1968 and the vengeful resurgence of conservative expulsionism. Enoch Powell's public rearticulation of Britishness portayed it as terminally, culturally threatened and incapable of assimilating 'alien' people who were capable of embodying only socially corrosive 'alien' cultures. This should now be seen as part of the context in which the initial formulations of multiculturalism in Britain were inscribed as a further liberal reaction.

According to Floya Anthias and Nira Yuval-Davis, by the 1970s,

> Multiculturalism emerged as a result of the realization originally in the USA, and then in Britain, that the melting pot doesn't melt, and that ethnic and racial divisions get reproduced from generation to generation. Multiculturalism constructs society as composed of a hegemonic homogenous majority, and small unmeltable minorities with their own essentially different communities and cultures which have to be understood, accepted and basically left alone – since their differences are compatible with the hegemonic culture – in order for the society to have harmonious relations. (Anthias and Yuval-Davis 1992: 158)

Leaving aside for the moment whether this is the only way multiculturalism can or should be conceptualized, we can note the orientation of this third liberal response to marked cultural differences in Britain. Its incarnation of multiculturalism reworked the codification of national identity away from the previous liberal orientations. It changed the perspective from routinely tolerating the temporary social persistence of minority ethnic cultural differences, to actively valorizing their aesthetic permanence in the national way of life and psychological role in providing an important sense of self-worth for individuals from those communities. Within schools this was translated into debates and projects concerned with the pedagogy of respecting and learning about different cultures (Rattansi 1992). Although the popularization of school multiculturalism, as indicated in the 'saris and steel band' epithet coined to describe these showcases of culture, was underwritten by a crude anthropological taxonomy as its template, it did cast the remit of multi-culture as a dialogical mosaic rather than as fixed, monological co-ordinates. The discourse of multiculturalism was the culmination of liberal attempts to address the social accommodation of racially marked white/'non-white' cultural differences in terms that enshrined the values of liberty and tolerance for both the 'British' self and the Caribbean, Asian and African 'others'. But this meant that racism went unconceptualized and racial antagonisms were perceived as merely resulting from ignorance, personal prejudice or mutual difficulties of cultural adjustment between majority and minority cultures. By the late 1970s and early 1980s multiculturalism was increasingly under attack by the more radical project of anti-racism in education and local government generally, with its emphasis on tackling social inequalities (jobs and services) and injustices (policing, racist attacks) resulting directly from the problem of (white) racism and its British institutionalization as a relation of power (cf. Brah 1996). Multiculturalism was excoriated for having nothing to say about racism and for placing its faith in social transformation in a simple change of heart or a change of mind by people somehow learning to live in each other's shoes. Or as Phil Cohen puts it:

> The multicultural illusion is that dominant and subordinate can somehow swap places and learn how the other half lives, whilst leaving the structures of power intact. As if power relations could be magically suspended through the direct exchange of experience, and ideology dissolve into the thin air of face to face communication. (Cohen 1988: 12–13)

The criticisms of mosaic or liberal multiculturalism on this point are legion (Rattansi 1992). The 1970s had seen significant growth in electoral support for the politics of the Old Right embodied in the National Front, while the New Right, having gained the intellectual leadership of the Conservative Party, reactivated anti-immigration sentiments as the bedrock of a shored-up British defence of heritage and identity. With the election of the Conservatives in 1979 and the 'authoritarian–populist' (Hall 1988) birth of Thatcherism during the 1980s, the discourse of 'race' became socially polarized. It revolved around the transformative ideas of anti-racism in local politics contra-posed to central state-led consultations on racial harmony that assumed an invariable relation between tight immigration control and good race-relations. As a consequence, multiculturalism's ethnic emphasis on the autonomy and celebration of cultural identities was demonized by the Left as a dangerous distraction to the anti-racist struggle and by the Right as a virulent undermining of the British way of life (Brah 1996). Between 1980 and 1985, in the wake of urban uprisings against policing in British cities of Black settlement, a radical politics of anti-racism expanded in generational scope and visibility.[8] It comprised Black and Asian community organizations, civil liberties groups, the urban Left in various Labour local government administrations and committed activists in some trade unions (Ball and Solomos 1990). Although the ideals of multiculturalism seemed passé, questions of ethnicity and cultural difference did not disappear. They were, rather, reconfigured institutionally within local government and the voluntary sector in the liberal discourse of equal opportunities, which was seen both as an adjunct to and autonomous from the project of anti-racism. The discourse of equal opportunities, particularly under the influence of the Labour-controlled Greater London Council led by Ken Livingstone (1981–86), expanded the meaning of cultural differences and social inequalities beyond 'race' and ethnicity to include gender, sexuality and disability (Mercer 1994). In the relation between local government and the voluntary sector, a cultivated politics of identity began to change the terms of political discourse (Bhattacharyya 1998). By 1986, despite the publication of the Swann report, the culmination of a long government inquiry into the education of ethnic minority children in Britain which espoused the importance of teaching all children to understand the meaning of a multicultural society (Brah 1996), a self-proclaimed multiculturalism as a broad political imaginary had all but dissipated.

Not that the fate of anti-racist politics was to fare much better. In the transition from the late 1980s to the early 1990s, from the Thatcher years of populism to the Major years of depression, public espousal of anti-racism was attacked across the political spectrum. From the Right as the preoccupation of 'Loony Left' Labour councils, as socially divisive and ultimately un-British (Solomos and Back 1996); and from the Left as socially divisive, doctrinaire and an unnecessary electoral liability (Brah 1996). Since that time, up until the publication in February 1999 of the MacPherson public inquiry into the racist murder of Black teenager Stephen Lawrence,[9] the question of racism had virtually been eliminated from the vernacular of British public culture. Despite the best efforts of local community organizations in highlighting the rise in racist attacks, continuing deaths of Black people in police custody and punitively unjust asylum and refugee laws, racism had become a non-issue in the public sphere. It had been folded back into the unsayable, unplayable 'race card'. But the representational landscape of Britain in the 1990s had changed and was changing. Ethnic diversity was prominently valorized in the food-scape, Indian and Chinese cuisine were now unquestionably 'British'. Urban ethnicities were increasingly penetrating media culture, not only was the 'ethnic look' in, *whiteness* was becoming mimetically ethnicized or, at any rate, commercially exoticized through eclectic forms of cultural appropriation, especially from 'eastern culture'. An acquaintance with Black musical fashions and sporting performances had become almost *de rigueur* among popular British youth cultures, now some of all 'our' heroes, if not our best friends, were Black. At the same time, in matters of religious and cultural affiliation Islam had become a more visible street presence than Christianity in many British cities and could no longer be represented as a generationally specific cultural affectation. As never before, distinct locations in Britain could now be promoted as tourist and business attractions on the strengths of their cultural diversity. The 1980s obituary on multiculturalism seemed exaggerated if not premature. As if reincarnated, it had 'been transformed in 1990s Britain into a part of a more liberal version of the heritage industry' (Bhattacharyya 1998: 263). Although it is also worth considering that the undoubted commodification of 'non-western', 'non-white' cultural differences and their dissemination as signs of style, exoticism, pleasure and connoisseurship, was more populist than liberal, more capitalist than constitutional, more ethnographic than historio-graphic; nevertheless it does seem right to insist that in 'some arenas multicultural thinking has seeped in as common sense' (Bhattacharyya 1998: 252). But once again we must observe it left the question of racism untouched.

Race-relations and Post-colonialism

The story I have told about the strange death of multiculturalist Britain is now, various nuances aside, standard fare in the writing on this period. Critical analyses generally establish an isomorphic relation between the *multicultural* as *a* signifier and *multiculturalism* as *the* signified. In this way, having been conceived as the accommodation of majority-white-indigenous and minority-'non-white'-immigrant cultures, the concept of multicultural-ism is treated as an essentialist category, where its meaning is invariant and trans-contextual. However, it was not because of its apparent weak liberal credentials compared to the radical qualifications of anti-racism that multi-culturalism as a political discourse in Britain was profoundly untheorized; that related to a failure to consider the discourse of multiculturalism as itself susceptible to the logic of the multicultural or the 'multi' (cf. Brah 1996). This meant questions concerning the possible diverse logics of the multicultural, or the mutually contested contexts in which they can be signified, generally failed to attract significant theoretical attention from the usual suspects (never mind others) in sociology, cultural studies and political theory. The discourse of multiculturalism that sprang up in Britain during the 1970s and 1980s was generalized as its only possible conception, rather than particularized as one among many possible conceptions. Perhaps we ought to remind ourselves that the 'post-war British discourse of multiculturalism emerged following the labour migrations which brought workers from the former colonies to perform low waged work in a period of economic boom and labour shortages' (Brah 1996: 228). Does this not suggest we need to think about the enduring post-colonial impact on the configuration of cultural differences within Britain as a 'diaspora-space'?[10] Or maybe that we need to consider the contested cultural meanings of an ambivalent juxtaposition between the end of the British Empire in the post-war period and the rebirth of Britain as a post-colonial nation? I am arguing for a return to questioning the relationship between the formal process of decolonization, the retention and/or dislocation of an imperial culture, post-war migration and the ensuing politics of racism and anti-racism. We should bear in mind, of course, that at the point of entanglement of these diaspora formations is the conjunction of 'race' and ethnicity inscribed as *the* cardinal cultural difference in Britain. This recurrently poses questions about the meaning of social representations and national identity, despite its apparent minority or peripheral status in the conventional scheme of things British. With hindsight it is clear this is what is signified as multiculturalism in Britain during the 1970s and 1980s, albeit in a diminished form. Although constrained within a liberal discourse of integrationism, it was in effect a *post-colonial* articulation of racialized designations in cultural differences. At the very least, then, we need to consider the contestation of multiculturalism in Britain as symptomatic of an unresolved post-colonial condition following decolonization, the dismantling of the British Empire and post-war migration from the erstwhile colonies.

What I am describing as Britain's unresolved post-colonial condition is generally eclipsed by a highly dubious yet conventional race-relations narrative of governance. That imperial themes of governance persist in the British race-relations narrative which primarily organizes the response of state instituitons to questions of 'race', ethnicity and cultural identity is a remarkable feat of survival. The ubiquitous race-relations narrative incorporates yet disavows its indebtedness to a racist discourse, structured discursively around a racially unmarked (i.e. white) *British* perception of the problem of national identity induced by post-1945 *non-white immigration* from the New Commonwealth. It both assumes the natural existence of discrete, biological and culturally incommensurate communities known as 'races' (Barker 1981; Miles 1993) and identifies the problem of 'race', not as racism but as the condition of being the racialized other, that is, 'non-white' (cf. Gilroy 1987; Small 1994). The imperial assumptions of the race-relations narrative are woven through a reinvention of British nationalism which occurs in the 'common sense' of the post-war/post-colonial period (Hesse 1997). The race-relations narrative implicitly and systematically questions the coherence and legitimacy of 'non-white' Britishness as well as the pervasiveness of white British racism. First, there is a narrow temporal framing of political and social developments associated with 'race' and racism to the post-1945 world, 'the forgetting of empire' (Hall 1978). Second, a reduction of the themes and issues to the dislocating impact of 'non-white' immigration and its accommodation or rejection by the so-called indigenous British. Third, an insistence that whatever problems arise are due to difficult or disharmonious relations between the 'races'. Fourth, a conception of racism in the psychological terms of interpersonal prejudice and as the experience of minority status, thereby stripping it of its political, cultural and institutional dimensions. Finally, the race-relations narrative promotes the idea that each of these empiricist observations, in their respectively attributed statuses as ephemera, leave uncontaminated an indigenously liberal and tolerant British nation which is intrinsically uninformed by historically racist processes. During the post-colonial period, the national colonial past is collapsed into obscurity by the discrete chronology of apparently ahistorical dilemmas deposited by post-war immigration.

Understanding the meaning of the post-colonial in this analysis is now a critical requirement. Without wishing to diminish the complexity of the extant debate (Chambers and Curti 1996; Loomba 1998; Prakash 1995), I want to suggest we need to begin by marking a provisional empirical distinction between the colonial and the post-colonial. In my view the *empirical colonial* comprises the formal, institutional, racialized govern-mentalities of the imperial 'Age of Europe 1492–1945' (West 1990) and their corresponding elaborations and contestations. While the *empirical post-colonial* refers to the formal disestablishment of the colonial institutional arrangement, the official moments of decolonization and racial desegregation and their ancillary reverberations and reconfigurations. Although this is only partially satisfactory as an operational distinction, it is helpful to the extent that it can be retained in order to problematize the radical conceptual polarization between colonial and post-colonial. This is why I want to insist, beyond the seductive discreteness of this kind of empirical classification, that we understand post-colonialism conceptually as *a critical discourse on the contested meaning and nature of an undecidable post-coloniality*. Paradoxically, the idea of undecidability[11] here invites us to conceive of the post-colonial as a concept that has always been under intense interrogation due to the global incidence of disparate, agonistic, *unrealized, incomplete and interrupted* post-colonial settlements. In effect, we are required to question the very different social formations in which post-colonial conditions have been variously instituted and cultivated and/ or destabilized, and disavowed. I am arguing here for a globally specific understanding of the post-colonial. If we understand this within the determinate locations of western metropolises, it suggests the post-colonial can be taken conceptually to designate in the late twentieth century: discourses arising from those political and cultural movements inscribed in contestatory relations with racially exclusive, Euro-American hegemonic forms of governance. All of which have been *instituted in the incomplete, multiple transitions from western imperialisms to racialized liberal-democracies*. This is the unresolved post-colonial condition. Consequently, one way of reading the discourse of multiculturalism and its signification of 'race' and ethnicity as *the* cultural difference in Britain, is as a thematic that invites a series of differently inflected, political responses to a dislocating post-colonial condition, symbolized by the persistence of institutionalized racism within the quixotic universalisms of liberal-democracy. This really does require a more sophisticated comprehension of what is and can be signified by the politics of multiculturalism.

Multiculturalism Across the Atlantic

In contrast to Britain, the figuration of multiculturalism in the United States has produced much greater social reverberations and contested theoretical elaborations.[12] This is hardly surprising, considering that the main institutional sites for the multicultural debates in Britain were primary and secondary school education, while in the United States it was the university (Rattansi 1999). What became known as the 'culture wars' in the United states during the mid-1980s into the 1990s, politicized and expanded the concept of multiculturalism beyond the parameters of 'race' and ethnicity, into the discourses of gender and sexuality conceived as socially repressed cultural differences. The culture wars engaged and enraged university teaching, book publishing and public journalism. Stimulating a searing calling into question as well as the implacable defence of the cultural mainstream of the United States, the culture wars produced an impassioned politics of knowledge in which interrogations of the exclusionary racial, gender, sexual and class formations of the nation were reactivated as themes relevant not only to the democratic ideals of citizenship but to the epistemology of many academic disciplines. Once it was widely perceived that the western canon was under assault, this sparked a counter-reformation (see Berman 1992).

The discourse of multiculturalism in the United States touched political nerves which were irreducible to the nervous systems of either Left or Right. It has been variously lampooned as 'political correctness' (Berman 1992; Dunant 1994); the critique of the hegemony of 'dead white males' in knowledge production; or the attempt to overturn western civilization by substituting for the 'classics' lesser readings based not on scholarly values but on ethnic and gender proportionality (cf. Lefkowitz and Rogers 1996). More considered critics have seen in it a feverish post-modern embrace of relativism in knowledge (whether scientific or moral) and an irrational, ethnicized opposition to universalism which eschews a broad-based politics (i.e. organized against the social inequalities of material interests), favouring instead an identity politics organized around the virtues of cultural recognition (cf. Taylor 1992).[13] The trouble with criticisms of this nature is that whatever merits they contain are ill-served by their inability to distinguish exactly the object of their critique. That there are various multiculturalisms in the politics of multiculturalism is perhaps the chief contribution of the United States' experience to the debate (McLaren 1994a; 1994b; 1997), but this is not yet something that the critique of multiculturalism has managed to take on board. Or as Cynthia Willet puts it in an important anthology of philosophical arguments, *Theorizing Multiculturalism*: 'Multiculturalism has not yet been fully theorized. In part the lack of a unifying theory stems from the fact that multiculturalism as a political, social and cultural movement has aimed to respect a multiplicity of diverging perspectives outside of dominant traditions' (Willet 1998: 1).

Admittedly, this may be the over-idealization of a provisional and pragmatic set of circumstances but it does point to the need to understand the politics of multiculturalism(s) as articulating, in critique of dominant, oppressive traditions, different specifications of the logic of the *multicultural* in the fields of knowledge and representation. Understanding these dominant traditions within the logic of the multicultural suggests the need for coalitions and co-production in knowledge formation which takes seriously the 'local memories' and 'subjugated knowledges' (Foucault 1977) whose exclusion and repression shore up the dominant tradition as an unquestionably valorized (western) universal foundation. In the United States (as in Britain), it is the colonial institutions of the western foundation of power and knowledge which, despite concomitant developments in liberalism and subsequent formulations of representative democracy, have yet to experience significant decolonization. At its best, the politics of multiculturalism in the United States has raised serious doubts and consternation about the capacity of western nations attempting to represent cultural diversity and incoporate differences, as if this did not imply the need for a broad transformation of politics, education and social inequalities. Multiculturalism is now indeed enshrined as a western spectre that haunts the 'western spectacle'[14] of tidy, uniformed, nineteenth-century European nationalisms continuing to reside in modern western democracies. The United States is only the most globally visible and protracted example (Melzer et al. 1998). Perhaps this explains the observations of Joe L. Kincheloe and Shirley R. Steinberg when they write:

> In public discussion multiculturalism is a term used as a code word for race, much in the way that 'inner-city issues' signifies that race is the topic being referenced. Among many conservatives multiculturalism is a term of derision, deployed to represent a variety of challenges to the traditional European and male orientation of the educational canon. (Kincheloe and Steinberg 1997: 1)

It is certainly the political and educational dimensions of multiculturalism, socially unsettled in the ambivalent conditions of post-coloniality, which concentrate the minds of academics, politicians, citizens and migrants alike. Stuart Hall, in his Conclusion to this volume, provides a seminal theorisation of the multicultural question as a global and local terrain of political contestation, with crucial implications for the West, especially Britain. In the rest of this Introduction I want to say something about how its irrepressible, recurrent qualities can be understood in order to convey what I mean by multicultural *transruptions*.

Multicultural Transruptions

As we can see, a particular construction of 'race' and ethnicity and their contestation seems to be integral to the configuration of multiculturalism in the West. Britain is hardly immune to these political ramifications, although it remains to be seen how long British universities will continue to treat the issues raised by the post-colonial fall-out of multiculturalism as if they were simply detestable noises from across the Atlantic. Can we continue to ignore the legacy of the colonial formation of Britain, the incomplete process of decolonization which left white racism intact (see Hesse, this volume, Chapter 5), and the generational impact of post-war Black and Asian migration on the racially exclusive narcissism of the nation? In combination, these factors have increasingly generated an irrepressible conjunction of 'racial', ethnic and cultural dynamics which frequently exerts unexpected, unsettling effects on unreflexive British social institutions. It is no official secret, for example, that: Britain seems to be constantly surprised by the recurrent agency of Black and Asian people with political challenges and culturally popular movements; or that in every decade since the 1940s deep-seated racism is rediscovered in Britain by the media; or that for many social institutions the prospect of engaging dialogically with the social demands of cultural diversity rather than simply managing its aesthetics is deeply threatening; or that successive generations of diaspora-thinking, western-speaking descendants of colonial migrants and those from former colonies are still entangled in defining the meaning of their place in the nation. Whenever themes like these arise in British public life they tend to disrupt the normal transmission of everyday discourse: normal transmission cannot easily be resumed, if at all, in its racially exclusive forms. The tendency to switch channels rather than address what has arisen is as British as the Dunkirk spirit, while the desire to repress or disavow the interruption is as familiar as the British propensity to queue. This is what underwrites multiculturalism as a political structure of feeling in Britain in the post-war period. Although the explicit discourse may now seem an anachronism, the post-colonial contestation and construction of cultural differences which compelled the naming of multiculturalism persists, as it always did, fluctuating between the butterfly effect and a bombshell, in a disparate range of apparent settlements in the British way of life. What Britain experienced during the long second half of the twentieth century was a consistent series of unsettled formations in relation to the multicultural.

Our brief problematization of the incidence of multiculturalism in Britain should have alerted us to the importance of understanding the multicultural as inscribed in a complex series of historical and political transactions. What, however, brings the multicultural to prominence in the West is the persistence of the unresolved discrepancies of imperial cultures and incomplete decolonization in post-colonial times. These are initialized in 'race' and its perceived correlatives in ethnicity, gender, class and sexuality. Clearly, racism is a profoundly unresolved discrepancy. We need, however, to understand *discrepancy*, in precise conceptual terms (Hesse 1999a). By this I am referring to historical antagonisms and social inequalities which underline cultural differences that are represented as marginal or insignificant in dominant discourses; and are conventionally repressed as a subject for discussion or redress. Yet, paradoxically, the discrepant, while remaining unresolved, actually confirms the dominant discourse in its dominance. Or, as Toni Morrison puts it in a related context: 'As in virtually all of this nation's [i.e. the United States] great debates, nonwhites and women figure powerfully, although their presence may be disguised, denied or obliterated' (Morrison 1992: xix). As we shall see, it is the exposure of the discrepant that opens up the nation to different challenges, interrogations and representations. It is in the logic of this type of exposure that we can at last locate the meaning of multicultural transruptions.

The concept of *trans-ruption* is in some ways a companion concept to that of discrepancy. It requires that we understand the logic of what turns a discrepancy into a transruption. The latter describes interrogative phenomena that, although related to what is represented as marginal or incidental or insignificant, that is identifiable discrepancies, nevertheless refuse to be repressed. They resist all efforts to ignore or eliminate them by simply recurring at another time or in another place. Transruptions are troubling and unsettling because any acknowledgement of their incidence or significance within a discourse threatens the coherence or validity of that discourse, its concepts or social practices. In one sense there is something more here than a singular interruption or an ultimate disruption. Although these qualities are sometimes apparent, a multicultural trans-ruption is constituted by the recurrent exposure of discrepancies in the post-colonial settlement. *It comprises any series of contestatory cultural and theoretical interventions which, in their impact as cultural differences, unsettle social norms and threaten to dismantle hegemonic concepts and practices.* Trans-ruptions transcend or overcome any initiative to dismiss their relevance, and continually slice through, cut across and disarticulate the logic of discourses that seek to repress, trivialize or silence them. In the absence of effective or satisfactory resolutions, multicultural transruptions are simply recurrent.

Residual and Emergent Transruptions

Raymond Williams provides a useful way of clarifying the dynamics of multicultural transruptions. Williams introduced the concepts of the *residual* and the *emergent* as a way of explaining the incidence of two temporally different but contextually related cultural processes over which a hegemonic social order held little or no sway. These were 'movements and tendencies both within and beyond a specific and effective dominance' (Williams 1977: 121) which connected with the past as well as the future; in other words, marginalized, resistant, alternative, incorporative, cultural forms which recast, challenged and/or stretched the meaning of dominant forms of representation, while engraving their own significations on the social land-scape. Now, if we construe the multi-culture of transruptions in this way, counterposed, for example, to an imperial and post-colonial articulation of the British nation, then the different implications Williams attributes to the residual and the emergent can be used to deepen our understanding of the multicultural.

With regard to residual multicultural transruptions, these can be said to refer 'to that which has been effectively formed in the past, but is still active in the cultural process, not only and often not at all as an element of the past, but an effective element of the present' (Williams 1977: 122). Challenging colonial representations and racist regulations of 'non-European' others has a long imperial history, which resurfaces renarrativized in the contemporary idioms of the British way of life. The residual raises the theoretical difficulty of separating culturally particular articulations of the past from the dominant cultural institutions of the 'present'. It also highlights 'certain experiences, meanings and values which cannot be expressed or substantially verified in terms of the dominant culture', but which are 'nevertheless lived and practised on the basis of the residue -cultural as well as social- of some previous social or cultural institution or formation' (Williams 1977: 122). Part of the difficulty with the dominant cultural formation of Britain is the inability or reluctance of its institutions to accept that European racism was and is a constitutive feature of British nationalism. While this remains unexamined, resistant to decolonization in the post-colonial period, it continues to generate a myriad of resistances and challenges to its historical formations. These dislocate the narration of Britain as a serialized essence, articulating the story-lines of a nation that is diversely politicized and culturally unsettled. Residual multicultural transruptions are constituted as forms of disturbance and intrusiveness by those resurgences of meaning, arising from the imperial past. They continually put in question, particularly in unexpected places and at unforeseen times, matters deemed in hegemonic discourses to be settled, buried and apparently beyond dispute.

Our examination of the meaning of multicultural transruptions needs also to be aware of what is coming into view, *emerging*. Williams suggests the emergent may be difficult to distinguish from 'some new phase of the dominant culture' (Williams 1977: 124) or the merely novel; but, once recognized the emergent is nevertheless 'substantially alternative or oppositional'. If the mosaic or liberal multiculturalism of the 1980s which attempted to specify how 'ethnic minorities' *ought* to be integrated into 'Britishness' was a 'new phase of the dominant culture', then what might be termed emergent multicultural transruptions? For me this refers to those recurrent practices and discourses arising directly from the post-war migrations and corresponding statist attempts to manage and deflect unresolved post-colonial discrepancies through the narrative of race-relations. Another way of thinking about this suggests that multicultural transruptions are resoundingly emergent in relation to the insufficiencies, distortions and shortcomings of 'British' theoretical, political and policy attempts which treat as real an *apparitional post-imperialism*.

The apparition of post-imperialism is the horizon of the unresolved post-colonial condition. It arose following the apparent demise of the European grand narrative of a progressive modernity. This had conventionalized the western regulation and designation of the 'non-European' other as unquestionably culturally inferior and politically pathological from the sixteenth century to the middle of the twentieth century. However, from the 1960s onwards this ceased to be representationally acceptable in the global terms of international relations, national sovereignties and what is domestically referred to in the West as race-relations. But the colonial tenor of racism remains conventionally determining in the parochial reconstruction and social stratification of western nations inhospitable to the rights, representation, citizenship and migrations of 'non-white' or 'non-European others'. Perversely, this is what marks the Eurocentric designation of the manner in which the European culture of racism is accorded coherence only in relation to the discredited, past histories of the imperial past. Hence, the contemporary implications and consequences of racism are mostly disavowed in western idealizations of social diversity and celebrations of cultural difference in the democratic nation. The disavowal of racism reinforces the apparition of a post-imperial phase of liberal-democracy; it eclipses any exposure of its failure to produce it. The problem is that where economically inegalitarian, racist formations are unsuccessfully concealed and subsequently exposed, the western 'promise of democracy' (Derrida 1994) is compromised by the revelations surrounding the unresolved ethnic antagonisms of its post-colonial conditions. The promise of democracy is subject to indictment as a foundational ruse by emergent multicultural transruptions.

Although the emergent may sometimes be complicit with what the 'dominant has effectively seized' as the 'ruling definition of the social' (Williams 1977: 124), the transruptive dimensions of the multicultural are effectively resistant to this. Critical representations of the emergent multicultural specularize 'areas of human experience, aspiration, and achievement which the dominant culture neglects undervalues, opposes, represses, or even cannot recognize' (Williams 1977: 124).

Diaspora Formations, Cultural Entanglements

The thematics of this book are organized around the meaning of multicultural transruptions. The conceptual potency of these transruptions lies in the recurrent force of their irrepressible quality of interrogation. While the conjunction of 'race', ethnicity and cultural differences persists in thrall to post-colonial discrepancies, the impossibility of ethnically cleansing multicultural transruptions from the political imaginaries of the western nation is equally apparent. *Un/Settled Multiculturalisms* suggests, using Britain and its cultural spheres of influence as its main example, that late modern western and western-influenced 'non-western' societies can no longer be thought of as either discrete or unitary national formations. We need conceptual tools and forms of analyses which are sufficiently nuanced to take into account the post-colonial formation of cultural differences and the social and demographic changes which seem diversely historicized, discursively globalized and intensely localized. In an exploratory attempt to address this contextual and constitutive *multicultural-scape*, the contributions span different types of cultural, social and political analyses. Loosely organized around the social scientific implications for studying contemporary meanings of the post-colonial West (e.g. Britain) and formations associated with its erstwhile imperial locations (e.g. United States, the Caribbean, South Africa), the book is divided into two thematic sections. The first section, 'Diaspora Formations', discusses the post-colonial impact of culturally different historicities and political-spatialities on conventionally western national configurations (e.g. Britain) and conventionally western conceptualizations (e.g. liberalism). The general idea of diaspora formations is both cartographic and dispositional (cf. Cohen 1997). Cartographically, they describe the migratory contours of particular communities from a historical place of domicile to geographically different places of generational settlement. Dispositionally, they refer to the implications of transnational 'elective affinities' (Hesse 1999b) animating communities that invest in imagining themselves as part of a diaspora. Diaspora formations currently define the post-colonial sense in the proliferation of and interaction between cultural differences that shape the transnational configurations of dispersed histories and identities within and against the cultural legislation of the western nation.

In Chapter 2, S. Sayyid develops a distinctive theory of the logic of diaspora as both 'anti-nation' and 'anti-global'. The importance of this contribution lies in its exposure of the waning hegemonization of the idea of the political exerted by the 'Westphalian order'. This describes the political construction of a world governed by the international relations established between European nations following the diplomatic termination in 1648 of the Thirty Years War (i.e. thirty consecutive years of religious wars in Europe). The Treaty of Westphalia established the sovereign, independent (European) nation as the basic political unit in international law. According to Sayyid, the Westphalian model, having endured for the greater part of political modernity, is now coming under increasing interrogation from diaspora formations. Because these are located both inside and outside the (western) nation, they cannot be integrated into its cultural protocols and therefore prevent the closure of the nation and its equivalent identification with the site of the political. Arguing that the transnational organization of 'Muslim subjectvities', the '*Umma*', can be understood as part of the political logic of diaspora, Sayyid re-describes a world marked by two global forms of decentring: the decentring of the West and the decentring of the nation-state.

The relocation of political logics is a dominant theme in Chapter 3, in which Brett St Louis takes elegant issue with the transatlantic commodification of the Black body and the commercialization of Black performance in sport. He evokes the diasporic ambiance if not the terminology of the Black Atlantic (Gilroy 1993a). St Louis's argument is that the meaning of Black sporting performances tends to transcend their national locations. This diasporic integument implies contested racialized and colonial histories which dominant sociologies of sport effectively ignore. The sociologists' conventional focus on questions of social structure elides the aesthetics and politics of the 'poetic imperative' of Black sporting performance. This is not to be confused with a fixation on the body evidenced in corporate advertising; its obsession with regulating the exotic and pleasure inducing corporeal surfaces of Black bodies as symbols of 'natural' power, strength and grace (without the distracting intrusions of reflexivity induced by the 'burden' of the mind). For St Louis, recognizing the institution of the political in Black sporting performances lies in exorcising the mind–body split projected on to Black people and recognizing the 'poetic imperative', the desire to play dialogically to the imagination of a constituency.

A less poetic, more mundane, though no less complex type of performance is analysed in Chapter 4 by David Parker, where the Chinese 'takeaway' is the setting for a remarkable theorization of routine cross-cultural contestations which are depicted as part of a 'diasporic habitus'. Although Chinese food has now become inseparable from a 'British' culinary sense of place, and the Chinese takeaway is as much a British institution as the adopted 'cup of tea', Parker argues that the apparent 'welcoming of the food migrants bring can sit alongside the disavowal of their distinctive social and political claims'. At the same time, the familiar, everyday encounters with white customers across the counter in the takeaway, while seeming to 'exemplify peaceful multicultural coexistence', often embody 'deep structures of racialized domination'. There is within the 'contact zones' established by the myriad of these socio-economic transactions a recurrent struggle over the place of the Chinese in Britain and the meaning of British Chinese identities, exemplified in face-to-face experiences with racial harassment and the passive, sexualized constructions of the Chinese reinforced by the orientalism of a 'celebratory multiculturalism'. This micro-formation subsists alongside the 'power geometries' of the diasporic habitus which contextualize Chinese takeaways as various nodal points in transnational networks of social space across western culture. Parker develops Bourdieu's concept of habitus in order to explore the racialized nuances of 'globalization, migration and the commodification of cultural difference' in their impact on the Chinese diaspora in Britain.

The theme of diasporic nuances is taken up in Chapter 5, where I question the conventional tendency to reduce the meaning of 'Black Britain' to post-1945 Caribbean migration, popularly symbolized by the arrival of the *Windrush* in 1948. What concerns me is how to understand Black Britain as a post-colonial formation. Its incidence, in the twentieth century at least, requires us to analyse not only continuities and discontinuities in the regional and national formations of Black Britain, but the changing economies of British racism, from their colonial to post-colonial signatures. In this context what I describe as the '*Windrush* symbol' becomes an impediment to critical thought in so far as it is conceived as an originary moment of Black Britain. I suggest that the historical continuities of Black sea-faring populations, evidenced only too clearly in the 1948 'race riots' in Liverpool, provide examples of British conditions of urban racism that pre-dated the post-war period. As an alternative and complement to the *Windrush* symbol, I analyse the meaning of the 1945 Pan-African Congress in Manchester, highlighting its contribution to a 'Black poetics of post-colonialism'. In this political landscape the particular impact of the African diaspora on the meaning of Black Britain is defined as a 'logic of diasporicity', which comprises an interface of diverse 'intra-nationalisms' and 'transnationalisms'.

Part II of the book, 'Cultural Entanglements', introduces a series of contributions concerned with post-colonial cultural differences. Inscribed as marginal or minority concerns in dialogues, interactions and representations, these are cultural diffferences which do not fit dominant national categories or social conventions of analysis and tend to be silenced, devalued or misrecognized. Yet at the same time they are tied into larger cultural formations, raise critical issues about these formations and require forms of analysis that can negotiate contingent and multiple vectors of meaning. The idea of cultural entanglement is taken from the work of Edouard Glissant (1989). Glissant uses it to convey the extent to which cultural formations are always marked and wrought by multiple intersections of engagement in the absence of any single or unique location of origin (see also Hesse 1999a). Culture in this view is constitutively cross-cultural, inescapably dialogical, fissured by movements and developments which frustrate the desire for absolute coherence and a singular rootedness. Glissant suggests it is the imperial formation of the West which, as part of its colonial governance, attempts to institute the 'reality' of discretely-formed, nationally monological cultures. Consequently part of the task of post-colonial theory and practice is to show how the meanings attributed to distinctions between relational cultural identities, like the 'West' and the 'non-West' are not distinctions that preceded actual cultural contact. In order to understand the significance of contestations or antagonisms generated from cross-cultural formations, we have to return to these points of 'entanglement'. Consequently, all the contributions in this section address the recurrence and consequences of different points of cultural entanglement.

A key illustration of this approach is provided in Chapter 6. Claire Alexander develops a powerful reading of the mesh of pathologizing discourses that during the 1990s invented the 'New Asian folk devil' from the media 'discovery' of the Asian 'gang'. These images were reworked ideological borrowings from extant 'Black folk devil' descriptions. The latter, dating from the 1970s, portrayed African-Caribbean men as constitutionally criminal and socially threatening. In her analysis, Alexander observes that the contemporaneous performances by young Asian men of their own sense of masculinity increasingly unsettles and destabilizes dominant conventional, 'British' definitions of Asian men. This leaves much media and academic discourse unable to explain these seemingly unwarranted departures from 'raced' expectations of social behaviour. Reviewing the dynamics of 'race', ethnicity, generation and gender, Alexander suggests that much of the analysis in this area tends to conflate the categories rather than discern the meaning of their intersection in contested cultures of entanglement. Illustrating her arguments with a pointed discussion of her ethnographic research, she provides an important alternative reading of young Asian masculinities which nuances rather than sensationalizes, and analyses rather than pathologizes the shifting complexity of their social lives.

By way of a gender contrast, Denise Noble in Chapter 7 provides a fascinating set of conceptual insights into the 'race', gender and sexual performativities of Black female consumption of Jamaican Ragga music. This musical culture, otherwise known as dance-hall, emerged during the 1980s as the rhythmically faster and lewd or 'slack' successor to the roots and culture idiom of reggae. The latter was popularly symbolized by Bob Marley and Burning Spear throughout the 1970s in Jamaica and Britain. According to Noble, it is possible to see in Ragga culture an outrageously ambivalent mix of sexist lyrics from male DJs (with regular disclosures of rampant homophobia) and the enthusiastic participation of revealingly attired, sexually gyrating young Black women. However, without these women dance-hall experience simply would not happen. Rather than present these women as cultural dupes, Noble unravels the entangled formations of dance-hall culture's gendered and sexualized disseminations. In particular she notes that although the predominantly male DJs talk in their songs directly to the women, as active consumers the women construct readings of the music which 'subvert by playing with and within its heterosexist authority'. While the culture of Ragga itself in dominant discourses is conventionally portrayed as the site of conflicting directions in Black popular culture, between the profane and the sacred, Noble argues that a profoundly gender-specific discourse disrupts this. Consequently, Black women are implicated in a sexual economy of erotic desire and the desire for respectability.

Respectability in its nationalist incarnation is a pervading theme of Chapter 8, where Roiyah Saltus-Blackwood provides a compelling political account of the underlying issues entangled in the 1995 referendum in the Caribbean island of Bermuda concerning independence from Britain. She is concerned to explore why the colonial legacy is constitutively disavowed in the contemporary Bermudan political discourse, despite the fact that white oligarchic rule continues to mould the future imaginaries of the island. Saltus-Blackwood argues that the differing and oppositional political campaigns around the referendum were distinctly united by coalescence around the lexicon of unspoken assumptions that 'race' and the colonial legacy were not legitimate, substantive themes for political discourse. Suggesting that the 'identity of Bermuda lies somewhere between the formation of an extant British colony and an ex-British colony', she questions what kinds of national representation are possible in post-colonial or quasi-colonial formations. Saltus-Blackwood reminds us of the establishment of Bermuda by the English as a slavery plantation colony in 1612. She traces the sustained development of white oligarchic rule from this point into the twentieth century when racial desegregation and a universal franchise were finally instituted after long-drawn-out political struggles. The occasion of the independence referendum is used by Saltus-Blackwood to identify a political lexicon of silence regarding Bermuda's colonial entanglements, underpinning efforts invested in denial which result paradoxically in referencing the contemporaneity and relevance of 'race' within political discourse.

On the face of it, it is virtually impossible to talk about South Africa without invoking thematics of 'race' explicitly and transparently. In Chapter 9, Zimitri Erasmus explores developments in differential racialization and power-knowledge relations in the academy of post-apartheid South Africa to develop an intriguing theorization of the meaning of cultural entanglements. Ersamus identifies continuities between apartheid and post-apartheid in 'struggles over racialized identities'. She argues these struggles are framed by 'entanglements of blackness, whiteness, colouredness and africanity' on the one hand, and the entanglements of post-apartheid South Africa, 'cross-cultural histories and national identity' on the other. However, bestriding this context is the hegemonic Black/white binary that reminds us of the governance of 'white interpretive authority' and 'white silence' in the processes of knowledge production and the empowerment/limitations of oppostional and redemptive 'Black essentialisms'. With regard to racialized western knowledges, Ersamus narrates the occasion of a university seminar discussion of Saartjie Baartman (a Khoena woman, whose body was a living exhibit in Paris and London in the second decade of the nineteenth century). Using this as an exemplar of the dynamics of racialized constructions of knowledge in the social sciences, she questions the dismissive, unscholarly response by white academics to academics of colour who critique colonial formations in the social sciences. In exposing the 'entanglement of white-centred knowledge with the race privilege of whiteness', she stresses the importantance of not 'recentring' whiteness, or leaving it unmarked. Different issues are raised by the question of 'Black essentialisms' which in affirming a hegemonic identity beyond fragmentation are also complicit with 'cultural essentialisms' and 'biological determinisms'. For Erasmus, the concept of 'Hi-bredie-ty' which she translates as an embedded entanglement in 'whiteness, blackness, colouredness and africanness', is a precursor to a different way of being 'Black'.

The various consequences and implications of the multicultural themes and transruptive effects discussed in the contributions to this volume are take up by Stuart Hall in the Conclusion. Hall invites us to reconsider the multicultural question and the question of multiculturalism as inescapable conditions of global, post-colonial times. Hall provides a unique theorization of the difference between the multicultural as an 'adjectival' distinction and multiculturalism as 'substantive', in order to capture the constitutive degree of non-fit between the former as a signifier and the latter as a signified. Surveying the impact of the imperial legacy and the cultural 'hybridization' of modern western identities, Hall provides a seminal historical dénouement of the meaning of the multicultural in the West. He critically assesses the implications of racisms and cultural diversities for the coherence of liberal-democracies which have so far failed to bring these complex civic considerations within the remit of the protected rights of citizenship. Hall's analysis of the 'multicultural question' is intended to 'underwrite a new strategic approach to multiculturalism', where it becomes possible to 'effect a new and radical reconfiguration of the particular and the universal, of liberty and equality with difference'.

Between Cosmopolitanism and the Multicultural

Not since the 1980s, when some semblance of these issues was ventilated in the major cities as a sustained questioning of the British urban way of life, has it been possible to envisage a legimitate debate about the redesign or branding of British national identity for the twenty-first century. However, the enthusiastic suggestion that the election of the New Labour government in May 1997 inaugurated this as an open possiblity invites more cynicism than celebration when we consider its media election campaign. Broadly speaking, the election campaign was fought by all the main political parties as if Black and Asian people did not exist. Frequent appeals to and claims on behalf of the 'British people' were made as if whoever the British people were, they had remained and would continue to be the same. The only public, explict references to 'race' came visually from the British National Party in their election broadcast as a way of marking the decay of British society and the corrosion of true British identity. Yet it was the case that when the BNP reiterated references to the 'British' people, there was little to distinguish them from Labour, Conservative or Liberal Democrat intonations. Because explanations were never provided and qualifications seemed unnecessary, these formulations were susceptible to being read as appeals to white people (cf. Gilroy 1987).

Of particular significance was Tony Blair's well-publicized attachment to British patriotism, evidenced in the election broadcast which appropriated the symbol of the British bulldog for Labour. It was an outstanding example of an essentially backward-looking, racialized exclusiveness. If any of our memories serve us correctly, the British bulldog does not just symbolize the British Dunkirk spirit during the Second World War, it also symbolizes the ethos and toughness of Britain's imperial identity overseas. This, taken together with a lack of discussion surrounding the Union Jack's contested signification, catapulted televisual representations of New Labour into the old racist position of British identity as white identity. At the same time, ideas concerned with tackling racism or developing cultural diversity socially remained as they had been throughout the 1990s, politically proscribed. It took the campaigning struggles of the Lawrence family and their supporters in relation to the racist muder of Stephen Lawrence to challenge and change the stranglehold of this racialized moratorium.

It was not until the beginning of the year 2000 that questions of racial equality and cultural diversity found their way once again, albeit ambivalently, on to the British public agenda following the publication of the Lawrence inquiry in 1999. Currently, it is uncertain whether the usual discovery hysteria that accompanies the public exposure of racism in Britain (which occurred in an unprecedented manner on this occasion) will produce any long-lasting social changes. It is also evident that the government of New Labour has largely continued to forge its policies within the anachronistic race-relations narrative. It differs very little in the traditional approach to the racialization of immigration, scoring high on nationalism for its punitive measures on refugees and asylum-seekers and higher still for its morally authoritarian 'law and order' policies. These will probably guarantee the support of floating Conservative voters everywhere well into the next decade. There are, however, precarious and unexplored discontinuities as well as rigid continuities between New Labour and the previous Conservative regime. Certainly, the former Conservative governments would not have commissioned the public inquiry into Stephen Lawrence's death; nor would they have accepted the appellation of 'institutional racism' to describe the 'collective failure of organizations' (Macpherson 1999) to meet the needs of Black, Asian and other communities in Britain. But for all New Labour's emphatic yet hesitant espousals of 'racial equality' and 'cultural diversity', the question remains, what vision of the British nation is intoned here? How will public institutions respond and what political sense of community is being evoked? There is a danger that an unreflexive sense of cosmopolitanism rather than a critical sense of the multicultural may well be guiding the official British path to the brave new globalized world of the twenty-first century.

Anthony Giddens, the social theorist most associated with New Labour's quasi-ideological commitment to the 'third way' as the 'renewal of social democracy', gestures unmistakably in this direction. Giddens argues in favour of a cosmopolitanism which embraces heterogeneity, while recognizing the importance of national soildarity. He contrasts this with what he describes as the 'radical multiculturalism of the libertarians, and some on the left' (Giddens 1998: 132) which is attached to 'cultural pluralism' at any cost, irrespective of a wider, shared collectivity. Here we have the assumed universalism of cosmopolitanism confronting the attributed particularism of multiculturalism, both of which 'merge around the question of immigration' (Giddens 1998: 136). But it is this very polarity which replays the discrepancies of western formations that arrange the global order in naturalized terms of unmarked and marked identities, where the former lack a ethnic enunciation and the latter comprise little else. It is alarming how easily Giddens reprises the nationalist exteriority between indigenous and immigrant communities. Despite the generation of diverse British-born and British-settled identities, he seems able only to comprehend a racialized national formation of white hosts and 'non-white' visitors, where racism arrives mysteriously with the ethnic visitation, unmarked by a colonial historicity. Giddens's inabilty to think the multicultural beyond the interrogation and regulation of the racialized 'other' is exemplified where he argues: 'the aim of multiculturalist politics is entirely laudable – to counter the exploitation of oppressed groups.' This, he suggests, cannot be done 'without the support of the broad national community, or without a sense of justice that must stretch beyond the claims or grievances of any specific group' (Giddens 1998: 133). And if the 'broad national community' disavows the incidence of racist oppression or indeed its own implication in its constitution, as may well happen with the concept of institutional racism in Britain, what then?

The construction of multiculturalism as an immigrant or ethnic minority interest seems to run counter to the ethics of cosmopolitanism, where heterogeneity implies at some point the dissolution of an essentialist distinction between fixed majorities ('broad national community') and permanent minorities ('specific groups'). The legacy of an unreconstructed British nationalism deforms this cosmopolitan vision precisely because it precludes the contestability of the 'broad national community' as an idea, where it is either culturally diverse or it is racially exclusive. Giddens seems to assume the inevitability of the latter. Yet it is possible to read the politics of national formations subject to cultural diversity otherwise. It has been suggested by a French thinker, Alain Touraine, though still within the *us/them* paradigm, that it is misleading to think in terms of an absolute radical separation between democratic and ethnic conceptions of the nation. Political discourses can be mobilized in terms of that distinction, such that it becomes possible to argue that 'newcomers' to the nation 'must also become part of a memory, and must then transform it through their presence' (Touraine 1995: 298). This implies that participation in the construction of national identity, by those whose histories signify the impact of diaspora formations and/or contemporary implications in cultural entanglements, cannot be accomplished through the imposition of an 'intangible history lesson which has become a nationalist mythology'. Consequently, contrary to the idea of a cosmopolitanism residing above the fray, this suggests that 'collective memory must be a living memory that is constantly being transformed' (Touraine 1995: 298) by all those residing within its social gestation.

Ultimately this is where we need to locate the contributions in this book. They pose the question of the multicultural and its transruptive effects in a variety of conceptual ways which have direct implications for social scientific and political discourses. Multicultural transruptions have powerful social and epistemological dimensions, which are increasingly deeply unsettling and at the same time resonant with creative and emancipatory possiblities of settlement. The discourses that have continually denied the contested significance of the multicultural in western formations as well as the global social order during the twentieth century are uninspiringly threadbare. It is now time to weave narratives out of other scenarios, other tales and multiple accounts.

Notes

Many thanks to Paula Williams for her research, S. Sayyid for incisive insights, Stuart Hall for contested conversations, Zimitri Ersamus for telling observations, Claire Alexander for critical responses and David Okefuna for the sustained commentary.

1. Important interventions have been staked out in educational studies (Kincheloe and Steinberg 1997), media studies (Shohat and Stam 1994), cultural and social theory (Goldberg 1994; Lemert 1993; McLaren 1995), political theory (Gutman 1992) and philosophy (Fay 1996; Willet 1998).

2. I use Foucault's concept of 'governmentality' (Burchell et al. 1991) in a racialized sense to convey the political, regulatory and representational dimensions of European/ white racism in the West. It describes the relation between power and knowledge that is used to sustain and govern the racialized (globalized and naturalized) distinction between European/'non-European' or white/'non-white' as the ontological basis of primary and secondary social designations. Racialized governmentalities structure and underwrite the social technologies of racialized inclusions (hierarchical forms) and racialized exclusions (segregationary forms). This is the political meaning of racism. Elsewhere I have referred to its specific operation in Britain as 'white governmentality' (Hesse 1997).

3. *Guardian*, 8 October, 1997.

4. *Independent*, 8 October, 1997.

5. I address the problems of this concept below.

6. In British political discourse the idea of the 'race card' refers to any intervention (or 'play') that intentionally raises the question of 'race' (whether to condemn racism or promote it) in any capacity, in order to make a party political point or gain a political advantage. Following the Smethwick by-election of 1964, which the Conservative candidate Peter Griffiths won using the slogan, 'If you want a nigger for a neighbour, vote Labour', it was tacitly agreed among the major political parties to keep explicit references to 'race' out of electoral politics (see Solomos, 1993). It was felt that references to 'race' tended to exacerbate matters. Of course this had the discursive consequence of making it virtually impossible to discuss the meaning of racism in the British public sphere.

7. 'Powellism' refers to the ideas, themes and arguments promoted by Conservative MP Enoch Powell during the 1960s and early 1980s, which powerfully portrayed the British nation as under siege and in danger of terminal racial contamination and cultural liquidation by 'non-white' immigrants and their generational descendants. Powell's ideas were infamously amplified in his 'rivers of blood' speech in Birmingham in 1968, attracting almost equal measures of support and condemnation. He was subsequently sacked from the Conservative cabinet by Prime Minister Edward Heath (see Gilroy 1987; Solomos 1993).

8. The politics of anti-racism in Britain was profoundly initialized in urban form during the 1970s in response to the National Front, racist immigration controls, racist attacks and oppressive policing (see Sukrah 1998). It also produced the anti-racist, political category of 'Black' which linked together the oppositional identities of Africa, Caribbean and Asian communities (see Brah 1996).

9. In April 1993 Stephen Lawrence (aged eighteen) was stabbed to death by five white youths in the south London borough of Greenwich, where other racist murders and assaults had occurred in the early 1990s (Hesse 1997: 101–2). The metropolitan police spectacularly failed to treat Stephen's death as a racist murder, ignored many anonymous witnesses who indicated the identities of the assailants, preferring instead to

question Stephen's Black companion on the night, Duwayne Brooks. Between 1993 and 1998 Stephen's family spearheaded a campaign to bring Stephen's killers to justice; this included a failed attempt to take a civil action against the four white youths alleged to be involved in the murder. In 1997, following the election of the Labour government, the Home Secretary Jack Straw, after meetings with Neville and Doreen Lawrence, the parents, agreed to establish a public inquiry into Stephen's death and the police investigation. The inquiry was conducted throughout 1998 under the leadership of Sir William Macpherson and reported in February 1999. Its condemnation of the police's failure to investigate Stephen's death effectively, to treat racism seriously and the subsequent police cover-up of this failure, was unprecedented. It also identified the existence of institutionalized racism in the Metropolitan Police force. Although its definition of institutionalized racism as 'unwitting' and 'unconscious' was conceptually insipid, nevertheless it marked the first ever public acknowledgement of 'institutional racism' in a major state institution in Britain. (See Macpherson 1999.)

10. Avtar Brah has usefully introduced the concept of 'diaspora-space' to convey the socially 'inhabited' conditions where the entanglement of identities constructed as 'indigenous' and 'immigrant', national and transnational constitute the 'point at which boundaries of inclusion and exclusion, of belonging and otherness, of "us" and "them" are contested' (Brah 1996: 209).

11. Undecidablity is a concept taken from the work of Jacques Derrida (see Laclau 1996). It describes formations of meaning which are unframed, resist translation or singular definition, are ambiguous or equivocal, hence undecidable, and for which a decision has to be innovated in order to establish a meaning that can be put to work.

12. See, for example, Foster and Herzog 1994; Goldberg 1994; Kincheloe and Steinberg 1997; McLaren 1997; Melzer et al. 1998; Willet 1998.

13. Charles Taylor (1992) has made an influential theoretical case for understanding the politics of multiculturalism as a culturalist 'politics of recognition'. The idea that people from particular negatively ethnicized or racialized communities or excluded groups are profoundly concerned about being recognized in terms of identities chosen by them rather than forced upon them is, of course, indubitable. I think Taylor is mistaken to limit the politics of multiculturalism to this condition of the desire for recognition. He fails to consider as constitutive of its politics, the objective of questioning the conditions in which certain hegemonic institutions or dominant practices arrogate to themselves a culturally exclusive right to adjudication. Whether on the worth/value of 'other' cultures, adjudication retains the power and assumption of the authority to confer recognition. I call the response to his western formation a 'politics of interrogation' (see Hesse 1999a).

14. By 'western spectacle' I am referring to the institutionalization of a conceptually panoptic vision in media culture and academic discourses. This affirms the perspectival assumption of a white European subject gazing on a world in which the historical consequences of European imperialism and contemporary implications of Euro-American racism have been either erased from view or spectacularly sanitized. (See Hesse 1999b.)

Part I

Diaspora Formations

2

Beyond Westphalia: Nations and Diaspora: the Case of the Muslim *Umma* – community of believers.

S. Sayyid

Even though 'the nation' was invented perhaps only two hundred years ago, as an invention it has proved to be fairly durable and highly mobile. Its durability is manifested by the way in which it has continued to undermine empires and other forms of political community. Its mobility is shown by the way in which it has spread to cover all parts of the planet. Despite its apparent success, however, there are reasons for thinking that the days of the 'nation-thing' are numbered. Samuel Huntingdon's much hyped *The Clash of Civilizations* sums up the anxieties about the nation, by arguing that nations are being replaced by quasi-primordial constructs such as civilizations. Despite the problematic nature of defining a civilization, what is clear is that these entities are the manifestations of an 'a-national logic'. Despite the many difficulties with Huntingdon's thesis, it is interesting that there is an implicit recognition of the relationship between the nation and the form that the political has taken. This means that the question of the nation also involves the question of the political itself.

The 'nation-thing' was conceptualized as a homogenous indivisible body. Recent critiques of the logic of the national have highlighted its empirical deficiencies (multiplicity of identities); its ethical difficulties (the possibility of genocide and totalitarianism); and its theoretical limits (the impossibility of eradicating difference) (see Held 1995; Anthias and Yuval-Davis 1992; Smith 1991; Bauman 1989). These studies have been very important in undermining the logic of the national and suggesting a multicultural alternative. That is, a normative stance arising out of the recognition and celebration of the variety of cultural forms and practices that exist within the body of the nation. Critics of normative multiculturalism point to the way in which such valorization may lead to the Balkanization of the nation.

The political is founded upon the distinction between friend and enemy (Schmitt 1996: 28). This enemy is a collective enemy. For the friend–enemy distinction to operate, there must be a capacity for combat (Schmitt 1996: 32). This capacity means that within the political there is the possibility of war as a means of negating the enemy. War is a group activity, and since the invention of the nation it is an activity restricted to the national. This notion of the political does not necessarily involve the nation. Since the invention of the nation, however, most political conflicts have taken the national form. Either the conflict has been visualized as a conflict between nations or it has assumed the form of the nation. The friend–enemy distinction not only constructs the political but also ensures that the political takes the form of the national. Thus, any attempt to contest the logic of the nation implies a transformation of the political. In other words, the relationship between the Westphalian model of political order and contemporary identity formation requires an examination of the nation and its future. In the rest of the chapter I want to examine this implication by focusing on contemporary Muslim subjectivity.

Over-stating the Nation

The assertion of Muslim subjectivity presents a serious challenge to the idea of the nation. As Manuel Castells writes: '[F]or a Muslim, the fundamental attachment is not to the watan (homeland), but to the *Umma*, or community of believers, all made equal in their submission to Allah' (Castells 1997: 15). I want to explore the implications of this watan/*Umma* distinction here and in the following section. Castells' reading of Muslim subjectivity reproduces orientalist and neo-orientalist accounts of Islam.[1] As a consequence, he positions Islam as an anachronistic presence in today's world, almost a monolith in a world of flows. It is also interesting that he perceives that Muslim identity is articulated in terms of a diffuse Islam rather than a spatially bounded unit.[2] The effect of this is to include Islam as a reaction to the world of flows where 'the search for identity becomes the fundamental source of social meaning'. For Castells, an uncertain world produces crises that require the solitude of 'primary identities', be they religious, ethnic, territorial or national. This is interesting because the way in which we have talked about collective identities has relied on the use of stable bounded spaces. Castells' general argument is that, for a variety of reasons, we are now living in a world of flows. He argues that these flows are unsettling because they disrupt the continuities that allowed collective identities to be formed, maintained and projected.

Globalization is one way of summing up the transition to this world of flows. It is a process that is intrinsically linked to the formation of dislocated communities; populations that no longer fit within the Westphalian 'container'. The container is unable to contain not only because of increased mobility but also because its own walls are becoming blurred. It is possible to identify five main processes characteristic of globalization.

1. There is the emergence of a global civil society. Not only do we have a proliferation of NGOs which operate across national state boundaries, we are also seeing the beginnings of an attempt to construct a 'consensus' on issues such as human rights, economic management, gender issues and so forth. The institutional framework for this consensus is provided by elements that are not restricted to a particular national space: these elements often take on roles such as 'intellectual and moral leadership', often highly critical of Westphalian notions of state sovereignty.

2. The emergence of supra-national state-like formations such as the European Union also points to a way in which the Westphalian container is being superseded. One can note similar tendencies in the formation of NAFTA and ASEAN. These 'superstate' structures serve to undermine the relationship between national forms and sovereignty. In the European Union we see the attempt to articulate a pan-European identity which subsumes (to some extent) the national identities of member-states.

3. The rise of cosmopolitan centres such as London, New York, Paris and Los Angeles provides the terrain where many of the trends associated with globalization can be manifested. Not only are these world cities nodal points in the international economy, but they are also the spaces in which attempts to articulate a global culture are sited. These global cities are, to a large extent, cut off from (or at least have an exceptional relationship with) the nation-states in which they are situated. In many ways, however, they have a distinct identity.

4. The generalization of the experience of distant travel (whether it takes the form of labour migration or the compulsory movements of refugees, or tourism) has created a situation in which very large numbers of people are on the move or have moved. In this moving, one can trace the implosion of the western colonial empires as well as the imperatives of the world economy.[3]

5. The development and increasing integration of the world political economy acts to suture disparate economies and societies and, at the same, limits the ability of nation-states (with few powerful exceptions) to regulate their economies.

It is in the context of these processes of globalization that the need to find a vocabulary to describe political/cultural communities that transcend the limits of the Westphalian model becomes necessary.[4] One such community is that of the Muslims.

The Muslim *Umma*

There are three factors that point towards the formation of a Muslim *Umma*. First, there is the phenomenon of the assertion of an explicit

Muslim subjectivity. This process has reached all Muslim communities. There are no significant Muslim communities in which more visible indicators of the assertion of Muslim subjectivity are absent. Second, Muslims are heavily represented in various migrant communities throughout the developed world. This has occurred partly because of migration that has been attendant upon decolonization, but it is also the case that since 1979 a large percentage of refugees have been Muslims. Third, like most recent migrants, Muslims have tended to concentrate in urban areas. These areas are in the nodes of the new developing planetary networks (Castells 1997). The net effect of these developments has been to produce situations in which Muslims from different traditions converge around commonalties. This juxtaposing of various Muslim populations has the effect of producing the conditions for the articulation of a Muslim *Umma*. Islam interrupts the logic of the nation by highlighting the problem of integration – i.e. how to include various populations within the boundaries of a nation – and at the same time it focuses on the problem of their loyalties to an edifice larger than the nation. In other words, Islamism undermines the logic of the nation and at the same time it seeks to transcend the logic of the nation. How can we conceptualize this collective? What kind of a structure is the Muslim *Umma* (a community of believing women and men unified by faith and transcending national state boundaries)?

The Muslim *Umma*, however, is not the nation writ large. One of the main qualities that distinguishes the nation from other forms of collectives is its limited and restricted nature. The nation is at best an enterprise based on an exclusionary universalism. It is a bounded entity; it is not open to everyone. Thus, the problem of integration has poignancy for the nation in a way that it does not for other groupings. Unlike other formations, the nation does not imagine itself to be a composite or *mélange*. The only universalism that the logic of nation can articulate is one that is based on exclusion rather than inclusion. The universal nation can be an exceptional grouping, an incarnation of all that is considered to be great and good; it can be infinite in a temporal sense, but spatially it has to be bounded, it cannot expand for ever.[5] The idea of the *Umma* rejects all such limits, its universalism and implicit expansionism is constantly re-iterated. Clearly, the *Umma* is not a nation.

Nor is the Muslim *Umma* a common market. It has been pointed out many times, despite pious statements that occasionally emerge from organizations such as the ICO, that Muslims do not trade with each other, nor do they co-operate with each other about other economic matters. We cannot conceptualize the *Umma* as a structure arising out of economic integration. The unity of the *Umma* is not built upon trading contacts and global networks of labour and capital flows. This is not to deny that such flows exist, as the relationship between the Gulf States and Muslim labour-exporting states (such as Egypt, Bangladesh, Pakistan and Yemen) is clearly based on such flows. These flows are not, however, strong enough or extensive enough to suture the *Umma*.

Nor is the Muslim *Umma* a common way of life or a linguistic community. There is no doubt that once upon a time an argument could have been made for the *Umma* to be seen as a collective based around a fairly homogenous, elite culture. Books of *fiqh* collected in Delhi would be commented upon in *madrasas* in Maghreb. Arabic functioned as the *lingua franca* of the elite. There are still some practices which are uniform among Muslims (e.g. all Muslim pray towards the direction of Mecca). However, it is difficult to conclude from these examples that that which constitutes the unity of the Muslim *Umma* is its uniform way of life. (Of course, it is precisely this idea of a Muslim/Islamic civilization that animates people such as Huntingdon, but like all attempts to conceptualize a civilization as a unity, these flounder since they rest upon an eclectic collection of observable and generalized features).[6]

If the Muslim *Umma* is not a nation, a common market or a civilization, is it anything at all? Does not the difficulty of identifying the *Umma* suggest that the idea of a Muslim identity is nothing more than a chimera? Analysts have tended to treat 'Muslims' as a phenomenon of other more sturdy bases of identity formations (such as class, kinship, caste and ethnicity). This analytical tendency is not only the product of orientalism, but also of the way in which nationalist discourses within Muslim communities have served to undermine the idea of a distinct Muslim identity. If Muslim identity is so fragmentary, how can we conceptualize it? One way might be to think in terms of a Muslim diaspora.

Redemption Songs

'Diaspora' may be used in a descriptive manner to refer to an empirical situation in which settler communities are relocated from their ordinary homes. Extrapolations from the experience of the Jewish and African diasporas have become templates for the understanding of what constitutes a diaspora. Both involve the forced mass removal of people(s) from a homeland to places of 'exile' and the construction of cultural formations premised on territorial dispersal and political fragmentation. As one study of the impact of diaspora on international relations considers: '[M]odern diasporas are ethnic minority groups of migrant origins residing and acting in host countries but maintaining strong sentimental and material links with their countries of origin – their homeland' (Sheffer 1986: 3).

The notion of diaspora rests on three co-ordinates: homeland, displacement and settlement. In other words, a diaspora is constituted when communities of settlers articulate themselves in terms of displacement from a homeland. The homeland acts as a horizon for the community, enabling it to construct its collective subjectivity. A diaspora is formed when a people are displaced but continue to narrate their identity in terms of that displacement. For example, the Jewish diaspora is possible because, unlike other groups that were deported by various ancient conquerors (Assyrians, Neo-Babylonians), the Jews managed to maintain their collective identity even when they were territorially displaced and politically subordinated. The pre-condition for diaspora is the articulation of a demotic ethnos (or, if you prefer, nationalism) that is a mechanism to bind a community in terms of its vertical linkages. This is the reason why diaspora refers to Jewish experiences because it is one first instance when a demotic notion of ethnos was circulating (Armstrong 1983; Smith 1995). The Jews were not the only people deported *en masse* by the Assyrians and the Neo-Babylonians; what distinguishes their experience, however, is that they continued to hold on to their 'Jewishness'. The Jewish diaspora is made possible by the development of a proto-nationalism, which prevents its assimilation into other cultural formations.

The idea that a nationalism of sorts is a pre-condition for the construction of diaspora is given additional credence by the way in which diasporas tend to take the form of the nation (for example, Palestinians, Armenians, Assyrians). In other words, diaspora refers to a nation in exile. The boundaries that the discourse of nationalism draws around a community is what prevents the dissolution of that community once it is displaced from its locality. Nationalism constitutes both nations and diasporas – that is a peoplehood which is territorially concentrated (nation) and territorially displaced (diaspora).

Such a view of diaspora, however, would be only partially adequate to account for the African diaspora. Of course, there are many examples of nationalist or proto-nationalist discourses among the African diaspora, which correspond very closely to the 'classic' definition of diaspora (narratives that are organized around the co-ordinates of a homeland, a displacement, and a horizon of return either as a redemptive gesture or an empirical possibility). There remains, however, the suspicion that in the case of the African diaspora we are dealing with a process that is not simply a nation in exile. Paul Gilroy's (1993a) notion of a 'Black Atlantic' suggests a more complicated cultural formation that cannot be adequately described in such terms.

Attempts to broaden the notion of diaspora usually take the form of trying to include another population group alongside the classical exemplars of diaspora. So, for example, there is an attempt to speak of an Irish diaspora or a Greek diaspora and so on. While these accounts seek an empirical enlargement of diaspora, they do little to extend it theoretically. The theoretical weakness of the category of diaspora has been the subject of a recent article by Floya Anthias (1998).[7] I want to draw out some of Anthias' concerns as a prologue to suggesting why it may be helpful to think of the Muslim *Umma* as a diaspora.[8]

Anthias argues that diaspora is another way of bringing essentialized notions of ethnicity in the guise of hybridized and syncretic formations. It is possible to identify three main criticisms that she levies against the current conceptualization of diasporas. First, she feels that diasporas, by focusing on soldarities based on transnational commonalities, inhibit the possibility of intra-national trans-ethnic alliances (Anthias 1998: 577). Second, she believes that diasporas, rather than transcending ethnicity, are actually continuations and extensions of ethnic identification (pp. 558, 563, 568, 576). Third, she believes that the focus on diaspora forms part of a post-modern neglect of issues such as gender, class and the internal divisions that the notion of homogenous diasporas cover up (pp. 558, 560, 564).[9] In other words, Anthias contends that the way in which diaspora is commonly used takes no (or little) account of issues of gender or class and continues to be locked in an ethnicity framework. It is useful to divide these specific criticisms into two main arguments: there is a theoretical argument about the nature of identities and their relationship to diasporas and, at the same time, there is a political argument about the way in which valorizations of diasporas undermine the possibility of intra-national co-operation among various ethnicized communities.

I have a number of difficulties with Anthias' discussion, primarily because of its contradictory and inadequate theorization of collective identities. At one point Anthias criticizes the way in which writers on diaspora seem to focus on the homogenous nature of ethnic ties, ignoring the way in which these ethnicities are riven by divisions and differences; however, at the same time she argues that class and gender are important dimensions that diasporas do not take into account. Although no one could really disagree with such a position, the problem is that 'class' or 'gender' are no more cohesive or homogenous than 'ethnicities'. Ethnic unities may be class-divided and gendered, but genders may be ethnicized and class-divided, and classes are gendered and ethnicized. Gender, ethnicity and class, however, are not some kind of 'holy trinity' of secularized social science – the spirit of which can be seen behind every other form of social identity (i.e. identities based on the profession of faith) – and they do not exhaust all ways of categorizing social identities. It is not helpful to think that these are permanent concepts, the building blocks of collective identities. Sometimes, the critique of essentialism has the effect of turning all social identities into façades, behind which one can find lurking the 'real' identities of class or gender or ethnicity. To borrow a phrase made famous by Clifford Geertz, it's 'turtles all the way down'.

Any attempt to think about social identities is based on an erasure of internal differences and divisions. In this, ethnicity is not exceptional: all attempts to articulate collective subjectivities (including class or gender) will try to erase its constituent elements in an attempt to produce an organic unity. Anthias seems to be aware of this, but appears to consider it to be a problem only when identity takes the form of ethnicity, rather than being a general phenomenon of identity itself. In other words, the formation of all identities is relational and exclusionary. Identities based on faith, gender, class, culture (or whatever) all have this exclusionary and relational logic. Anthias seems to give the impression that ethnic identities are based on 'division and difference' and in that they are somehow different from other forms of identification.

It is the case that the most common notions of diaspora are continuations of the ethnic framework, but it does not follow that other identity frameworks are somehow more real and more permanent than ethnicity. How populations are classified and formed into particular clusters is ultimately a political process. All social identities are heterogeneous since they do not have an essence that can guarantee their homogeneity. Thus, it would be impossible to ground empirically the homogeneity of social identities (hence, the various ethnographic studies within the field of ethnic relations will always be able to point to divisions and diversities). Homogeneity is an effect of articulatory practices, an articulation that rests upon exclusion and not the uncovering of some deep underlying essence. Having said that, one should not confuse the existence of social identities as being necessitated by some essence. The recognition of the in-essential character of social identities does not demand that we reject the possibility of all social identities (or, more problematically, that we maintain that social identities which we do not agree with are mere fictions, or that we argue that only social identities which take particular forms – i.e. ethnically based – are essentialist).[10]

I agree with Anthias when she argues that just because a group of people hail from a particular place does not necessarily mean that they then constitute a 'valid sociological category'. The validity of sociological categories, however, cannot be the product of a practice external to the process by which identities are articulated. Diasporic identities have significance to the extent to which they appear in difference discursive practices. One has to recognize that diasporic imaginings can have an empowering effect: for example, Marcus Garvey and Malcolm X saw in the possibility of diaspora a way of 'out-flanking' some of the constraints on African-

American communities. Similarly, the idea of Muslim subjectivity within North Atlantic plutocracies owes its emergence to the possibility of making links between and beyond the sites in which Muslim settler communities have been ghettoized.

Further, I would agree with Anthias when she makes a distinction between diasporas which are simply extensions of ethnic frameworks, and diasporas as conditions (this a distinction that I also find useful). While I agree with much of her criticism relating to the difficulty of conceptualizing diasporas as a condition, I do not think that the attempt is so flawed that it needs to be abandoned in favour of a 'valid sociology'. What is required is an attempt to articulate diasporas as political formations in the context of the erosion of the Westphalian order. In the case of the Muslim experience (which, like all collectives' experiences, is riddled with division and diversity but still forms a unity), the category of diaspora as extended ethnicity is inadequate. While it is the case that there are many Muslims living as minorities throughout the world, the idea of a diaspora demands both a displaced population and a homeland – the point from which the displacement originates.[11] Such a homeland is clearly lacking in the Muslim case. We Muslims do not have a Zion – a place of redemptive return.[12] Also the universalist urge within many Muslim discourses makes it difficult to locate a unitary point of origin, and so there is no homeland, imagined or otherwise. In addition, there is no founding act of displacement. For the Muslim *Umma* is not only reducible to displaced population groups, it also includes the Muslim population in Muslim countries. It is for this reason, therefore, that the notion of diaspora seems an unlikely metaphor for describing the Muslim *Umma*. Thus, to read the Muslim experience as diasporic requires the reconceptualization of the notion of diaspora from demographic to political. Given these limitations I would like to suggest another way of understanding diaspora. It is possible to expand the idea of diaspora beyond its descriptive core, and there are a number of notions implicit in the descriptions of diaspora that would allow us to reconsider the idea of diaspora as a political formation.

Diaspora as an Anti-nation

Earlier I made the point that diasporas were dependent upon the discourse of nationalism. Without a form of nationalism it would be difficult to construct a diaspora. The idea that a diaspora is a nationalist phenomenon is, however, not the only way in which this phenomenon has been described. Diasporas have also been considered as *anti*-national phenomena. Unlike the nation with its homogeneity and boundedness, diaspora suggests heterogeneity and porousness. Nations define 'home', whereas diaspora is a condition of homelessness; in the nation the territory and people are fused, whereas in a diaspora the two are dis-articulated. The diaspora is not the other of the nation simply because it is constructed from the antithetical elements of a nation, it is, rather, an anti-nation since it interrupts the closure of nation. The existence of a diaspora prevents the closure of the nation, since a diaspora is by definition located within another nation.

The Jewish experience of diaspora acts as an illustration of the anti-national character of diaspora. Hannah Arendt (1973) shows how the parvenu/pariah distinction underwrote Jewish integration into European society during the period up to the Second World War and its aftermath. Arendt argues that Jews had two main subject positions open to them. One was based on assimilation. That is, the Jew became part of the 'host' society as an exceptional Jew. Somehow, one was a Jew in an exotic sense but, at the same time, was not a Jew. The other option available was that of total alienation. A Jew who was totally distinct from the 'host' did not belong to that society. The figures of parvenu or pariah both have problematic relationships with the idea of the nation, as both suggest that the nation is not home. The nation is not the place in which one's identity finds affirmation through the daily mundane rituals of life. The parvenu as a figure of obscure origins and recent recognition is a figure who is not settled. She arrives from unknown place, she gains prominence without trace, and she is clearly an exception to the rest of her 'race'. The pariah as a figure is clearly and unambiguously someone who is not at home – an outcast. Arendt's reflections on the relationship between identity and belonging after Nazism point to the importance of a notion of home as a way in which the nation sutures the subject. It is the nation as home that acts as an arena for our everyday practices, practices that give focus and meaning. If identity is 'a way of life', then the nation, by providing a home, is the stage upon which a particular way of life is enacted.

Those without homes face the prospect of trying to enact their 'way of life' off-stage. This is a task that they can accomplish only by using either a strategy of alienation and thus becoming a pariah, or by using a strategy of assimilation and thus being considered parvenu. In this sense, those members of a diaspora have a paradoxical relationship to the nation. On the one hand, they demonstrate the possibility of the strength of a nation in their attempt to maintain the sense of nationhood in the context of territorial dispersal. On the other hand, they point to the inability of a nation to be completed by making it difficult to erase difference. It is in this sense that the notion of diaspora is deployed as the antithesis of the nation. Members of a diaspora have an undecidable relationship with the idea of nations and homes; for example, Arendt's opposition to Israeli statehood stemmed from the privileging of 'Jewish homelessness' which allowed Jews to escape the blinkers of belonging to a single nation. In other words, the condition of homelessness is seen as a way of escaping the limits of ethnocentrism. Similarly, Gilroy evokes the 'Black Atlantic' as countering both what he perceives to be the cultural absolutism of black nationalism and closure of the western project. The Black Atlantic emerges as the name of a space that inhabits the West and that also transcends it. This use of diaspora as anti-nation, as a presence which subverts, hyphenates and hybridizes national identity, points to the impossibility of constituting a nation.

It is this undecidability that Arendt privileges in her account of the Jewish experience. Similarly, Gilroy in his description of the Black Atlantic makes an appeal to the experience of the African diaspora as constituting a marginal (undecidable) position within western modernity – being in the West but not of the West. Both Arendt and Gilroy see in the possibility of 'not-quite being a nation', a position that subverts absolutism. In these notions of homelessness there is a certain pathos. Homelessness suggests the possibility of being hyphenated and hybridized. If we understand a diasporic formation as being an anti-nation, then it becomes clear that what is involved in a diaspora is the deconcentration of power and subjectivity. In other words, the concept of diaspora dis-articulates the relationship between the political and the national. The nation focuses power and subjectivity; it makes the national subject the locus of power. Diaspora problematizes the possibility of establishing a relationship of coherence between power and subjectivity. What is of critical importance in the formation of a diaspora is the extent to which power and subjectivity are dispersed. This suggests that, in many ways, diasporas do not require the trinity of displacement, settlement and homeland. From this perspective, it would be possible to conclude that we are living in an age in which nations are being replaced by diaspora; that is, the dream of homogenous, hermetically contained spaces is being replaced by the idea of hybridized, porous collectives that flow and overflow through any attempt to contain them. However, I would suggest that such an understanding fails to acknowledge the nature of diasporic logic and fails to acknowledge the unevenness by which nations are transformed into diasporas.

The logic of diaspora is paradoxical. On the one hand it emphasizes the possibility of a nation in even the most difficult circumstances where the Westphalian order does not apply. On the other hand, it suggests the impossibility of a nation by preventing the nation from being fully formed, by deferring the moment of closure and absolutism. If diasporas are nations without homes, than the process of homelessness is not generalized; some nations are less likely to be homeless than others. If homelessness is a consequence of the way in which relations of power and collective sub-jectivities are dis-articulated, then this process is intrinsically political. It is a reflection of broader global struggles. A flavour of these struggles can be gleaned from recent publications such as *Jihad vs McWorld* (Barber 1996).

McDonalds@Mecca: Being at Home in the World

In this book, Benjamin Barber makes a distinction between the forces of global disintegration captured in the banalized idea of Jihad and the idea of global integration represented by the metaphor of an American fast-food chain. This dichotomy tends to suggest two different conceptions of the articulation of power and collective subjectivity. One, the road of Jihad, suggests the prospects of 'retribalization' and Balkanization: a global Hobbesian war against all, in which narrow particularities rage against modernity, against technology, against pop culture and against integrated markets – against the future itself. The road of Jihad seems to point to an attempt to assert nationhood (i.e. ideas of collectivities bound by cultures of authenticity and the exclusion of the possibility of heterogeneity).

In opposition to the idea of Jihad, we have McWorld, a place of

shimmering pastels, a busy portrait of onrushing economic, technological and ecological forces that demand integration and uniformity and that mesmerise peoples everywhere with fast music, fast computers, and fast food – MTV, and McDonald's – pressing nations into one homogenous global theme park, one McWorld tied together by communications, information, entertainment, and commerce. (Barber 1996: 4)

Although this global theme seems to promise heterogeneity, the form that this globality takes excludes that very possibility. In other words, the homogeneity associated with McWorld is culturally marked and as such it is more like the homogeneity associated with 'narrow particularism' writ large rather than an escape from particularisms. In this sense, McWorld is the latest trope in the history of exclusionary universalism that has characterized the western enterprise. As Geyer and Bright (1995) point out, it is this strange mixture of universalism and exclusion that has underwritten the West's relationship to the Rest and it continues to do so. McWorld is based on the domestication of difference and its reduction to superficialities. Underlying the diversity of surface effects is the idea of homogeneity founded upon the recognition that underneath our cultural skins we are all the same. The form this sameness reflects is our common unity based on our being human. This makes possible our concerns for the 'starving' in the Third World, it makes possible our demand and extension of human rights across the planet. It is only by focusing on our common humanity that we can avoid the tribalism promised by the advocates of Jihad. The snag with this comforting vision is that the notion of what the common human is, what constitutes those values and beliefs that arise from our common humanity and those that are incidental to essential humanness, tend to correspond also with the boundaries of the Enlightenment project. In other words, features that arise from common humanity too often become conflated with features associated with a particular cultural formation. Thus, the West becomes the only place where a human can be truly human, freed from the veneers of superstition and retrograde cultural practices; humans can express their humanness. This conflation of what is essentially western with what is essentially human is what excavates the heterogeneity from the globalization of McWorld. McWorld emerges not as a 'rainbow' formation where all human cultures find a home, but, rather, as an attempt to make the whole world a home for one way of life, one cultural formation. The difference between McWorld and Jihad comes down to matter of scale rather than of content, for both projects seem to be about making the world familiar. Making the world a home.

If, as a Believer (female or male), you go on *haj*, you may travel to the Red Sea port of Jeddah, from there you will take the road that has taken many believers before to the Holy City. The road leads up to the Haram; opposite the Haram there is an air-conditioned shopping mall; inside the shopping mall, the weary pilgrim who comes from far away will find a McDonalds fast-food restaurant. As in any other shopping mall in any other city, you are never far from a McDonalds. If the city that will not admit any others than believing women and believing men will admit a McDonalds – is not the Believers' world already lost?

Of course, it is possible to argue that the establishment of a fast-food chain does not really tell us very much about the ways in which global, cultural identities are being transformed. If chicken tikka masala can emerge as one of Britain's most popular dishes, then the appearance of a McDonalds chain in Mecca is equally insignificant. Why consider McDonalds to be more of a sign of cultural imperialism than General Motors or Sony? Is it really possible to make such sharp distinctions between those goods that are considered to be the carriers of cultural values and aspirations and those that are mute on this point? Surely, we have seen that even the Taliban came to recognize that it was not 'television' that was demonic or Western, since, once they captured Kabul and they began to broadcast their own programmes, their attitude to television changed.

The most common way in which a particular form or cultural object is given a specific identity is by privileging its moment of origin. The problem with such an approach is that it tends to confuse historiography with history. For example, most accounts of democracy see the process beginning in Ancient Greece (Athens being the model), developing in Europe and finally reaching its fullest form in the North Atlantic plutocracies. Such a sequence ignores the arbitrariness of constructing an origin from many beginnings and it ignores the possibility of other kinds of narratives that could reconstruct democracy as originating from other sites (for example, Sumerian city-states). As the furore over *Black Athena* suggests, the idea of specific historical trajectories is important in establishing the identities of forms and objects. I want to suggest that one sign of being at home is that the narratives that tell tales of origins are also narratives that project one's identity backwards. In other words, being at home means the world is familiar to us, because its institutions, rules and its complex web of relations are the same discursive productions that articulate our identities in terms of being 'at home'. There is then a sense of belonging that is produced through various hegemonic discursive practices. Being at home becomes a condition of the way in which these hegemonic narratives seem to be products of the articulation of our identity. In other words, it is not just that hegemonic practices are considered to produce our identity, but it is when our identity is manifested in those hegemonic practices that we can be considered to be at home. That is, when the world seems to be our mirror.

What I am suggesting is that being at home is no longer simply an empirical experience of the kind that, it is argued, becomes rarer as international movement is further restricted due to tighter immigration controls. Just because the movement of people is becoming rarer, it does not mean that more people are settled. The process of globalization is an attempt to make a home for some. This settlement implies that others have to be unsettled. In other words, does the redeployment of the Westphalian order and notions of diaspora on a planetary scale transform the rules by which we could conceive of diaspora as merely 'ethnic minorities' harking back to the lands of their origins? Diaspora is a condition of being homeless: that is, of being displaced and territorially diffused. But if this process is global, then the only way one can maintain the idea of a diaspora is to make the effects of global displacement specific rather than general. Global displacement is not a culturally neutral activity: the process of globalization imposes displacement upon some cultural formations by settling other cultural formations. This means that the logic of diaspora has a cultural specificity (arising out of current historical circumstances). The logic of diaspora includes those who are articulated as homeless in this world – that is, those for whom the global hegemonic order is not an echo of their subjectivity. The logic of diaspora is then not simply an interruption of the logic of the nation, it is also an interruption of the global hegemonic order: the logic of diaspora is culturally marked. It is this cultural marking which prevents the logic of diaspora becoming simply a synonym for an anti-nation. The logic of diaspora is not only anti-national, but, in present circumstances, when a particular national formation takes a global form, it also becomes anti-global.

In other words, the logic of diaspora cannot escape the most fundamental distinction: the distinction between the West and the Rest. It is this distinction that underpins the post-colonial world. Attempts to overcome the West/Rest distinction by pointing to *empirical multiculturalism* (that is, the existence of many cultures and the impossibility of thinking of one culture) and valorizing hybridity (the normative celebration of multiculturalism) fail because they ignore the way in which the West/Rest distinction is played out as the distinction between the hegemonic and subaltern and between the culturally unmarked and culturally marked. In the rest of this chapter I want to see to what extent this diasporic logic can help us to locate the Muslim *Umma*.

The *Umma* and Diasporic Logics

Earlier, I argued that the Muslim *Umma* could not be seen as a nation or a common market or a civilization. It can be argued that since the abolition of the Caliphate in 1924, the Muslim *Umma* has been increasingly parcelled out into 'nations' which, while consisting of Muslims, are not a reflection of a Muslim subjectivity (Sayyid 1997: 52–83). The nationalization of the Muslim *Umma* took place in two distinct domains. First, there was development of nationalism within the Ottoman Empire that helped to undermine the Ottoman state. This nationalism had two distinct phases. One was the phase when non-Muslim minorities within the Ottoman Empire began to demand rights of national determination. The second phase was the development of nationalism among the Muslim communities of the empire. These communities began to identify themselves as Turks and Arabs rather than Muslims and, as a result, the 'a-national' logic of Islam was replaced by national logic. In this set of circumstances, nationalism emerged in clear opposition to Islam. The second arena for the development of nationalism was among the Muslim subjects of the European empires. Decolonization often took the form of struggles of national liberation in which nationalism was articulated in opposition to European imperialism and thus its relationship to Islam was more ambivalent. Both these forms of nationalization raise doubts about what exactly the Muslim *Umma* is. It is not clear what kind of relationship is constitutive of the Muslim *Umma*; in other words, what kind of networks or interactions would have to exist for us to accept that there was a Muslim *Umma* and that it had an existence that was not merely rhetorical. There are three main reasons why many consider the idea of the Muslim *Umma* to be little more than an exercise in wish fulfilment.

First, it is pointed out that political projects based on the discourses of Muslim subjectivity have failed to make any headway in the Muslim *Umma*. The nationalist regimes of *dar-ul-Islam* continue and the Islamists have been unable to dislodge them even in Algeria or Egypt. The hegemony of the 'moderates' in post-Khomeini Iran is further evidence that even the regime most clearly identified with the articulation of a transnational Muslim subjectivity has retreated from its support of the idea of a unified Muslim *Umma*.[12] Second, arguments regarding the integration of Muslim communities into the global economy are seen as signs of the waning significance of Muslim identity. For example, it is argued that the Islamist rejection of modernity flies in the face of the desire of Muslims to have television, Coca-Cola, 501 Levis, McDonalds, etc.[13] Third, it is argued that any idea of the Muslim *Umma* is undermined by internal conflicts between Muslims. For example, the war between Iraq and Iran, Iraq's invasion of Kuwait, sectarian conflict in Pakistan and even among Muslim communities living in the North Atlantic plutocracies.

These ideas of what should constitute a Muslim *Umma* tend to under-theorize what exactly is involved in the construction of a collective identity. For example, the idea that unless there is total agreement among Muslims it is impossible to think of a unified Muslim presence would seem to suggest that a unified collective is possible only in conditions of unanimity. That is, a set of conditions in which there should be no possibility of a friend–enemy distinction and the impossibility of the political. Not only is such a set of affairs unlikely to be found among Muslims, it is debatable if it can be found in any other cultures or societies. The lack of unanimity does not prevent us deploying the category of Europe, even though in the last 100 years, intra-European conflicts have been responsible for over 50 million deaths. Muslim unity is thus possible in the absence of unanimity.

The notion of diaspora that I am advocating for the Muslim is not based on ethnicity (in the form of a common descent from an originary homeland). Nor is it merely metaphoric in the sense of trying to come to terms with the mismatch between peoples and places. I do not make the claim that Muslim identity is organic, but I do argue that, for various reasons, it is the subject position that currently has greater prominence than other forms of identification for those who describe themselves or are described by others as Muslims. I am also aware that there are many among those who would be constituted as Muslims who would reject the political significance of that appellation and who would refuse to accept the idea that there is a Muslim *Umma*. The idea of the Muslim *Umma* is an attempt to come to terms with the limits and the crisis of the nation-state. As forces and developments associated with globalization have weakened the institutional rigidity of the Westphalian state, cracks and gaps begin to appear in the international state system that provided the terrain for politics. Given the mobile and constructed nature of social identities, these fissures within dominant institutional forms of the nation-state have allowed different kinds of collectives to be articulated, taking advantages of these gaps. These formations seep through the Westphalian edifice, creating political formations that are neither in nor out of the nation-state, but that have an undecidable relationship to it. In this sense, diaspora is the name of this undecidable political formation.

This logic of diaspora suggests an attempt to create a full subjectivity in the form of the nation in the context when the nation cannot be completed. The Muslim *Umma* also points to a political project which, if successful, would produce a cultural formation which would be as remarkable or unremarkable as the Chinese or European but which would remain open, unable to construct itself around an ontological premise. The nationalization of the *Umma* was an attempt to destroy the possibility of the Muslim *Umma* as a universal cultural formation. Processes associated with globalization have lead to the denationalization of peripheral nation-state forms at the same time as the expansion of the central nations. The Muslim *Umma* occupies an undecidable position. Being clearly located within the periphery, it is subject to a process of denationalization, but this denationalization opens up the possibility of the reconfiguration of a cultural formation that is less and less particular and more and more universal. The inability of the Muslim *Umma* fully to articulate itself as universal means that it is caught in the logic of diaspora. The *Umma* interrupts and prevents the nation from finding closure and at the same time it points to another nation that will come into being at some point in the future. In this, the *Umma* is becoming – it is a horizon as well as an actuality. The current world is characterized by two types of decentring. There is the decentring of the West that marks the end of the Age of Europe and there is the decentring of the peripheral nation-state that is associated with globalization.[14] It is in this nexus between these two forms of decentring that we can locate the Muslim *Umma*, and it is this location which gives its diasporic form.

Notes

1. Castells places Islamist movements within the genre of religious fundamentalism and suggests that the latter has been present 'throughout human history'. While we

should not take this hyperbole too literally, it is clear that Castells' definition of fundamentalism has been taken without reservation from the flawed 'Fundamentalism Observed' project, which sees fundamentalism as a species of dogmatism that has been a constant in human history. Following this observation, Castells (1997) argues that 'Islamic identity is constructed on the basis of a 'double deconstruction' (p. 15) in which subjects must deconstruct themselves as national citizens or ethnic groups and '[W]omen must submit to their guardian men'. Castells refers to *Surah* IV, v. 34 as a way of justifying this claim. Of course, it is equally possible to pluck other verses from the Qur'an to demonstrate that the Qur'an is one of the few sacred texts that makes continual and frequent references to 'believing men and women', 'believing woman and man', and so on.

2. Castells also seems to conflate Ali and Hussein, by giving the date of Ali's assassination as the date of Hussein's martyrdom.

3. The collapse of the Soviet Union and its attendant population movements being the latest episode of western decolonization.

4. Mandaville 1998: 19. Mandaville's paper is an insightful overview of some the consequences of the erosion of the Westphalian order within the International Relations community.

5. Even the United States, which many would consider to be the most universal of nations, endeavoured to fulfil its manifest destiny – a destiny that was still bounded by the oceans.

6. See Hodgson's (1988) discussion of the difficulties of identifying civilizations.

7. Given our very different epistemological starting points, rather than engage in point-by-point analysis of Anthias' argument, it seems that what I should do is tell a more general story that will by-pass the points that Anthias makes and, at same time, make clear why I think that the notion of diaspora is useful for understanding the current status of the Muslim *Umma*.

8. Of course, one of the difficulties of someone like me engaging with someone like Anthias is that we belong to different epistemological tribes, we anti-foundationalists do not share the confidence in the neat separations that fundamentalist foundationalists have in positivist sociological categories, nor do we think that we can legislate the use of 'sociological categories'.

9. This one-sided anti-essentialism is fairly common; for a critique of this tendency see Sayyid 2000.

10. As Anthias correctly points out. See Anthias 1998: 561.

11. See, however, Yasin Aktay's use of the concept of diaspora to refer to Islam-orientated groups in Kemalist Turkey and their attempt to 'return' to the 'fundamentals' of Islam (Aktay 1997: 149–280).

12. See, for example, Roy 1994.

13. See Sayyid 1997.

14. It is in this sense that 'reflexive globalization' allows us to see the Western spectacle. See Hesse 1999a for an elaboration of this point.

Readings within a Diasporic Boundary: Transatlantic Black Performance and the Poetic Imperative in Sport

Brett St Louis

West Indians crowding to Tests bring with them the whole past history and future hopes of the islands. English people, for example, have a conception of themselves breathed from birth. Drake and mighty Nelson, Shakespeare, Waterloo, the Charge of the Light Brigade, the few who did so much for so many, the success of parliamentary democracy, those and such as those constitute a national tradition. Underdeveloped countries have to go back centuries to rebuild one. We of the West Indies have none at all, none that we know of. To such people the three W's, Ram and Val wrecking English batting, help to fill a huge gap in their consciousness and in their needs. (C. L. R. James 1994: 233).

In *Beyond a Boundary*, C. L. R. James asks the question: 'What exactly [is] art and what exactly culture?' (James 1994: 151). This can be extended to ask: what exactly is sport? Placing this addendum within oppositional political strategies and the theorization of 'race' alongside cultural processes and production demonstrates a series of epistemological and critical gaps. Offering a cartography of black social and cultural criticism, Paul Gilroy reminds us that the creativity of music within black strategies of resistance and acculturation within the West has, contrary to the role of Christianity, 'been less extensively commented upon' (Gilroy 1997: 104). If music has been under-examined as a creative form of black resistance, then sport in terms of cultural embodiment has arguably been ignored to an even greater extent. In this vein, the work of C. L. R. James illustrates the significant role of a rerouted bodily symbolic power. It not only expresses insight into anti-colonial struggles, it also highlights the imperatives of formulating a national culture and identity in the West Indies. In this way, James delineates within a sport like cricket a contested space which spurns the cathartic comforts of constructing a mythologized, homogeneous social condition attempting to erase all traces and resonances of a European past. For James, the critical interrogation of the meanings of culture and identity in a national, post-colonial locale necessitates the recognition and acceptance of historical antecedents, however traumatic or unpalatable they may be, as a means to evading the psycho-social dangers of a selective amnesia.

In stark contrast to this, much of the sociology of sport has productively concentrated on its immersion within distinct social structures (Brohm 1978; Hargreaves 1994; Cashmore 1996; Houlihan 1997; Polley 1998). Similarly, the sociology of 'race' and sport has occupied much of the same structural terrain (Cashmore and Troyna 1982; Williams 1994). In her insightful critique of the film *Hoop Dreams*, bell hooks (1996) paints a picture of the mirage of professional sport reinforced by overwhelming structural obstacles facing the inner-city black youth looking towards the seductive promise of the field. It appears that there cannot be a poetics of sport: poetics are attached to the cultural as cerebral, for which the physicality of sport is too base an enterprise. With great originality in *Beyond a Boundary*, James seeks to establish an outline for sport, and cricket in particular, not only as cultural production but as a 'legitimate' art-form. He sees an aesthetics within cricket that, attached to a humanist Marxism, offered possibilities for the redemption of human creative impulses marginalized within the tumult of modernism. However, his project has been much maligned, reproached as politically irresponsible in its aesthetic transcendence of structural and material social reality (Wynter 1981; Surin 1995; Tiffin 1995).

In this chapter, I resurrect and expand James's project to draw a set of insights into the expressive as well as the oppressive aspects of sport. First, I engage the exoticized construction of black performance as connected to a carefully constructed commercialism that strategically places the image of the black body at the vanguard of a rearticulated capitalism. Second, I uncover the separation of mind and body alongside 'race' as a crucial generating aspect of both hegemonic and oppositional discourse, precluding the positioning of sport as either cultural or radical performativity. Exploring the trajectory at which 'race' engages discourses of sexuality and drug abuse, I point to the strategic moments when the category of 'mind' is invoked in order to demonstrate an 'errant' blackness. Third, I extend the separation of mind and body to examine its incorporation into discourses of 'nation'. Finally, developing a concept of the poetic imperative and using the story of Matthew Bondman from *Beyond a Boundary*, I connect sport as cultural production and performance to some highly influential contemporary work that disrupts the understanding of ideological flows as unidirectional from hegemonic core to social subject (Gilroy 1987, 1993a;

Hall 1992; Mercer 1994). I seek to show that through engaging sport and the meaning of representational images of black performance, we can open a significant space for political engagement.

Packaging and Unpacking Black Performance

Thinking of sport in tandem with the slippery discourses of globalization, the figures of black performativity stand as cultural icons. Watching news footage of various 'Third World' natural and social 'disasters', it is not uncommon to be struck by the images of people wearing Chicago Bulls jerseys – usually Michael Jordan's number 23 – or the strips of various European football teams. However, as performance has become increasingly commercialized through an escalating culture of the body, we can also witness globalization's fault-lines. The downturn in sales and projected income from sportswear in Britain interrupts the image of the omnipotent marketing of sports through clothing. Expanding the perception of this constricted commercial horizon, the peripheral figures on the newsreel lack the income, disposable or otherwise, to represent a viable and sustainable market for western sporting equipment and apparel. Additionally, an important western cultural shift is taking place. In one of the most effusive marketing slogans of recent times, Nike invited us to 'just do it'. This mantra of 1980s drive and boundless self-sufficiency has been recently replaced with the more tactile coaxing of 'I can', arguably an attempt to reflect a more 'caring 1990s', recognizing obstacles in the way that require some negotiation. Reworking the doctrine of a work ethic with an emphasis on its capacity to cleanse us of the stresses of (post)modern life, much of this contemporary genre of advertising confronts process instead of an exalted production. It is no longer simply a matter of 'doing it', but *how* we do.

As performativity becomes a focal point of representing and marketing sport, the figure of the black sports person is shifted to a different cultural position. If market saturation is to be reached through expression over achievement, what better than the compelling image of exoticized black performance to convey this shift. So, in a Nike television commercial featuring heavily in the run-up to and during the 1998 football World Cup, we see the heavily romanticized images of carefree, naturalistic Brazilian footballers unable to contain their expressive urges while at an airport. They do not play football merely as a means to alleviate the boredom of being held in transit, they play with a certain *style*. To a seductive samba sound-track, these Brazilian artistes glide around the glistening chrome airport terminal, incorporating its functional appendages into their performance. Providing stark relief and performing dazzling tricks in the close vicinity of fellow travellers (us) they display a performativity that allows them to transcend the boredom and monotony of the advanced civilization that envelops us, resonant of what Aimé Césaire recognized as 'blue steel piercing mystic flesh' (Césaire 1995: 115). The primacy of process over result is emphasized in the ending of the advert. The last shot at 'the airport' hits an impromptu goalpost, to the nonchalant disdain of an young boy watching the display. The shot is taken by the young Brazilian global Nike 'poster-boy' and 1998 FIFA World Footballer of the Year, Ronaldo Luis Nazario de Lima or, simply, 'Ronaldo'. Ronaldo's human frailty, confirmed by the young boy, is supplemented by another series of Nike advertisements. Extolling the naturalistic joys of expression, these adverts featuring a multicultural group of footballing 'stars' parading as 'average', fallible 'guys' (us) are a clever rearticulation of brand re-inforcement. Footballing superstars presented as inept figures soothe our fear of our own inadequacies. If the black Frenchman and AC Milan midfielder Ibrahim Ba is rather clumsy after all, then our own lack of co-ordination does not disqualify us from being capable of playing for the Milan giants. Ultimately, the message is a simple and timeless marketing ploy: we can express our originality and non-conformity through allegiance to a particular brand.

Questioning the salience of certain debates on globalization, John Street (1997) suggests that many of its discourses apolitically suggest the emer-gence of a confident transnational popular culture. Conversely, in pointing to the operational structures of dominance within globalized popular culture, Street opens the door for standard Marxian questions on the relations of production. Therefore, even if globalization alternatively means selecting from an array of multicultural forms and styles through a trans-national medium, the construction of the representational images of these forms and styles conceals a particular axis or generative force. At this point, 'race', and the figure of the black sportsman as the messenger of this return to naturalism, become highly significant. Within a Eurocentric capitalist logic immersed in the cerebral, images of fluent naturalism cannot be expressed through whiteness; German footballers cannot offer a con-vincing representation of marauding free-expression within the cathedral of western civilization. Their archetype is one of Teutonic efficiency and technique. German skills, unlike those of the boys reared on the Copacabana beach – not the *favellas* of Rio de Janerio and São Paolo – are worked on, developed, and not innate. Similarly, the beautiful Nike cinematography of Michael Jordan dunking a basketball where time and space are arrested would not work in the same way with, say, his white Chicago Bulls team-mate Tony Kukoc. The messengers of an elegiac, carefree, romantic performativity are best represented in the figures of blackness. As James

Baldwin (1995) and Frantz Fanon (1986) remarked, the construction of blackness as the 'other' allows for the white recognition of discontentment and unease in a non-threatening space. Alongside this, in attempting to sell an aesthetic and physical aspiration, competence neither sells nor is sexy, but at the same time functionalism cannot be discarded. The figures of blackness offer a means to represent an elemental performativity that rearticulates but does not fundamentally disturb the foundations of capitalist logic. We express our naturalistic non-conformity through allegiance to a particular brand.

In Spike Lee's film *Do the Right Thing*, the character of Vito rationalizes his racism alongside his repulsion and compulsion towards Black people, by explaining that his favourite basketball player and actor are Michael Jordan and Eddie Murphy because they transcend their blackness or, in other words, they are packaged in a manner that makes them palatable to him. Safely conveyed to Vito's television through fibreoptic cable and acceptable to commercial stations, Jordan and Murphy contrast the transgressive 'niggers', undiluted by corporate America, who patronize his father's pizzeria. This tense cohabitation of attraction and repulsion demonstrates the complexity of the trajectories at which 'race' and desire intersect (Carby 1986; Fanon 1986; Young 1995). Within the representation of black sporting performance, 'race' and desire become complicated further by consumption. Especially in advertising, where desire is complicitous with consumption, romanticized Brazilian marauders and the gravity-defying Jordan are desirous images that impact on our lives through consumption or its potentiality. However, I want to suggest that this position is too straightforward and rather simplistic. Within this discourse, the relationship between desire and consumption becomes an a priori link, but which comes first, desire or consumption? Or, rather, is desire reducible to consumption?

Jean Baudrillard (1998) has been one of the most influential critics of the developing phenomenon of consumption within our contemporary historical phase of late-capitalism or post-modernism. Within the advent of post-industrial western societies, Fredric Jameson (1991) notes the movement of capitalism towards the cultural arena, creating (western) societies fixated with the 'spectacle' disseminated through a burgeoning media industry. Attendantly, the post-Second World War discourses of 'leisure-time' facilitated through time- and labour-saving consumer durables opened a discursive space for what Baudrillard (1998) calls the 'rediscovery' of the body. Within contemporary structures of production and consumption, Baudrillard notes that the body has become represented as both capital and fetishized object. Mirroring Pierre Bourdieu and Michel Foucault, Baudrillard suggests that the emergent narcissistic discourses, far from being self-generated, are a means of regulating social subjects through the

external controlling of their bodies. In this conceptual schema, the pack-
aging of black performance represents a double-bind. Watching the 1997
NBA College Draft on television, I was struck by the similarity between
the sight of a huge gathering of awkward-looking young black men in ill-
fitting suits awaiting their turn to be selected by future paymasters and the
parading of livestock on market-day. This selection process, a procedure
that hooks (1996) likens to the selection of slaves, sustains the lives and
imaginations of millions of young African-American males. Walking on to
the stage after selection, their nervousness and self-consciousness was
manifest. Even the swaggering bravado that some found was rendered
almost comical by their ill-fitting suits, their now unwieldy bodies placed
in stark contrast to the power and dynamism that they display on the
court. In this scenario it is easy to read the control of young African-
American men through their bodies. However, reading Baudrillard, this
control is discursive. The television audience complete the double-bind,
for even if they do not share a dream of playing in the NBA, the elevated
standard of physicality on display becomes surreptitiously linked to their
own self-perception and consumption. What happens the next time the
viewers receive junk-mail inviting them to join a gym at a special introductory price? What happens when they next see a magazine for sale
bearing the secret to achieving a 'six-pack' stomach? What happens when
they see the next commercial for dietary aids or easy-assemble, convenient
and cheap home exercise equipment?

The arguments of Jameson and Baudrillard appear compelling but, as
I mentioned above, there is a tendency to conflate desire with consumption.
Critiquing Gilles Deleuze and Félix Guattari (1977), Robert Bocock argues
that while we become socialized into capitalist consumption, it is mechan-
istically reductive to ignore that 'People are symbol-producing, symbol-
consuming, creatures' (Bocock 1993: 84). If it is symbols that are desirous,
then our interpretation of these symbols becomes crucial. Therefore, we
must ask whether the symbols of black performance are monolithic in their
meaning, or do they yield hermeneutic spaces that in turn offer the possibility for multiplicitous meanings? I want to argue that these deterministic
discourses of capitalist consumption do not account for the possibility of
alternative discourses of black performance. While Baudrillard recognizes
the 'recovery' of the body as a project for social control, the historical
separation of mind and body remains largely unadulterated. The capitalist
formation of consumption informing the culture of the body encourages
us to think critically about our bodies as a *discrete* entity, but not to think
critically about the epistemological and political algebra of this doctrine of
physical reformation. Additionally, this mind/body split regulates the
specific trajectory at which 'race' enters the discourses on cultures of

performance, irreducible to a unified social mechanism exercised through consumption. Desire articulated through images of black performativity provides certain exoticized, sexualized and infantilized representational images of blackness, separated in their specificity from consumption, that reiterate and reinforce social and global stratification and racism.

'Race', Mind, and Body

The national and cultural discourses that underpin the commercial representations of blackness on the sports field combine aspirational imagery with the maintenance of historical racialized discourses. Idealistically, within the tenets of consumption, the 'body' offers the inhabitants of the West a route towards redemption from the price of its technological advancement, the prison of standardization and bodily conformity. Anyone who has regularly commuted into a city centre to work becomes accustomed to the same faces, standing in the same position on the platform each morning. As our bodies are herded into train carriages and shuffle along pavements in oblivious unison, our minds are elsewhere. Within this discourse our bodies may be imprisoned but our minds are our own, they are free. The representational images of black sports people are the other side of the coin. Cavorting in an ecstasy of naturalistic physicality, these carefree dark bodies have no need for 'mind'. The freedom of play, childlike in its expressive enthusiasm, and being deeply instinctual, has no need for contemplation or cognitive action. Within the deployment of this paradigm, the durable Cartesian mind/body dualism, the figures of blackness are a perfect testament.

While blackness is 'body' but not 'mind', its 'otherness' is demonstrated as not only phenotypical contrast but also as a potent hyper-physicality. This discourse is not new but, as hooks (1996) notes, can be genealogically traced from that of the sturdy slaves fit enough, unlike the indigenous populations, to plough, sow and reap the soil of the Americas. The innocence of childhood encapsulated in the black body at 'play' also yields aspects of the incomplete mental, emotional and behavioural development of the former. Within the figure of the black sportsman, the mind/body split is enhanced: superb body, unstable mind. For examples, we need only think of the myriad stories of the intractable Ian Wright and Mike Tyson in constant contravention of their respective sporting, and sometimes legal, authorities. Revisiting the Nike airport scene, the French footballer Eric Cantona – also contracted to Nike – appears, sitting on board a plane on the runway. Renowned for his flamboyant skill and incendiary temperament – represented as a Gallic archetype – a besuited Cantona sits reading a broadsheet newspaper, his tranquil moment of intellectual contemplation disturbed fleetingly by the rampant naturalism of Brazilians introducing their enactment of an uncontrollable footballing vision to the runway.

Within this arena of an exalted physicality, sexuality looms large if only just beneath the surface of consciousness, as also noted in some psycho-analytical discourses on consumption. Extending the scope of the mind/body split, black performativity does not just appropriate images of black-ness as body within the public sphere, but incorporates the private. The sexual connotation of black performance recalls historical mythologies and pathologies of the black hyper-sexuality (read animalistic) attached to the practice and justification of the rape and lynching of black women and men (Carby 1986). Therefore, within an increasingly integrated media, black sportsmen are hyper-representations of the sexual preoccupation of the black body that lurks threateningly within all black men, evident in a range of examples from Mike Tyson to Clarence Thomas to Michael Jackson. The connection of blackness and sexuality within sporting repres-entational images can be read as a means to display black sexualities that are always 'errant', outside of what is considered 'normal' in prevalent social discourses. I am not suggesting that black representational images ought in turn to reiterate 'normality', but instead note their use as 'other', ratifying the sanctity of a 'standard' heterosexuality. Black heterosexuality becomes represented as the uncivilized animalism that white western society has managed to transcend by cultivating 'mind' and the human faculty of reason. Therefore, even though the expression of heterosexuality is, in general terms, 'normal', the specificity of black sexuality read from sporting representational images demonstrates instinctual, unpoliced primal urges that are uncivilized and injurious to a cohesive civil society.

There are certain moments when the black male body becomes re-articulated with a certain emasculating ambiguity, also evident within the sphere of sexuality. Stuart Hall (1997) points to a Pirelli advertising poster featuring the African-American sprinter Carl Lewis on a track wearing full race clothing and women's stiletto-heeled shoes under the caption, 'Power is nothing without control', as offering an ambiguous representative image of black masculinity. However, remembering the British decathlete Daley Thompson's offensive and juvenile wearing of a T-shirt asking 'Is the world's second-best athlete gay?' on his lap of honour at the 1984 Olympic games and the public speculation over Lewis's sexuality, the fact that Pirelli featured Lewis and not Ben Johnson, Linford Christie or an anonymous black male model is significant here. The overt message of the advert – 'Power is nothing without control' – would not have been altered were a female sprinter featured instead of Lewis. The portrayal of the articulate Lewis, a graduate of the University of Texas at Houston, as 'body' in the charged context of an ambiguous sexuality and on the track in the 'set' position demonstrates the fixation with the 'errant' sexualization of the Black body.

As black performance is encoded with a sliding 'errant' sexualization, the issue of drug abuse supplements the repertoires that emasculate and invalidate the black body. Additionally, the theme of drug abuse provides a critical juncture where a non-infantilized mind enters black performance and the exoticized monumental potency of the black body becomes demonized through this sudden introduction of 'mind'. No longer rendering black performance as independent of or devoid of mind, the western discourses that have constructed the supremacy of the black body enter an introspective critique, questioning the very representational image that it has created. The omnipotence of the black body becomes a fallacy, sullied and falsely sustained by the misappropriation of advanced chemical technologies. The ignoble drug-test failure and demonization of Canadian sprinter Ben Johnson at the 1988 Seoul Olympics provides a stark example of this. The uncovering of Johnson's 'cheating' led to his emasculation, the magnificence of his black body as 'body' rudely interrupted by the imprudent intervention of his unstable mind. The frailty of black 'mind' introduces not only a discrepant rationality, but also an inherent immorality and lack of ethics, making the 'other' unsuited for civilized social congregation. Forming the basis for eugenic theories of black criminal congeniality, opposing the ethically vacuous capitalism that Richard Wright famously paints as the generative impluse for his murderous protagonists in *Native Son* and *The Outsider*, the genetic material of black people becomes incompatible with advanced, civilized society.

This invalidation of the black body is not confined to men. The *Guardian* obituary of Florence Griffith Joyner in the late summer of 1998, 'Drama, dazzle and the doubt', concentrated on the suspicion of drug-taking that surrounded her achievements.[1] This is interesting reading when one considers the reaction, that same summer, when the president of the International Olympic Committee, Juan Antonio Samaranch, initiated a debate about the possible relaxation and regulation of hitherto proscribed performance-enhancing drugs. Samaranch sparked a ripple of moral panic on the sports pages, some indignant riposte but nothing approaching the vilification of Johnson or the bitter tenor of the remembrance of the tragically short life of Griffith Joyner. The other major drugs-in-sport story of the summer of 1998 was the uncovering of widespread and systematic drug abuse by many teams and cyclists on the Tour de France. Media reaction to this was mixed, certain strands even flirting with the idea floated by Samaranch. Towards the end of the Tour, Duncan Mackay wrote in the *Guardian*: 'admiration must be the emotion that most television viewers experience as they watch the Tour de France. Pity might be more appropriate. For within five or 10 years some of the cyclists could be seriously ill – or even dead.'[2] While the culture of drug abuse in sports is here rightly heralded as a human tragedy, the failure to extend this lament and human consideration to Ben Johnson and Florence Griffith Joyner is significant. The cyclists on the punishing terrain of the Tour de France exercised a warped logic: 'living now paying later: buying success on hire purchase.'[3] Supported by the justificatory comment of a drug-using cyclist on the 1996 Tour, 'If you're in a war and everyone is using machine-guns, you need to go out armed with at least a pistol,'[4] the warped logic is a logic none the less.

In this section I have largely talked about the separation of mind and body in the dominant representations of black sporting performance. But how do we argue against this? How do we instigate alternative decodings of representational images and symbols of black performance that challenge and surpass these hegemonic discourses? The project of thinking about and discussing black performance requires a significant reconsideration of our conception of physical production. Even in challenging Eurocentric western discourses and revealing the racialized pathologies attached to the black body, the separation of mind and body is deeply entrenched in our epistemological assumptions. It is easy to distil a discussion of Michael Jordan to his 'body', even when arguing against the reification of the representational image of him. Jordan, as 'body' in his Nikes fashioned by 'innocent' and 'dexterous' juvenile and female hands in the sweatshops of South-East Asia, can be easily dismissed as the pawn of capitalism's 'mind'. However, whether coming from a concerted political position, and/or as black people, one of 'race', some of us can criticize Jordan because we are 'black mind'. We have transcended our bodies, and in developing our minds we have rid ourselves of the taint of our bodies. We have graduated to the seriousness and sagacity of 'mind' and left our bodies behind.

Returning to the relationship between desire and consumption outlined above, there is a certain 'relative autonomy' that is lost in the privileging of material outcomes over physical process and performance. If our contemplation of black performance is distilled to its positioning within social structures, we cannot wholly understand the significance and meaning of the performance itself. In saying this, I want to suggest that sport presents a *potential* space for the fusion of mind and body and not its separation. The footballer, tennis player or wide receiver awaiting or anticipating the ball has to know where and when to run. Their physical abilities must be allied not only to a spatial awareness, but also to a heightened imaginative concept of the potentiality of space. Running needs to be timed strategically in order to correspond with the anticipation of a possible future occurrence. A prematurely executed run and the footballer is offside or the wide receiver allows the cornerback the time to 'drop deep', negating the desired outcome. This is an issue of technique, not mere brute physicality. Technique as mental understanding of a physical practice provides a synthesis of mind and body. Linford Christie did not 'run' down the track, but was acutely aware of applied bio-mechanics. He knew precisely what his arms and knees had to be doing, the correct position for his hips, and that, in true dialectical fashion, he had to relax and 'try less' in order to run faster. When we witness the encampment of Kenyan distance runners on the medal rostrum at major international games, we are seeing not the manifestation of 'natural talent', but the result of the unity of physical ability and mental preparation.

In some quarters, however, this synthesis of mind and body in technique may appear somewhat mystical or even utilitarian. Pierre Bourdieu points to the illusory and phantasmical formation of the *game* that draws on the insiders' discourse of having a 'feel for the game', a phrase which in itself, 'gives a fairly accurate idea of the almost miraculous encounter between the *habitus* and a field, between incorporated history and an objectified history, which makes possible the near-perfect anticipation of the future inscribed in all the concrete configurations on the pitch or board' (Bourdieu 1990b: 66). Additionally, this sensory perception of the game also gives it an 'objective sense' in that the individuals encountering this discourse uncover a sense of order and rationality in its construction, creating 'the effect of consensual validation which is the basis of collective belief in the game and its fetishes' (p. 66). Concretizing the abstractions of the game within society, Bourdieu suggests that it cannot harvest a radical humanism as it depends on bad faith in that the followers of the game cannot bring their consciousness to bear on the field which, exhibiting the power of discourse, always interpellates its imperatives through them: 'agents never know completely what they are doing [and] that what they do has more sense than they know' (p. 69).

However, this structuralist discourse offers a foothold for the contingency of a relative autonomy within sport, as Bourdieu recognizes that all social orders systematically use the body and language to collate and activate certain ideological directives. Therefore, the significance and potency of 'collective ceremonies' (the game) not only create representations of the group, but also construct social formations through the 'symbolic power' of the body that generate belief and behavioural patterns. We can either go down Baudrillard's path of inextricably connecting the 'symbolic power' of the body to hegemonic repertoires, or we can seek to excavate relatively autonomous discourses of black performativity. This is not to say that bodily symbolic power of black performance bears the indelible hallmark of a triumphalist resistance, but to suggest that eliciting meaning from social practices is a struggle that ultimately privileges neither individual subject nor state power. The oscillating fortunes of this struggle over the symbolic power of the body are best seen and understood in the connection of black performance to discourses of 'nation'.

Representing 'the Race' and Nation in Mind and Body

The fusion of mind and body in black performance that challenges its Cartesian separation most often becomes apparent when the resonance of the performance is extended outside the field. As mentioned above, it is easy to criticize Jordan's complicity with the exploitation of female and child labour. While not seeking to excuse or condone this, we may also ask whether Pete Sampras, also a 'Nike-man', is confronted with this same political responsibility. With his successes understood as examples of naturalistic physicality, Jordan's failings become representative of larger social issues and introduce his 'mind' into the discourse. Asking why Jordan bears the weight of widespread political criticism for the policy of his paymasters, criticism that his corporate colleague Sampras is somehow exempt from, connects to Hazel V. Carby's (1998) theme of 'race men'. Carby offers an insightful commentary here, mapping the weight of prospective social redemption that is placed upon the bodies of representative men. In this sense, as a black cultural figure, Jordan's body becomes inherently politicized and bears a representational responsibility and burden.[5]

The discourses of nation that are attached to sport are subject to a certain slippage as they can be deployed both to representations of femininity and masculinity. However, while the 'race man' is prescriptively invested with the capacity to critique and re-create the nation, the connection of women on the field to nation is more passive and descriptive. While Jordan is implicated in and bears the responsibility of addressing global inequality, Florence Griffith Joyner's *Guardian* obituary hints at the pivotal role of her domestic struggle, the social deprivation of childhood and subsequent hardship. Reading that she 'was the seventh of 11 children … [and] started running at the age of seven and competed until 1979 [aged 20], when she had to give up her college career to support her family,' we enter a familiar stereotype of the struggles of the urban black underclass that invite and explain, if not justify, the racialized particularity of moral weakness. We may recall that after winning the 1994 Commonwealth Games 400 metres title representing Australia, Kathy Freeman's lap of honour holding aloft the flag of Aboriginal peoples made far less of a political impact than the infamous image of Tommie Smith and John Carlos standing on the medal rostrum, black-gloved fists raised to the sky at the 1968 Mexico City Olympic games.[6] The way that 'race' is articulated with 'nation' in these examples of masculinity and femininity is significant in its demonstration of politicized symbolic power residing in men while the resonance of women's performance is both depoliticized and localized, confined to the domestic sphere where possible.

When the *fusion* of mind and body in black performance is engaged *within* the field, it can tend to relate to material outcomes, success or failure, largely the latter. This is especially evident in the problematic conflation of 'race' and nation in sport which is fought out over the contested terrain of citizenship. The sight of successful black British track and field athletes on a lap of honour draped in the Union Jack is contrasted with the questioning of the national commitment and authenticity of the unsuccessful. The perceived underachievement at international level of the footballer John Barnes and the cricketer Devon Malcolm has, in certain media circles, often been attributed to their being born outside Britain. Within this discourse, their disconnection from the soil of Britain at birth lessens their investment in the national 'cause'. Chris Searle points to this discourse and, in particular, to Robert Henderson's 1995 article 'Is it in the blood?' in *Wisden's Cricket Monthly*, as a part of a wider racist English discourse within the same historical moment, complemented by the Metropolitan Police's 'Operation Eagle Eye', which targeted black youth 'as the prime cause of London street crime' (Searle 1996: 50).[7]

However, this discourse of blood as an inextricable signifier of nation is used strategically. Notably, the underachievement of the white South African middle-distance runner Zola Budd, imported with offensive haste in time to register for the 1984 British Olympic team, escaped the critique attached to John Barnes and Devon Malcolm. In contrast, Budd was cast as a young, vulnerable athlete, traumatized by her collision with the American favourite Mary Decker Slaney in the Olympic final and placed under intolerable stresses by the rabid anti-apartheid lobby, which sought a public statement of her position on South African racial politics. In steadfastly refusing to comment on apartheid, Budd's position was received as defensible and indeed laudable in her principled intention to keep politics and sport separate. With the articulation of whiteness and sport transcending the crude intrusion of politics, the acceptable circumstances for linking politics, nation, and sport are evident when 'race' becomes 'visible'. This strategic slippage becomes glaringly evident as Searle recalls the Conservative Party politician Norman Tebbit's notorious 'cricket test': 'you are only truly English if you support England at cricket when they are playing against the national team of your country of origin, be it Pakistan, Sri Lanka, India or the West Indies' (Searle 1996: 46). This unqualified ethnocentrism can be linked to the signification of the pristine 'Nike airport' which offers a metaphor for the centrality of the metropolis, the space from where its tentacles reach out to the peripheral locales. The airport reminds us of the Euro-American axis on which our multicultural world revolves. That the multicultural nation is predicated on certain metropolitan premises is manifest as Searle notes that, for Henderson, 'the oppression and exploitation of Empire and colonialism are "post-imperial myths" purveyed by "Negroes" and "Asians"' (p. 46).

The articulation of discourses of 'race' and nation within sport are, however, not always constructed negatively. But the absence of negativity does not inherently imply positivity: representations of sport and Black performance have long been used as a means to paper over the cracks of social cleavages. In the aftermath of the French victory in the 1998 football World Cup, Nick Fraser suggests that: 'The triumph of France's multi-ethnic football team has united the nation ... it could be the start of a new era.'[8] Interestingly using a metaphor evoking Carby's (1998) concept of the cricket field as a space where men embodying the nation engage in battle, Fraser likens the excitement in Paris to the day of liberation from German occupation in 1944. Fraser recovers a French national unity sealed by the diverse ethnic origins of the team extending from France to the Basque country, Armenia, French Polynesia, Senegal, Ghana, Algeria, Argentina and Guadeloupe, against the grain of French far-Right racism. The fraternal possibilities of multicultural France presented by the success of the national football team united the nation behind the Tricolor, which overnight became the property and pride of a cohesively heterogeneous people. The script continues to read that the nation realized its triumph drawing on the racial and ethnic mosaic that it had previously mis-understood as divisive. The key factor here, which is totally overlooked, is the World Cup-winning *success* of the French team, and on home territory as well. Had they lost, maybe defeat would have been, even at least partially, attributed to an inchoate team lacking an authentic Frenchness around which to solidify and congeal. To drown out the newly formed multi-cultural choir's rendition of *La Marseillaise* with a sombre song, bell hooks' (1996) commentary on the overall scope of the film *Hoop Dreams* shrewdly notes the constricting effect that competition and success within a culture of domination can have on the meaning of sport, its message, and capacity to inform radical social transformation.

Against these compelling examples of the manipulation of the symbolic power of the body it is difficult to wrest black performance back towards a politically oppositional stance. Allen Dunn (1998) claims that in *The Rules of Art*, Bourdieu outlines a science of aesthetics that attempts to strip away the mystical powers and category of genius that are conferred upon certain individuals in performance and creation, and that the meaning of aesthetic symbols is subject to certain historical shifts. Significantly,

Dunn raises the possibility that Bourdieu can be read more optimistically than he intends, linking Bourdieu's normative ideal of freedom to 'the possibility that an aesthetics of the future, whether scientific or not, might be more than a meditation on a world of constraints and illusions' (Dunn 1998: 89). It is important to understand this within the setting of a post-colonial national identity which not only acknowledges the formative influences of the metropolis, but inherits the complex entanglements of western culture. Symptomatic of this setting are crises and contradictions within metropolitan civilization itself. I now want to turn to the concept of the poetic imperative to illustrate these crises and contradictions and the obstructions that they present for comprehending the symbolic power of Black performance.

The Poetic Imperative and the Art of Resistance

At the beginning of *Beyond a Boundary*, James draws a compelling insight into the power of cricket as a site for artistic production and the profound effect of this production in addressing and fulfilling the aesthetic imaginings and longings of the spectators and the larger community. Introducing us to Matthew Bondman and his family, who lived next door, James depicts them as the antithesis of the puritanical reserve of the Jameses, from whom they rented their home. James remembers Matthew Bondman as an aggressive young man with an anti-social demeanour: 'He was generally dirty. He would not work. His eyes were fierce, his language was violent and his voice was loud. His lips curled back naturally and he intensified it by an almost perpetual snarl. My grandmother and my aunts detested him. He would often without shame walk up the main street barefooted' (James 1994: 3–4). However, Matthew Bondman represented one of James's first profound experiences of the 'personality in society', for while the young James was disturbed by Bondman's talent for invective and aggressive behaviour, it was his cricketing 'alter ego' that captivated James and rendered the memory with an intensity and acute resonance: 'For ne'er do well, in fact vicious character as he was, Matthew had one saving grace – Matthew could bat. *More than that, Matthew, so crude and vulgar in every aspect of his life, with a bat in his hand was all grace and style*' (p. 3, emphasis added). The problematic that confronted James was the disparity between Bondman's aggressive persona within the larger society and the grace with which he expressed himself at the wicket. How was it that Bondman could be such a transgressive social personality in combination with his archetypal expression of the quintessential *English* game? In confronting this question, it is possible to initiate the recognition of the 'relative autonomy' of the aesthetic realm and its informative role in our political understandings of sport and the representational images of blackness.

While both the wider society and the wicket are social spaces, the latter opens up a distinct expressive possibility for Bondman. This distinct facility can be recognized within an articulatory mode that I call the 'poetic imperative'.[9] This poetic imperative refers to the capacity and compulsion of an individual to create moments of artistic beauty, or as James and the aestheticians might say, 'significant form'. The purpose of the poetic imperative is to invest certain individuals with the capacity *and compulsion* to create these moments of significant form, but only in that they express it to a mass of people not solely comprised of members of an elevated social class. The ability to comprehend the articulation of significant form ought not to depend on an extensive technical or bio-mechanical knowledge. The recognition and comprehension of significant form is represented as a human reflex that is individually determined, both within and outside dominant social discourses and structures, attempting to evade the ascriptive and hierarchical tenor of perfection as promoted by the Spanish Falange. For example, the variety of specific inflections that comprise the execution of a cover-drive or, indeed, an absorption of its totalized performance, can be regarded as beauty or the articulatory moment of significant form. However, while James attempts mystically to collectivize a specific instinct-ive human reflex, I want to trace how taste and discretion are constructed within society and are ideological in formation.

There are certain constructed criteria of taste that confront the con-centrated observer of human movement (Bourdieu 1984). For some it may be a specific choreographed gesture within modern dance or ballet; for myself, the British sprint hurdler Colin Jackson in full flight or the West Indian batsman Carl Hooper driving off the front foot are beautiful and moving sights. To the observer, and maybe especially to the experienced one, each protagonist's movement is as intrinsic as a signature, the inflection applied to the execution of the generic action capable of moving us. Critiquing Kant and neo-Kantian concepts of autonomous 'taste', Bourdieu argues that the senses and tastes – including that of beauty – of the 'socially informed body ... never escape the structuring action of social determinisms' (Bourdieu 1977: 124). Bourdieu's proposition is problematic only in the sense that it assumes that the only possible outcomes of 'social determinisms' are negative and oppressive. However, Bourdieu's pessimism can be challenged if we rethink the deployment and agency of the body in terms of performance as *articulation*.

According to Stuart Hall, the concept of articulation

asks how an ideology discovers its subject rather than how the subject thinks the necessary and inevitable thoughts which belong to it; it enables us to think how an ideology empowers people, enabling them to begin to make some sense or intelligibility of their historical situation, without reducing those forms of intelligibility to their socio-economic or class location or social position. (Grossberg 1996: 142).

Therefore, for Hall, the way that discursive formations are constructed does not denote inevitability, they are *not* necessary and, therefore, can be transformed. Encountering the meanings and understandings of black performance within sport, I want to argue that through applying the concept of the poetic imperative we can begin to conceive how the internal discourses of sport regarding 'race' and performativity can be articulated in different *ways*. In order to outline this project, I want to return to the prototypical socio-poetics of sport, C. L. R. James's *Beyond a Boundary*.

Situating cricket as a important signifier in the anti-colonial struggle, James illustrates the political role of black performativity, a performativity that nevertheless has an aesthetic relative autonomy. Writing on a highly charged symbolic encounter during the West Indies' cricket team 1963 tour of England, James notes the articulation of the poetic imperative:

> There was another stroke that I remember in the Oval match by the little wicket-keeper, Murray. He came in and Trueman or somebody bowled him a short ball. And then he got back on his right foot and put him through extra-cover to the boundary. *Soon he was out but that stroke had been made.* (James 1986: 144–5, emphasis added)

The historical and geographical context of this moment is extremely significant. West Indian nations are beginning to gain independence. The scene is Kennington, in the heart of the heart of the metropolis, five years after the Notting Hill riots, and five years before Enoch Powell's 'rivers of blood' speech. Historically, the organization of West Indian cricket had reflected colonial power, therefore the symbolism of winning a test series in England would have contributed towards exploding the myth of the superiority of empire.[10] However, alongside the social meanings of the match – its social determinisms – James isolates the creative moment, the expression of the poetic imperative, with relative autonomy, from the material symbolism of the match: '*Soon he was out but that stroke had been made.*' When Murray batted, the match and the series win was far from certain yet, despite not being a specialist batsman, he strove to express himself in a creative manner, to articulate a moment of beauty that both he and the assembled crowd could understand, each in their own specific way.

This may appear contradictory to my critique of the possible subversive symbolic power of the French World Cup-winning football team, but there are two reasons for suggesting otherwise. First, it was an event within a historically established and evolving discursive counter-narrative to the authority of empire. Second, and significant to the articulation of the poetic imperative, the aesthetic relative autonomy of the performance relegates success to the status of a peripheral discourse. The hegemonic discourse of competition and success has often been used to negate the emancipatory possibilities attached to Matthew Bondman's performance outlined above (Wynter 1981; Surin 1995). Resolving the disparity between Bondman's aggressive behaviour and his stylish strokeplay at the wicket, Sylvia Wynter and Kenneth Surin offer different but generally socio-economic explanatory arguments founded in his social marginalization. For Wynter, Bondman inhabited a liminal space directly transmitted from the social conditions of plantation society where the creativity of the slaves was obstructed in order to maintain the primacy of their capital value, proscribing 'their living their own radical historicity' (Wynter 1981: 59). Employing a different emphasis, Surin notes that his social marginalization limited Bondman's artistry to the wicket. Bondman, like other black West Indian batsmen, was not allowed to build a world but could only 'testify with his bat to the absence, in the prevailing social and political realms, of that world which would come to exist once West Indian government became a reality' (Surin 1995: 315–16).

Conversely, I argue that these critiques of Bondman are flawed in at least one crucial sense: they evade the question of why did he bat in the manner that he did? And what specific meanings were attached to his performance within his community? Noting Bondman's aggressive personality, he might have been expected to attempt to expel the ball to the boundary with all the violence that he could summon. Additionally, regarding his batting as an expression of the poetic imperative, Bondman initiates a subversive redirection of the ideological flows of the archetypal expression of English colonialism. James illustrates how the symbolic power of Bondman's performance was separated from the constricting discourses of competition and success:

> When he practised on an afternoon with the local club people stayed to watch and walked away when he was finished. He had one particular stroke that he played by going down low on one knee. It may have been a slash through the covers or a sweep to leg. But, whatever it was, *whenever Matthew sank down and made it, a long, low 'Ah!' came from many a spectator, and my own little soul thrilled with recognition and delight.* (James 1994: 4, emphasis added)

James then continues, broadening the symbolic power of Bondman's performance:

Matthew's career did not last long. He would not practise regularly, he would not pay his subscription to the club. They persevered with him, helping him out with flannels and white shoes for matches. I remember Razac, the Indian, watching him practise one day and shaking his head with deep regret: how could a man who could bat like that so waste his talent? (James 1994: 4).

It is deeply significant that the people assembling to watch Bondman were prepared to do so in a non-competitive context – they came to watch him practise. That is to say that, ultimately, they desired to witness the creative moment of significant form that would move them to the core of their own existence. This communitarian impulse is questioned by Althusser's anti-humanism, which argues that the notion of a universal essence of man suggests an *'empiricism of the subject'*, necessitating each empirical human subject carrying the entire human essence resulting in an *'idealism of the essence'* (Althusser 1969: 228). However, I would argue that understanding Bondman's artistic production through the poetic imperative allows for the discernment of a singular expression to be filtered through the particularized and differentiated nuances of each specific observer. There is something to see and be moved by only if one sees it. In discovering a moment of beauty expressed through Bondman, the crowd witnessed and encountered significant form in its relative autonomy. The symbolic power of Bondman's performance was removed from the exclusionary, competitive sphere that it occupied within a wider, material social situation that orients the representative image towards externally regulated consumption. Understanding this communal observation as a political act, rearticulating the colonial tenets of cricket as promoting the absolute authority of rules and process, the articulation of black performance under a non-stratified and exoticized gaze takes on new ideological meanings.

As the 'code' of cricket is often collapsed into a category understood as Bourdieu's 'structuring action of social determinisms' – fairness, manners, the rule of law and process – this tends to be a matrix for comprehending representational images of the body on the field. However, in cricket, as in sport in general, I want to argue that there is a subsidiary code, a relatively autonomous aesthetic code articulated through the poetic imperative that can harvest counter-narratives. I want to suggest that the resistance to this subsidiary code within James's cricket writing is generated by the historical bourgeois taint that contaminates aesthetics, rendering it antagonistic towards an oppositional political project. However, this resistance constructs and fixes the project of an oppositional politics to the terrain cultivated by capitalist state power. The demands of inhabiting this space lead Helen Tiffin into reiterating the hegemonic dualism of expressive performativity and social structure in her critique of the political possibilities of aesthetics whereby 'individuals have creative moments which lift them, with one stroke or ball out of the realm of social reality and into art' (Tiffin 1995: 367). Reading cricket as generated by a singular code, a colonial moral and ethical directive, Mark Kingwell (1995) recognizes 'taste and discrimination' as an enclosed, historically static discourse, exclusive to the moneyed classes while the working class is solely defined by its relations of production. Therefore, even if we want to think in the classical Marxist binarisms of class and social position,[11] working–class radical self-activity is confined to the economic sphere, its entire ontology is collapsed into the experience of waged–labour, the only relations of production that concern it are economic.

Understanding representional images as 'produced' and implicated in the structural formation of society, then, their relations of production may offer an insight into critiquing and dismantling oppressive social structures. Returning to the example of Matthew Bondman, we can ask: why ought he to have packaged his artistic production for articulation in an externally regulated space? Bondman's subversive ownership of his bodily production also grounds the slippery concept of 'agency'. Recognizing his body as an entity that he could control within an alienating society, Bondman realized the reconfigurated cultural capital of its attendant production, rejecting the regimentation and commodification of his artistry that submission to organized competition meant. In refusing to enter a rarified social space that he was summoned to in order to perform only to be returned to his sub-stratum, Bondman rejected the coercive moral and ethical code of cricket. Expressing himself within cricket's aesthetic code meant that its emancipatory possibilities afforded him the opportunity to realize his highest creative aspirations as well as repelling the seductive promise of transient class elevation.

Conclusion

The political task for the poetic imperative is to uncover a method for reconfiguring the symbolic power of the representational images of (black) performance. Historicizing fine art, Jean Baudrillard (1981) recognizes the illegitimacy of the copy as a modernist discourse whereas in the nineteenth century the copy had its own value. Baudrillard points to the importance of the signature as the legitimizing factor of the artistic medium with modernity where the sign denotes the subjectivity of authenticity that objectifies social consensus and commercial value. In terms of sport, bodily lines of significant form are 'signed copies', the signature lying in the specific inflection of the performativity. A redirected reading of sporting representational imagery can be observed that contests the reduction of an oppositional politics to solely addressing industrial concerns with increased pay, better conditions of employment, shorter work hours and a culture of leisure-time. The recent developments at the Wimbledon lawn tennis championships, where the balls have been made lighter in order to counter the tedium of the insistent brutality of the men's game offer a case in point. The popular disenchantment with the incessant 'serve and volley' tactic of the men privileging crude power has led to a greater interest in the women's game, where creative skills and artistry illustrating significant form remain prevalent. The Brazilian public disappointment with their pedestrian victory in the 1994 football World Cup after a twenty-four-year wait provides another expression of the critical understanding of form over content. Historically and contemporaneously, there is a political struggle evident in the moments when jazz ceases to be 'dance' music and becomes an art-form, and when drum and bass music provides the sound-track to television adverts. Just as these forms of black and 'urban' cultural production are labelled as 'subcultures' when in fact the commercial centres of authenticated culture are in their slipstream, we can also ask what did multiculturalism mean when we witnessed the careful racial manicure of 'Cool Britannia'? The ascension of a non-rugged muscularity opens up sport in the structural sense as the old dualism of mind and body becomes pressurized. However, this is only part of the struggle. We need a socio-poetics of sport that will critique racist and sexist representational images of performance as well as transforming the social structures and meanings.

Notes

1. *Guardian*, 22 September 1998.

2. *Guardian*, 19 July 1998.

3. Ibid.

4. *Guardian*, 18 July 1998.

5. In a significant intervention, Stuart Hall notes 'the end of the innocent notion of the essential black subject' (Hall 1992: 254), reminding us that political mobilization around blackness and black readings of representational images need not necessarily yield a progressive perspective.

6. Obviously, the juxtaposition of these two political acts of dissent are situated in separate and distinct historical moments. However, accepting the historical specificity of the transnational political ferment of 1968, the issue of Aboriginal land rights and reparations in Australia is a bitter ongoing dispute. The lack of attention to the political content of Freeman's gesture was significant as it represented a marked contrast to the typical practice of the winners' uncritical shrouding of themselves in their national flags.

7. Even though I have moved back in time to another historical moment, Operation Eagle Eye's predecessor, 'sus' – the law enabling police to stop and search subjects on the (non) suspicion of criminal activity – was a highly politicized marker of the systematic harassment of black youth during the 1970s–1980s along with other expressions of state and ruling-class racism.

8. *Guardian*, 15 July 1998.

9. My usage of the phrase the 'poetic imperative' as an articulatory mode within a socio-poetics of sport, rerouting the meanings of representational images of black performance, is differentiated from its deployment as a part of the political and philosophical teachings of the Falange in Spain under Franco. Richard Wright quotes the Falange's usage of the poetic imperative as: 'An inward force that always leads us to prefer the beauty of things ... [and that] all that is beautiful tends towards perfection and in choosing the beautiful we also choose what is perfect' (Wright 1995: 277–8).

10. The explosion of the myth through cricket had begun with the famous 1950 West Indies 3–1 series win in England. For narratives on the social meanings of this victory, see Phillips and Phillips (1998).

11. Drawing on Gilroy (1987) and Mercer (1994), the poetic imperative can be applied outside the crude binarisms of black/white, left/right and monolithic class distinctions.

The Chinese Takeaway and the Diasporic Habitus: Space, Time and Power Geometries

David Parker

> Many years ago we copied your porcelain and called it China. We adopted your passion for tea. And more recently, the local Chinese restaurant has become a familiar feature of life throughout this land. (HM Queen Elizabeth II, *Guardian*, 20 October 1999)

The Queen's welcoming remarks to the Chinese President Jiang Zemin, at a state banquet during his visit to Britain, indicate how just how deeply select signifiers of China and Chinese culture have permeated British life. Whether in promotions for McDonald's Lemon McChicken, advertisements for Tango soft drink, or the tired routines of stand-up comedians denouncing MSG-laden Chinese food, the Chinese presence in Britain is recurrently reduced to the willing provision of everyday staples, and thus celebrated with orientalist condescension as an example of a dormant and pacified contribution to a successful multicultural society. In what follows I attempt to theorize the everyday dynamics sustaining these constructions. By developing Bourdieu's notion of the habitus, I interrogate the overlooked power geometries underlying routine forms of racialization in the Chinese takeaway.

Every night, throughout Britain, the contact zone of the takeaway counter is not only a site for the enactment of racial and sexual harassment, but also an indicator of the stubborn resilience of a specifically British Chinese diasporic habitus. Consequently, this chapter endeavours to show how Chinese takeaways are crucial constituents of what Avtar Brah has termed 'diaspora-space', being 'a point of confluence of economic, political, cultural and psychic processes ... where multiple subject positions are juxtaposed, contested, proclaimed or disavowed' (Brah 1996: 208). For as well as facilitating a redefinition of British popular food culture and thereby national identity, they are nodal points in the global networks of the Chinese diaspora which 'cut across Western social space' (Allen 1995: 132). By focusing on the Chinese takeaway as a familiar social setting characteristic of the British Chinese population, I respond to Ong and Nonini's call for analysts of the Chinese diaspora to engage with 'the hard surfaces of daily life' (Ong and Nonini 1997: 13). I highlight the routine reproduction of cultural differences through an everyday institution which appears to exemplify peaceful multicultural co-existence, but in fact embodies deep structures of racialized domination.

The key concept developed here is the *diasporic habitus*. This refers to the generative principles which produce the mundane practices sustaining the transnational networks and social locations that define a diaspora. The term 'habitus' arises from the work of Pierre Bourdieu. A selective appropriation of Bourdieu's concept has the potential to place space, time and everyday social practices at the heart of current discussions of diaspora. For the signal virtue of Bourdieu's work is its concern 'to analyse the ordinary experience of the social' (Bourdieu 1990a: 5). In this chapter I explore the 'ordinary experience of the social' from the point of view of young Chinese people working in Chinese family takeaway businesses in Britain. Accordingly, the work reported here develops out of previous research and an ongoing programme of interviews, correspondence and participant observation concerned mainly with young Chinese people in Britain (Parker 1995). Between 1990 and 1993 I talked with fifty-four young Chinese people throughout Britain; in 1995 and 1996 I revisited ten respondents and six new ones. I draw on these discussions here, partly through reporting interview material, mainly by imbuing my reflections with their observations.

There are four main arguments in the chapter. First, I discuss the ethnocentricity of terms which have been used to devise a phenomenology of globalization, in particular Doreen Massey's idea of power geometry. Her partial, almost throw-away, deployment of the Chinese takeaway from the customer's viewpoint vitiates an otherwise insightful formulation of how globalization is experienced. Second, I demonstrate how the Chinese takeaway has played a particular role in discussions of ethnic food in a version of multiculturalism which I propose to term *celebratory multiculturalism*. Once again the perspective of those working in the takeaway and the critical edge this experience may give are overlooked. Third, to rectify this I attempt to theorize the dynamics of the encounters within the takeaway. The concept of diasporic habitus forces a close investigation of how spatial relations, temporal rhythms and the embodiment of imperial legacies structure the exchanges between workers and customers. The recognition of distinct spatial perspectives and experiences of time is focused on and through the racialized body in routine interactions, encounters across the counter. Finally, the diasporic habitus does not simply give rise to a conformism which equips people for subordination, it also offers resources for the creation of a distinctively British Chinese perspective. The diasporic habitus as the embodied subjectivities poised between the legacies of the past, the imperatives of the present, and the possibilities of the future, can generate a powerful critique of the terms in which Chinese culture has been interpreted. I refer briefly to interview material and cultural production from an emerging generation who have grown up in the strategic location of the takeaway. Their verbal, poetic and visual representations dispute the dominant conception of the Chinese in Britain as a quiet, obliging and servile community.

'Chinese In Britain' or 'British Chinese'?

There is a tension in both popular and scholarly writing between a recognition of how Chinese food has transformed the British diet, and the recurrently contested presence of Chinese people in Britain. Such disjunctures are neatly captured in a line of thought initiated by Doreen Massey (1993). Writing about the changing sense of place in the contemporary world, Massey develops the idea of 'power geometry'. This is intended to capture the variable experiences of the forces of globalization felt by people in different social locations: 'different social groups have distinct relationships to this already differentiated mobility: some people are more in charge of it than others; some initiate flows and movement, others don't; some are more on the receiving end of it than others; some are effectively imprisoned by it' (Massey 1993: 149). Unfortunately, this recognition of how power geometry maps out distinct social co-ordinates is marred by the exemplification she elaborates. Massey chooses to highlight the plight of 'the pensioner in a bed-sit in any inner city in this country, eating British working class style fish and chips from a Chinese take-away, watching a US film on a Japanese television; and not daring to go out after dark. And anyway the public transport's been cut' (pp. 149–50). Even though Massey gives several examples of being 'on the receiving end' of globalization, I have always been troubled by the bathos of this extract, expressing as it does an implicit nostalgia for all that has changed in the pensioner's lifetime. Massey seems to empathize with the pensioner for whom the *Chinese* takeaway now providing the staple British dish signifies a reluctantly experienced cultural transformation of the nation. In a remarkably condensed passage, the Chinese takeaway is a metonym for the global influences assailing the bodily senses of the helpless pensioner whose ethnicity, in contrast to the artefacts itemized, is unmarked.

Massey's extract raises the question of how the relationship between British and Chinese cultural identities has been addressed in representations of Chinese migration to Britain. There is a split discursive structure oscillating between depictions of 'the Chinese in Britain' and an abstract conception of 'the overseas Chinese'. Both these extremes overlook an emerging British Chinese counter-narrative. Representations of 'the Chinese in Britain' take the form of success story narratives. These see Chinese and British culture as sharply separate; the former is welcomed as a cultural contribution from an unacknowledged position of dominance by the latter. The Chinese community is homogenized and Chinese culture in the form of food purveyed by ethnic entrepreneurs is cited as contributing to a harmonious multicultural society. The 1985 Home Affairs Select Committee Report on the Chinese in Britain is a prime example: 'we believe that the integration of the Chinese into British society could be one of the success stories on the road to a truly multi-racial society' (Home Affairs Committee 1985: lxxix).

A troubling consequence of such portrayals is the rendition of the Chinese in Britain as a self-sufficient enclave whose socio-economic location in the catering trade has isolated them from the pernicious effects of racial discrimination. One anthropological study commented: 'The catering establishments are virtual islands of Chinese culture in the larger British society, isolated pockets where the migrants can interact with the outside world on their own terms' (Watson 1977: 193). There is little recognition of the experiences of racial harassment to be reported later.

The second prevailing representational strategy locates the worldwide Chinese population in discussions of the part played by Confucianism and Asian values in entrepreneurial success. Depictions of the overseas Chinese as a globally mobile people who carry with them a fixed sense of Chinese identity have become popular in both business studies and less academic presentations (Seagrave 1996, for example). Here the Chinese diaspora is conceived economistically as a trading diaspora (Cohen 1997), a global chain of ethnic entrepreneurs. One eminent analyst emphasizes the role of the apparently enigmatic and secretive Chinese business network; 'as so much of their life is conducted in a dialect of Chinese, and as so many of their emotions are concealed from public view, they are less transparent than many other cultures' (Redding 1990: 41). These conceptualizations echo the classical racial theory of de Gobineau who, in the nineteenth century, described the Chinese as inherently disposed towards 'a steady but uncreative drive towards material prosperity' (de Gobineau, cited in Mosse 1978: 53). The discursive tone betrays an anxious admiration of the overseas Chinese and a thinly veiled fear of their success (see *The Economist* 1996). These formulations have a partial utility in recognizing the ubiquity of the Chinese diaspora (Hamilton 1996: 338). However, they are pitched at too high a level of abstraction to explore why specific cultural institutions like the takeaway came into being, and how they endure in far from propitious circumstances. They fail to register the critical possibilities engendered by Chinese transnational practices which cannot be neatly confined to the realm of economics.

What both the 'Chinese in Britain' and the 'overseas Chinese' depictions lack is a more nuanced investigation of emerging British Chinese experiences and sensibilities, many of which reflect on takeaway life from the hitherto unacknowledged vantage point behind the counter. Chinese takeaways in Britain embody a distinct power geometry, their workers occupying a unique position in social space. They serve mainly white, mainly male, often far from sober, customers in settings which through shop signs, menus, smells and sounds accentuate the display of a particular version of Chinese culture. Far from interacting with the outside world on their own terms, those serving on the counter have had to negotiate the very concept of the takeaway itself. Yet this very negotiation disturbs homogeneous conceptions of the British nation, reveals the logic underlying attempts to confine difference to the margins, and has been a formative British Chinese experience which contests the terms of both the 'Chinese in Britain' and the 'overseas Chinese' modes of representation.

The Takeaway, the Foodscape and the Ethnoscape

The Chinese takeaway must be conceptualized as a model of cultural appropriation and transformation which can illuminate how cultural difference is handled within the social logics of contemporary multiculturalism. There is an intimate connection between ethnic food, migrant communities and the discourse of 'cultural contribution' described above. Globally dispersed settlements such as the Chinese diaspora are positioned adversely by a distorted appropriation of the symbolic practices associated with the food they bring with them. These foods are marked as ethnic by the dominant and hailed as evidence of the openness of multicultural societies. Ethnic cuisine is read as a hopeful sign of intercultural accommodation; 'the most rewarding and easiest bridge across ethnic lines. It is a form of internal tourism [...] What more accessible and friendly arena of inter-ethnic contact could be devised than the ethnic restaurant?' (Van den Berghe 1984: 393–4).

The dynamics of this strictly limited openness to cultural difference can be explored by adapting Appadurai's model of the dimensions of global cultural flow (Appadurai 1990). Appadurai sets out a variety of 'scapes', imaginary landscapes, as heuristic devices for understanding the disjunctive flows structuring the contemporary world. These landscapes comprise imaginative resources for coming to terms with the flux and mobility of globalization. Of particular pertinence is the 'ethnoscape'.

Appadurai uses this term to describe 'the landscape of persons who constitute the shifting world in which we live' (Appadurai 1990: 297). Reworking Appadurai, the presence of Chinese takeaways in Britain for several decades could be described as adding new dimensions to the British foodscape, the culinary landscape of tastes readily available for purchase. However, this presence has implications which cannot be held within the horizon of the 'Chinese in Britain' discourse. That set of representations confines the impact of Chinese settlement to a reflavouring of the national palate, and ignores the impact this has on conceptions of national identity.

Modern societies are characterized by an intimate connection between alimentary imagery and national identity. Food as the source of nutrition and bodily sustenance symbolizes the vitality of the nation, and the culinary field is a crucial arena for assigning value to cultural practices and the social groups associated with them (Bourdieu 1984). One of the consequences of transnational migration is a change in both the range of foods consumed within a nation and the people bringing those cuisines; in short, both the national foodscape and the ethnoscape change. The variable relationship between foodscape and ethnoscape is a crucial element of competing national imaginaries in the context of multiculturalism. In particular, a welcoming of the food new migrants bring can sit alongside a disavowal of their distinctive social and political claims.

One response to the increased diversity of the ethnoscape is a broadening of the foodscape within the terms of a celebratory multiculturalism. This places different ethnic foods in a putatively non-hierarchical register of comfortably accommodated differences; an array of food choices to be gazed at, sampled and enjoyed at leisure (Hardyment 1995). The limitations of this perspective are revealed in a comment Hardyment makes in a discussion of Indian food in Britain: 'the answer to coping in a multicultural society is celebration of difference' (Hardyment 1995: 125). Multiculturalism here becomes a problem to be coped with by the offering up of cultural treats, thereby evading a more profound engagement with the possibilities for cultural transformation.

However, there is a different ethnoscape/foodscape relationship which moves towards a more contestatory vision of multiculturalism. This recognizes the 'transruptive' potential of these new presences. The general concept of transruption and its relationship to multiculturalism are outlined in the Introduction to this book. In this instance transruption refers to the redefinition of the very notion of British food. Far from being celebrated as different in themselves or exotic, for some, so-called ethnic cuisines now symbolize the British nation itself. So, from a South Asian diasporic perspective, Narayan states, 'many immigrants would describe the proliferation of interest in ethnic cuisines positively, as an aspect of formerly colonized outsiders infiltrating and transforming Western life – where, for instance, England would no longer be England without its Indian restaurants and grocery stores' (Narayan 1995: 76). In Britain the Chinese takeaway has a distinctive but analogous location in the redefinition of the post-war foodscape; as one report on the catering industry states: 'Chinese restaurants could now claim to be the archetypal British restaurant' (Economist Intelligence Unit 1993: 80). In both these examples, South and East Asian cultural forms have not only transformed themselves, and become established as distinctively English and British, they have thereby begun to transform the very meanings of those latter terms also. Unfortunately, this redefinition still attempts to contain the transruptive potential of an institution like the takeaway. It is only a partial recognition of the contestatory multicultural possibilities, for three reasons.

First, multiculturalism is held within the confines of service industries at the disposal of the dominant. Those who work in catering find themselves 'valued only in those areas of life where they are allowed to tend to the needs of the dominant group' (Wong 1993: 58). 'Their non-assimilation is highly selective and staged, ingratiating rather than threatening' (p. 56). The very concept of the takeaway is predicated on availability, deference, and a solicitous attention to customer expectations.

Second, the celebration of culinary diversity overlooks the discrepancies between national foodscapes and local ethnoscapes. Congenial invocations of the Chinese takeaway as a very *British* place must be tempered with a recognition that particular Chinese takeaways do not operate wholly on their own terms. There is a discrepancy between a willing acceptance of a more diverse national foodscape, and at times brutal resistances to the transformation of the local ethnoscape brought about by the associated migrations. Graffiti and other forms of racial harassment illustrate the sharp contestations of these changed ethnoscapes in neighbourhoods where the Chinese takeaway often stands alone as the only visible institutional embodiment of cultural difference (see Parker 1995: ch. 5).

Third, celebratory multiculturalism simplifies the terms of contact between cultures, overlooking the unequal terms of interchange between Europe and Asia in both past and present. It is no coincidence that the first encounter with Asian food arose from Britain's imperial adventures in India and East Asia. Narayan highlights the crucial issue: superficial interest in other cultures has all too often underpinned imperialism of various forms, in the case of food consumption an Orientalist 'carnal relish' (Narayan 1995: 80). The much celebrated transformation of the British foodscape cannot evade the deep-rooted inequalities of historical legacies. Eating practices encode social relations by harking back to imperial motifs of conquest, in this case the conquest and mastery of culinary difference.

As the ethnographic material reported later in the chapter and elsewhere (Parker 1995) attests, this structure persists in relation to Chinese takeaways today, in the form of a desire for digestible difference which is simultaneously gendered, racialized and sexualized. The very term 'takeaway' itself is suggestive as a metaphor for cultural appropriation and domination.

The work of engaging with cultural difference is done by the takeaway, the meat sliced into bite-sized portions, parcelled in disposable containers, made recognizable and palatable. This cultural work is always vulnerable to challenge through the invocation of an indigestible difference lurking unseen within the menu, as evidenced by the continuing urban mythology of cats and dogs being the raw material for Chinese food (see Dawson 1967; Parker 1995: ch. 4). Although in a modest way the takeaway menu acts as a microcosm for the development of new combinatory British Chinese cultural forms, it is important to note how takeaway food is derided for lacking authenticity, being full of monosodium glutamate and enjoyed almost with shame. For example, one food critic recounts the growth in popularity of Chinese food in this way: 'the taste for Chinese cooking had to be acquired, with the cheapness as the most obvious stimulant to the appetite' (Driver 1983: 80).

The takeaway cannot simply take its place in a comforting imaginary of celebratory multiculturalism, which jocularly disregards it as nothing more than a dietary supplement. Criticism of the Chinese takeaway as cheap, unsatisfying and trivial takes away the possibilities of viewing its location as precarious yet privileged; as offering the vantage point for a re-examination of the terms on which cultural differences are engaged in western multicultural societies. The optimism of the 'Chinese in Britain' model overlooks the partial and attenuated nature of the intercultural contact implied by the cultural contribution narrative. The 'success story' narrative of the Chinese and other ethnic entrepreneurs in Britain welcomes endeavour in spatially and temporally isolated socio-economic niches which service the consumption patterns of the dominant. Locating difference in dispersed, late-night eating venues keeps it manageable and confined. Absent in the culinary metaphorizations of celebratory multiculturalism is an understanding of how everyday encounters between Chinese people and their customers in catering establishments are structured. This is a prerequisite for the recognition of a contestatory multiculturalism, and can be grasped only by attending to the interactive dimensions of the takeaway.

The Chinese Takeaway as a Contact Zone

The very phrase commonly used to describe the purchase of food from a Chinese takeaway – 'Going for a Chinese' [sic] – condenses the hierarchical dimensions of the transaction. It combines a condescending demeanour with an appropriative dynamic which carries sexual connotations. 'Going for a Chinese' has become as integral a part of British daily life as 'going down the pub', and indeed the two activities are often closely related. This is evident from the spatial distribution of Chinese takeaways in Britain's towns, cities and villages. Chinese takeaways have installed themselves in the interstices of shopping centres; on street corners, road junctions, in between pubs and clubs. In previous work I explored the takeaway counter as a metaphor for the place of young Chinese people in British society (Parker 1994). Here I explore the spatio-temporal structure of the takeaway more closely and ask: what kind of 'contact zone' is the Chinese takeaway? As Mary Louise Pratt outlines: '"contact zone" is an attempt to invoke the spatial and temporal co-presence of subjects previously separated by geographic and historical disjunctures and whose trajectories now intersect' (Pratt 1992: 7). The precise terms of 'contact' vary markedly across different contact zones. Accordingly, the social settings where diasporic cultures and identities are displayed, circulated and refashioned need addressing more concretely. This can highlight the everyday practices of diaspora, the resultant experiences of space and time, and the differential power relations working through those spaces.

The Chinese takeaway is an exemplary contact zone with a direct enfrontment between worlds constructed as different. It is a liminal space of intercultural encounter containing two physical frontiers. First, that between the customer's body and the food consumed. Ingestion across this frontier is a visceral physical act which both depends on, and redefines, the boundaries between the inner and the outer, the domestic and the foreign, the tolerably exotic and the indigestible (Wong 1993: 26). Second, the frontier between the takeaway itself and the locality can be subject to vigorous contestation. Behind the glass shop frontage, the server sits on the counter in front of a hatch or other entry to the kitchen, relaying the orders to the back and the cooked food to the front. Many takeaways have glass partitions with one-way vision to enable the public area to be monitored from within the kitchen, it being imperative to control the takeaway from behind the counter. There is a pronounced physical barrier between the serving and cooking areas defined by the counter which mediates between the shop and the outside world.

In this context it is possible to compare the location of Chinese takeaways to Bell and Valentine's depiction of South Asian restaurants in Britain. They refer to the tradition of lager louts making their 'weekly pilgrimage at pub-shut times for chicken vindaloos all round' as 'one of the most ambivalent and troublesome' food production–consumption relationships (Bell and Valentine 1997: 174). The Chinese takeaway's spatial–temporal locations generate a different but at least as problematic a set of social relations which mark it out from other sites for the consumption of 'ethnic' food. By law the food purchased in takeaways has to be consumed off-premises, thus compared to Indian and Chinese restaurants where customers eat at tables, the encounters across the takeaway counter are more fleeting, under greater time pressure, and thus potentially more pointed.

The takeaway counter serves as the focal point for the power geometries operating between Chinese families and their customers. It is a pivotal location in the spatial-temporal constitution of the local ethnoscape. The particularity of one diasporic location is illustrated here: a potentially vulnerable stand-alone business trading on its cultural difference late at night with often just one server, invariably a young Chinese person, on the counter having to face mainly white customers.

JOHN: (aged 20, Manchester) You've got a business with massive windows and it's easy for them to just come back later with a brick.

DP: You can't really afford to alienate the customers then?

SUK HAN (aged 22, West Midlands): No, 'cos they all know each other, they all go down the same pubs don't they? They go down 'the Brit' [the British legion] or the working men's club, or they just live round here and know each other.

The hard surface of the counter can be a site for the 'brutal condensation of social relationships' (Lefebvre, quoted in Dear 1997: 57). The server on the counter bears the pressures of late-night neighbourhoods, being open to drunks, passing traffic and associated racist abuse that can result in direct acts of violence (see 'Racist Jailed', *Birmingham Evening Mail*, 9 April 1998).

In trying to understand these situations we reach the limits of what can be said with existing concepts. The term power geometry alone is insufficiently nuanced to deal with specific experiences of the matrix of power relations defined by the forces of globalization, migration and the commodification of difference. We need a more focused account of the racialized dynamics and inequalities guiding these processes and shaping contact zones such as the takeaway. This can be facilitated by deploying and significantly reworking Bourdieu's concept of habitus to produce the idea of the diasporic habitus. The term diasporic habitus refers to the schemes of perception, appreciation and action which govern everyday practices in diaspora. This concept can economically conceptualize the relationships between spatial proximity and social distance in an everyday setting such as the Chinese takeaway.

The Diasporic Habitus

An understanding of the concept of diasporic habitus requires a consideration of the general theory of practice within which Bourdieu develops the notion of habitus. Bourdieu treats social life as a mutually constitutive interplay of positions, dispositions and actions and the habitus plays a crucial role in linking these dimensions. It is particularly important to avoid conflating habitus and habitat. The habitus is not a physical territory. Bourdieu clearly distinguishes habitus from field. Field is Bourdieu's designation of social space and refers to the arena of struggle in a particular domain marked out by a network of objective relations between social positions. The habitus consists of the durable, transposable dispositions which govern how these positions in social space are taken up and occupied (Bourdieu 1990b: 53). The habitus is a 'set of acquired dispositions over time, a generative mechanism, between structure and practice' (May 1996: 130) which furnishes agents with what Bourdieu terms the practical sense, or 'feel for the game', required to adjust to ever-changing social contexts and become accustomed to their overall social position. This formulation usefully tries to capture how social action is simultaneously regulated and improvised, while neither wholly determined or spontaneous. However, the term habitus is deliberately vague in Bourdieu's work and requires operational refinement. Bourdieu's concept of habitus does not capture the lived experiences of racialized hierarchy; his topology of social space prioritizes the mapping of class positions, he does not give sufficient attention to the specific asymmetries of other social locations (see Cohen 1997; Connolly 1997; Reay 1995).

Both the advantages and the limits of Bourdieu's use of the term habitus can be gleaned from his most recent formulation (Bourdieu 1997). This defines habitus as the practical sense arising from agents' particular mode of exposure to the world. However, Bourdieu's work does not specify the non-class modes of exposure to the world defined by the habitus, hence the need to describe a specifically diasporic habitus. To be part of a diaspora is to be exposed to the world in a particular way, to be vulnerable to objectification, and be placed in a relation of immediate engagement, of tension and attention which makes sense of the world (Bourdieu 1997: 168, 170). The Chinese takeaway is a dramatic example of such a tense and potentially vulnerable engagement, of how what Bourdieu terms 'the most serious social injunctions' impose themselves not on the intellect but on the body (p. 169). Bourdieu provides many suggestive formulations such as these, but securing their insights requires the further specification of distinctions which cannot be reduced to the logic of reproducing class positions which dominates his vision of social life.

The term diasporic habitus facilitates the exploration of specific modalities governing the social practices of transnational collectives, operating 'away from home'. The takeaway itself is not a diasporic habitus, it is one of the contested sites of 'diaspora-space' (Brah 1996) where a variety of forces intersect to produce the power geometries defining globalization. These power geometries configure the distribution of locations in hierarchical social relations. However, what happens at those locations within diaspora space is governed by the dispositions of the diasporic habitus, the practical sense, or 'feel for the game', appropriate to that field. Within a takeaway there are recurrent interactions motivated by conceptions of cultural difference. The following issues arise. How are aspects of Chinese culture resignified and deployed in everyday social settings and practices? How do white customers gain the upper hand in takeaways? How is social vulnerability experienced? In particular how is it inscribed on, and felt through, the racialized body in an arena like the takeaway which through close proximity over the counter sells ethnically marked food?

The Chinese diasporic habitus may help answer these questions. It comprises those dispositions which flow through, and thereby constitute, the transnational networks connecting the globally dispersed Chinese population. What maintains a sense of 'being Chinese' through global displacement is the diasporic habitus. This is not a static governing origin, or the 'Confucian values' cited in the business studies literature (Redding 1990). The Chinese diasporic habitus consists of mobile, portable, transformative orientations: know-how, strategies whose practical operationalization varies between sites of transnational dispersal. This structure of dispositions underlies the transmission and reinvention of distinctive cultural forms and practices, including food, throughout the global Chinese population.

It is important to emphasize the difference the addition of a diasporic dimension makes to the concept of habitus. Bourdieu has a tendency to render social agents' habitus as automatically compliant with the imperatives of the field within which they operate. However, the diasporic social location adds an extra element which he cannot accommodate in his model: the stubborn commitments and resistances resulting from the differentially racialized embodiment of social inequalities. The habitus is defined in general terms by Bourdieu as 'the product of a historical acquisition which makes it possible to appropriate the legacy of history' (Bourdieu 1981: 305). However, the distinctively diasporic habitus arises from the necessity to recognize, and at times bear the burden of, radically differential histories. The dispositions of the diasporic habitus have to reckon with the legacy of colonization and how this provides white people with imperial capital. This form of capital comprises the accumulated privileges of imperial history, resources of power, which can be mobilized to the advantage of the dominant, almost without thought, in the most ordinary everyday exchanges. The Chinese takeaway offers an important illustration of the deployment of imperial capital in even the most familiar of settings. However, contrary to Bourdieu's conception of habitus, the diasporic habitus does not simply predispose those without imperial capital to a stoic and passive acceptance of the hand dealt to them in the social game in question. What we are beginning to see in the new generations of British Chinese is a struggle over the terms of occupation of diaspora space, and the formation of a British Chinese diasporic habitus. This can be discerned only through an exploration of the everyday racial harassment endured and resisted in Chinese takeaways.

Routine Racialization

Analysing social spaces such as the Chinese takeaway highlights how racialized inequalities and power relations are felt and reproduced in everyday transactions. I propose to analyse these encounters in terms of the endowments, comportments and deployments in play. Endowments are the financial, cultural and social resources held by social actors by virtue of past histories. Comportment refers to how these resources are 'carried' in the form of bodily mannerisms, postures and affectations. Deployments are the practical enactments through which endowments and comportments are expressed in verbal and physical activities. Studying how these three dimensions come together in the takeaway setting, it is possible to discern 'strategies of condescension, by which agents occupying a higher position in one of the hierarchies of objective space symbolically deny the social distance which does not thereby cease to exist ... one can use the objective distances so as to have the advantages of proximity and the advantages of distance' (Bourdieu 1990a: 127–8).

Here Bourdieu is referring to class hierarchies, but I propose a more explicit consideration of embodiment in face-to-face encounters across the counter. This enables the understanding of routine racialization which describes how, even where no explicit discriminatory intent is present, the everyday actions, reactions and demeanours of customers and workers in Chinese takeaways are shot through with the tension-laden objectifications of 'race'. These processes are governed by the dispositions of the diasporic habitus. This animates the possessions of transnational collectives into practices through embodied activity which strives to maintain dignity under duress. I will specify the three dimensions structuring these practices more closely.

Endowments Into each interaction in a Chinese takeaway 'individuals carry with them past and present positions in the social structures, marks of social position, social distance which can be manipulated strategically' (Bourdieu 1977: 81). Although Bourdieu's conception of multiple forms of capital is intended to encompass the cultural resources as well as the economic capital agents possess, it is insufficiently sensitive to the deep cultural histories that individuals can mobilize to their advantage in social interaction. In particular it overlooks what I've termed imperial capital, the legacies of imperial dominance in the form of conceptions of servitude and stereotypical deformations of cultural difference. A persistent theme in my discussions with young Chinese people is how customers in Chinese takeaways are inclined towards displays of superiority, armed with the knowledge that this is acceptable:

> TSEE SUN (aged 26, West Midlands): They tend to think as it's a shop they're consumers and they have the right to be abusive and that's their opinion. That's the Chinese takeaway – it's very much to do with the image the media portray throughout the years and they are still portraying. They should be servants like throughout the centuries quite a few films have Chinese characters and they're either servants or they're doing something strange and weird – according to the Western perspective … I think they still think they're the good old Great Britain, they still have that concept very strongly; those who walk into a Chinese takeaway.

Location in a racialized hierarchy is itself an endowment; for the majority of takeaway customers whiteness and masculinity combine to enable them to reap the continuing advantages of imperial capital. These endowments find expression in the bodily postures and demeanours of the customers and workers inside takeaways.

Comportments The term comportments refers to how endowments are carried in bodily mannerisms, non-verbal attitudes and bearings, which embody social differences and distinctions. Bourdieu's concept of habitus is intended to capture this neglected dimension of social practice, how 'social distances are written into the body, or, more exactly, into the relationship to the body, to language and to time' (Bourdieu 1990a: 128). However, as others have noted (Reay 1995), Bourdieu fails to address the particular corporealization of racialized inequalities, largely confining his attention to how class distinctions are embodied.

The Chinese takeaway with its close but fleeting encounters, both predicated on and structured by racialized differences, provides an important site for recognizing the role of the gendered, racialized and sexualized body in sustaining a specifically diasporic habitus. This is marked by the radically distinct stances and position takings on each side of the counter. The takeaway counter is subject to distinct power geometries, being a point 'where power reaches into the very grain of individuals, touches their bodies and inserts itself into their actions and attitudes, their discourses, learning processes and everyday lives' (Foucault 1980: 39).

The encounters across the counter are racialized, and these disparities and inequalities are felt bodily. The comportments of the takeaway customers betoken an exercising of sovereignty, perusing the menu in the manner of 'the socially informed body, with its tastes and distastes, its compulsions and repulsions' (Bourdieu 1977: 124). At one takeaway shop I observed subtle assertions of the ownership of the space on the part of white, male customers; their imposing presence as they walked through the door, the manner in which they leant on the counter. I noticed how the local evening paper on the counter was simply reached across for, picked up and read without the customers asking for permission. Prompted by this, the young woman behind the counter wrote 'Do not take away the paper' on the newspaper and observed, 'They keep taking it away. They rarely ask.' The asymmetry of the service relationship is expressed in the comportments of the takeaway staff: receptive and attentive, ready for orders and to cook on demand.

> FIONA (aged 23, West Midlands): Facing the people was the worst part – actually taking the order and you know you're scared to look them in the eye. And I'd feel my face was red all night … It was something you had to do, you had no choice.

This exposed positioning on the takeaway counter underscores a more general relationship between facialization and racialization. Facialization describes the process whereby facial features are fixed as the signifiers of racial difference. This is particularly the case for Chinese people, whose eye shape, hair colour and texture have always been accentuated in stereotypical representations such as the novelist Sax Rohmer's oriental villain Fu Manchu (Clegg 1994). The encounters across the counter in Chinese takeaways are particularly susceptible to the citation of this cultural repertoire. They require a face-to-face engagement where the server is on display, available for scrutiny from both inside and outside the shop. Where there is a young Chinese woman serving food to white men, there is an expected mode of presentation, ingratiating, subservient and passive. This is still circulated in contemporary culture, for example by the advertisements for Singapore Airlines which feature smiling stewardesses. Against this cultural backdrop, it is not simply the food itself that signifies cultural difference, but also the sexualized terms on which it is often exchanged through the bodily mannerisms in play over the counter.

Deployments The third dimension I am proposing is the analysis of deployments, how these endowments and comportments are activated and verbalized in practice. In observations I conducted in a takeaway in a Birmingham suburb I was struck by the subtle choreography of interchanges. Although there were some pleasantries, the verbal exchanges consisted largely of contact without intimacy, a cautious guarded proximity without reciprocity. Very little is said and yet a great deal is going on. At times there were noticeable hesitations before ordering, an inability to pronounce the dishes correctly, a desire to be steered to safe tastes. A marked reluctance to experiment on the part of several customers meant that many of the verbal exchanges involve the server 'reassuring the patron that the unsettling implications of eating ethnic can be arrested' (Wong 1993: 68).

Even without gross forms of verbal or physical harassment, the encounters in Chinese takeaways are routinely racialized. There is a recurrent mobilization of cultural stereotypes which even if it only exists as a potential constitutes power geometries defined by a 'flexible *positional* superiority' for the customer, 'which puts the Westerner in a whole series of possible relationships with the Orient without ever losing him the upper hand' (Said 1978: 7). Serving on the counter involves handling far more than a food for money exchange it entails a series of broader class, cultural and gendered relations. In addition to the cash nexus, there are ingrained cultural expectations in play, customers expecting an 'excursion that is at once adventurous and tame, leaving their sense of cultural superiority intact at the end' (Wong 1993: 57). This superiority is enacted through repeated, seemingly minor but cumulatively harassing acts. This sense of Chinese takeaways as a manageably exotic adventure for the largely white male customers is captured by a young woman's observation:

MEI HAN (aged 20, West Midlands): I don't like working Friday nights because there's this man who comes in and he keeps singing 'Suzy Wong, Suzy Wong … '

These four words condense decades of gendered, sexualized and racialized stereotyping: the feminization of the Orient, the sexual appropriation underlying the iconic white male's fantasy figure of East Asian femininity, these cultural legacies have to be endured for a few seconds every week. Takeaways are sites for the regular assertion of proprietorial rights over Chinese female bodies by white men, wilful transgressions of personal space. For example, in one takeaway I observed one male customer ruffling the hair and then holding the hand of one young Chinese woman while ordering his food. This is an example of how the endowment of imperial capital – the accumulated historical advantage of colonial power – can be deployed in the everyday encounters.

RAYMOND (aged 23, Warwickshire): In a way the English have a very imperial attitude, they want to dominate the world and think they should still
dominate the world; you just let them get on with it. Sometimes they would
talk down at you, they just treat you as if you don't know anything ... But
we can't throw it back in their face if they insult us or anything, you can't
because you'd push the business away and so you have to take it, always
subservient, basically it's their money.

In focusing on the takeaway as a contact zone, there is a danger of a
partial analysis which privileges space and the physical proximities of
interpersonal contact, and ignores the importance of time in the structuring
of the diasporic habitus. These deployments of imperial capital drive home
the importance of the regular return of customers being both the predicate
of the takeaway's success, and the defining feature of its vulnerable location.

Heterochronicity

A complete understanding of a contact zone like the takeaway requires
an appreciation of *heterochronicity*. This refers to the divergent temporalities, the multiple cycles, rhythms and trajectories which characterize
different life patterns in diaspora space. The importance of recognizing
particular temporal structures arises from the prevailing assumption that
globalization and postmodernity can be defined by the changing experience
of space and time (Harvey 1989 and 1996; Castells 1997). The dominant
concept for encapsulating this is time–space compression. Time–space
compression refers to the simultaneous quickening in the pace of life and
the overcoming of spatial barriers by the processes of globalization, and
how these processes bring together different worlds in the same space and
time. It is no coincidence that time–space compression is signified through
the proliferation of 'ethnic foods': 'Chinese takeaways, Italian pizza parlours
... the list is now endless in the Western world' (Harvey 1989: 300).

Unfortunately, as with power geometry, the insights promised by the
idea of time–space compression are impaired by the unacknowledged
perspective from which they are advanced. For example, when Harvey
calls for 'the study of how we cope with time–space compression' (Harvey
1996: 247), both who 'we' are here and what 'coping' signifies are not spelt
out, consequently debarring an account of the variable senses of time
operating across different social constituencies. This is particularly limiting
in the consideration of diasporas. For diasporic communities live particular
relationships to time. The very term diaspora implies the importance of
migration trajectories, historical memory and the reactivation of the old in
new contexts. In more mundane terms, an institution like the Chinese
takeaway, emblematic of the British Chinese diaspora, highlights the

distinct temporal structures governing the lives of different social groups. The takeaway is important as an example not simply of a contact zone, but also of the daily vigilance required to operate within a space of intercultural exchange which has to be protected against potentially violent assertions of proprietorial rights. These pressures cannot be understood through a universal designation of time–space compression. For some to experience the joys of fast food, those cooking and serving it have their pace of life disrupted, they surrender their time so others can save time. The Chinese takeaway sees a struggle over time as well as space. This is felt most keenly by the young people serving on the counter, due to the potential for racial harassment when working late at night. Understanding their distinct experiences requires a closer specification of the temporalities defining the takeaway.

To survive economically, a takeaway has to 'claim' a locality and become a nodal point in a network of nocturnal gender and class-specific pleasures. Catering for this pattern of demand imposes a particular rhythmic rigour. As Bourdieu argues:

> social disciplines take the form of temporal disciplines and the whole social order imposes itself at the deepest level of the bodily dispositions through a particular way of regulating the use of time, the temporal distribution of collective and individual activities and the appropriate rhythm with which to perform them. (Bourdieu 1990b: 75)

The temporal discipline of ceding time through labour to meet the consumption demands of others has been a defining experience for the families owning Chinese takeaways. Most are open at least six days a week, from five until midnight in the evenings, possibly one or two lunchtimes also. However, the disciplines on the diasporic habitus are not uniform for different generations. For the first generation need to respond to what Sau Ling Wong has termed 'Necessity' (sic) to refer to 'all the hardships, deprivations, restrictions, disenfranchisements, and dislocations' they have collectively suffered as immigrants and minorities in a white-dominated country (Wong 1993: 20). Central to Necessity is the stoicism of deferred gratification. Wong remarks: 'The parents' labours are meant to break the cycle of Necessity, to make possible the luxury of choice for the next generation' (p. 33).

In Britain the next generation of British-educated young Chinese has also suffered the blurring of boundaries between family time, leisure time and work time. A feature of the takeaway is the different experience of time on the different sides of the counter, a contrast felt most deeply by the young Chinese people serving their peers:

TSEE SUN: The takeaway trade influences most young Chinese people in that in a sense it takes away the time.

ALISON (aged 17, Merseyside): Here I was stuck in on Friday and Saturday nights, serving people who've been out on the town and having a good time; and that's when you start to get pissed off … at these times it made me hate being Chinese – I'd ask myself why couldn't I go out during the weekends or after school along with all my friends?

The takeaway work is hardest when others are at play; the pace of work behind the counter regulated by the leisure schedules of the locality. Being 'stuck' in a Chinese takeaway most nights, and in particular at weekends, brings home the marginal social location occupied by most Chinese people in Britain. But for the second and third generations, it can also sharpen a critical sense of how this position can provide resources for a specifically British Chinese recognition of the iniquities of racism:

TSEE SUN: As a takeaway you're somehow not really 'in' the society … I actually felt I'm trapped in this little hole full of uncivilized individuals and racist and ignorant people – white English people. That group of people often very sadly to say, I think they're so uncivilized, uneducated and they don't respect people as an individual; they just see Chinese people as a bunch of cooks who work in our country and provide a service for us as a servant as it were.

The local ethnoscape is temporally variable; a hierarchy of leisure with a racialized division of labour, defined by patterns of exposure and vulnerability. This is the routinization of racism: the reliance on recurrent custom limits resistance to harassment which comes to be regarded as routine. Yet the very need to survive in such circumstances has critical potential.

A Critical British Chinese Diasporic Habitus

It is no coincidence that several young British Chinese artists utilize their experiences of the takeaway within their work and turn the tables precisely through repeating and subverting the takeaway scenario. I will cite two examples here; Yeu Lai Mo's video installation, 'service, kissing, licking', and Linda Chui's poem 'West North' printed in the appendix to this chapter. The poem is written from the vantage point of the Silver Sea takeaway in north-west England. It sketches the defining features of takeaway life from the standpoint of having to serve on the counter, the power geometry of late-night opening. Located between five pubs, it draws in customers known by their bodily emissions rather than names. The English become the objects of scrutiny and are seen in a different light here: an invading force which is chronically inebriated, incoherent and potentially duplicitous. The use of Spanish and Chinese in the poem also turns the tables by leaving the reader to perform the work of cultural translation, the reverse of the demand placed on the takeaway to produce the immediately recognizable. Linda Chui thus brings into a play a distinctive British Chinese sensibility formed through being embedded in the locality, yet different from it. As she explains: 'I draw from many traditions ... Cultural affinities I think ... because I'm neither 100 per cent Chinese and I'm definitely not 100 per cent English ... the affinities are not black and white or clear cut.

Yeu Lai Mo's video installation, 'service, kissing, licking', is a more direct restaging of the takeaway encounter. As exhibited in the 'Number Six' show in London in March 1998, it consists of a short video which loops continually, played through the kind of portable colour television so often deployed in takeaways to entertain waiting customers. However, this performance sees the artist dressed in catering uniform silently offering in the starkest form what the white customer implicitly desires. Mouthing the usual 'Hello' and 'Thank you' greetings, she then goes on lovingly to kiss and finally lick the counter. Taken out of context, stripped of sound, offered in silence, the piece is a devastating and disturbing revelation of the expectations of service harboured by white male customers on entering takeaways.

These interventions mark two examples of an emerging sensibility which transcends the terms of the 'Chinese in Britain'/'overseas Chinese' binary structure of representations I described at the start of the chapter. They are British Chinese productions working through the experiences of facing up to regressive enactments of Britishness, revealing the takeaway to be a very British institution, but one felt through the body in radically distinct ways each side of the counter. The British Chinese diasporic habitus offers the resources to return the gaze back across the counter, unsettle the comfortable consumption relationships characteristic of celebratory multiculturalism and mark a British Chinese presence within an emergent contestatory multiculturalism.

Conclusion

This chapter has developed the concept of the diasporic habitus to conceptualize the everyday social practices sustaining a social setting emblematic of the Chinese diaspora in Britain, the Chinese takeaway. Prevailing conceptions of diaspora are overloaded with spatial metaphors and privilege the analysis of mutation and novelty in fields such as music, art and literature. Too often cultural theorists of transnational practices

prematurely favour the 'the quickened beat of improvisation' ...
'the glacial force of the habitus' (Appadurai 1996a: 6). By c...
concept of diasporic habitus focuses on the mundane. This is c...
spatio-temporally by the logics of practice within institutions ...he
Chinese takeaway central to its reproduction. Understanding the experience
of diaspora requires a penetration into everyday social interactions and
their continuing permeation by legacies of domination, inscribed on bodies
and surfaces of interaction like the takeaway counter.

Exploring these processes in a particular setting demonstrates that an
understanding of multiculturalism requires a much closer specification of
the perspective from which it is being understood. This entails a relativization of terms such as power geometry and time–space compression
employed all too loosely in depictions of globalization. The takeaway forces
us to consider power geometry and time–space compression in relation to
the pressure, vulnerability and racial harassment which arises from serving
food to white customers late at night.

In terms of one of this book's key concepts, why is an institution like
the Chinese takeaway *transruptive* of British national identity? Above all,
because however much it is derided or dismissed, the takeaway persists.
Chinese takeaways exemplify a modality of cultural recombination; what
have now become familiar forms of difference such as sweet and sour, chow
mein, are in fact not known in that form in China, but are *British* Chinese.
Although 'Having a Chinese' (sic) from one perspective appears familiar
and tame, it also carries seeds of cultural and social transformation, marking
the widespread insertion of aspects of the global into the economies of
pleasure and consumption which define the local neighbourhood. Far from
the Chinese catering business merely occupying an 'unobtrusive niche on
the fringe of the British economy' (Watson 1977), its geographical dispersal
and dependable availability are part of a wider post-war redefinition of the
British foodscape, one of the defining symbols of national identity. However,
it is crucial to advance beyond a celebratory multiculturalism which extends
a patronizing welcome to new culinary repertoires. The contestatory dimensions of multiculturalism become apparent only with a recognition that
changes in the foodscape wrought by the forces of migration cannot be
disassociated from changes in the ethnoscape. It is important to acknowledge
that takeaways 'make their living on the knife edge between novelty and
familiarity, risk and comfort'. Their battle with reluctant palates forms part
of a broader struggle to establish a viable presence (Wong 1993: 58).

The everyday encounters across the counter in Chinese takeaways have
given rise to modalities of survival which highlight the deployments of
imperial capital, and reveal the taken-for-granted orientalizing manoeuvres
which have for so long disfigured perceptions of Chinese culture. Chinese

prematurely favour the 'the quickened beat of improvisation' and overlook 'the glacial force of the habitus' (Appadurai 1996a: 6). By contrast, the concept of diasporic habitus focuses on the mundane. This is constituted spatio-temporally by the logics of practice within institutions like the Chinese takeaway central to its reproduction. Understanding the experience of diaspora requires a penetration into everyday social interactions and their continuing permeation by legacies of domination, inscribed on bodies and surfaces of interaction like the takeaway counter.

Exploring these processes in a particular setting demonstrates that an understanding of multiculturalism requires a much closer specification of the perspective from which it is being understood. This entails a relativization of terms such as power geometry and time–space compression employed all too loosely in depictions of globalization. The takeaway forces us to consider power geometry and time–space compression in relation to the pressure, vulnerability and racial harassment which arises from serving food to white customers late at night.

In terms of one of this book's key concepts, why is an institution like the Chinese takeaway *transruptive* of British national identity? Above all, because however much it is derided or dismissed, the takeaway persists. Chinese takeaways exemplify a modality of cultural recombination; what have now become familiar forms of difference such as sweet and sour, chow mein, are in fact not known in that form in China, but are *British* Chinese. Although 'Having a Chinese' (sic) from one perspective appears familiar and tame, it also carries seeds of cultural and social transformation, marking the widespread insertion of aspects of the global into the economies of pleasure and consumption which define the local neighbourhood. Far from the Chinese catering business merely occupying an 'unobtrusive niche on the fringe of the British economy' (Watson 1977), its geographical dispersal and dependable availability are part of a wider post-war redefinition of the British foodscape, one of the defining symbols of national identity. However, it is crucial to advance beyond a celebratory multiculturalism which extends a patronizing welcome to new culinary repertoires. The contestatory dimensions of multiculturalism become apparent only with a recognition that changes in the foodscape wrought by the forces of migration cannot be disassociated from changes in the ethnoscape. It is important to acknowledge that takeaways 'make their living on the knife edge between novelty and familiarity, risk and comfort'. Their battle with reluctant palates forms part of a broader struggle to establish a viable presence (Wong 1993: 58).

The everyday encounters across the counter in Chinese takeaways have given rise to modalities of survival which highlight the deployments of imperial capital, and reveal the taken-for-granted orientalizing manoeuvres which have for so long disfigured perceptions of Chinese culture. Chinese takeaways are difficult and dangerous work, tedious and tiring, requiring immense physical and symbolic labour. The diasporic habitus answers the question, how is this endured? For the diasporic habitus not merely generates the resilience to cope with the exigencies of social inequality and cultural stereotyping, but also offers sharp insights into the appropriative logic of celebratory multiculturalism. The Chinese diasporic habitus underlies the proliferation of Chinese practices and institutions which 'has engendered complex, shifting, and fragmented subjectivities that are at once specific yet global'; and 'multiple subjective senses of Chineseness that appear to be based not on the possession of some reified Chinese culture but on a propensity to seek opportunities elsewhere' (Ong and Nonini 1997: 26). The recognition of contestatory multiculturalism requires an engagement with the varied cultural habitus created while transported, as such opportunities have been sought by a growing transnational constituency. The Chinese takeaway is just one example of the spatial–temporal reconfiguration of the everyday and the transruption of the contemporary ethnoscape by new forms of diasporic habitus which are here to stay.

Appendix: from *El mar*

'West North' by Linda Chui (1995)

In daylight I look like a corpse
resurrected for Easter, but without
the smell of five-day rotting flesh
tombed up. It's Bank Holiday Monday
afternoon. I would really like to get out,
not just out of doors in these streets –

A nonchalant little town,
with its A6 jugular plan of pubs
from the *George and Dragon* to the
Rising Sun. There's the *Woodman* and
his neighbour the *Anchor* facing the *Grove Inn*,
and you can tell the whole damn place is ready
to flood with the Silver Sea flying salt
364 nights a year.

I am Lazarus, no, Elizabeth Tudor –
a real Lancastrian rose
with a face to launch the last bell invasion:

Diasporicity: Black Britain's Post-Colonial Formations

Barnor Hesse

The Black British subject is therefore born out of an imposed contradiction between Blackness and British-ness, British-ness being equated with white-ness in the dominant symbolic order. The Black British identity is one of many multiple identities emerging in the post-colonial era, both within the West and in the former colonies, and in the continuos human, cultural and material traffic between the two. (Mama 1995: 114)

Self-questioning seldom avoids an agonistic commentary on a relationship to an Other. When I was an undergraduate I found myself regularly teased by a Nigerian, an overseas student, who whenever he saw me would shout out, 'Black British, Black British!' It was an extraordinary feeling. I hated the epithet and yet I could not deny it. I opposed it but could not under-mine its imposition. I knew I was Black, I valued that social identity; I also knew I was British, I had abandoned myself to that contingency of birth. But when you put them both together, 'Black British', I was mortified. Blackness had an African, a Caribbean, an American accentuation; it even had a regional empathy with Liverpool, Manchester, Leeds, Birmingham or London. But ensconced as I was within the political and musical cultures of African-American funk (cf. Vincent 1996) and Jamaican reggae (cf. Potash 1997), there was little meaningful identification with Britain. Along with many of my generation, any ideas of national identification were submerged beneath investments in elective diasporic affiliations, the par-ticular Caribbean or African countries our families had migrated from and the distinctive, unquestionable attachments to the British cities we grew up in. Yet this still left undissolved an indelible, cultural birthmark that regularly induced others, if not ourselves, to question the *meaning of* and the *connection between* our Black and British identities.

Although since the late 1970s and early 1980s the relationship of Black people to the British cultural landscape has become more visible in its coherence and complexity, the idea of Black Britishness still retains the resonance of an oxymoron. Culturally, it appears to be no more than a balancing act between the racial exclusiveness of British nationalism (Gilroy 1987; Mama 1995) and the aspirational, transformative cultures of Black identities in Britain (Hall 1998; Sudbury 1998). However, even considering it as a *cultural* oxymoron (a routinely familiar, paradoxical enunciation), Black Britishness is a discourse whose increasing currency has yet to be conceptualized seriously. It is noticeable within the sound-bite proclivities of an unreflective public sphere that the mere evocation of Black Britishness manages to convey the profound impact of our cultural dynamics on the nation's popularization of itself, particularly in London, as either multicultural or liberal or simply *cool* (Phoenix 1998). No less apparent to the communities journeying under this nomenclature are the intimate ways variously dispersed forms of Black enunciation and representation are networked, cross-culturally, diasporically, and yet elaborate a personalized, British accentuation. Here the cultural theorist confronts two critical questions: what is signified by Black Britishness? What is the horizon of its signification? In this chapter my attempt to answer these questions explores the relationship between different contextual perspectives of Black Britishness in three main ways. My first concern is with the exclusive meanings of Black Britishness attached to post-1945 Caribbean migration to Britain, symbolized by the arrival of the SS *Empire Windrush* in 1948. The second discusses the significance of the post-colonial for understanding the configuration of Black Britishness and considers its possible symbolization around the 1945 Pan-African Congress in Manchester. The final part outlines a possible analytics of Black Britishness, defining its theoretical specificity by way of its intra-national and transnational relations with the African diaspora, that is to say, its logics of *diasporicity*.

Loose Ends: Unravelling the *Windrush* Symbol

By the time the *Windrush* arrived there were already Black communities who could trace their ancestry back a couple of centuries. But on 22 June 1948 the *Windrush* sailed through a gateway in history, on the other side of which was the end of Empire and a wholesale reassessment of what it meant to be British. (Phillips and Phillips (1998: 6)

During 1998 there was an unprecedented, public discussion of post-war Caribbean migrations to Britain since the docking of the *Empire Windrush* at Tilbury in 1948. In the course of what was celebrated as the fiftieth anniversary of the *Windrush*, that unremarkable former troop ship, the spirited, predominantly Jamaican, migrants and their year of disembarkment acquired an inspiring symbolic status.[1] Yet throughout the celebrations, *Windrush* as a symbol retained a curiously double-edged sensibility. Until its reappropriation, it had served for forty-nine post-war years, in periodic screenings of the contemporary newsreel, as the originary moment of Britain's national implication in the colonial demarcation of race-relations (see my Introduction, this volume). It had also symbolized, in the nationalist fears of the white racist imagination, a strange *coloured* trickle of immigration that became a Black flood of undesirability into British cities. At the same time these reified images formed an uncomfortable imprint on the Black gaze. The generational repetition of almost anthropological pictures, spoken over by the faintly imperial tones of an overbearingly English accent, evoked 'a curious clash between nostalgia and irritation' (Phillips and Phillips 1998: 2). As Mike and Trevor Phillips insightfully point out, irritation arose precisely because this constant, unchanging reference to the *Windrush* asserted 'over and over again, that Black citizens, the Caribbeans and their children, were unreconstructed newcomers, aliens for ever'. For forty-nine years *Windrush* signified in the public sphere the problem of 'race' and the racialized other.

Among others[2] Phillips and Phillips have made an impressive case for arguing that time has made it increasingly possible to identify a Black British appropriation of the *Windrush* as a symbol. It appears to mark a rather different relationship to an originary moment, 'as if the *Windrush*, in spite of time and distance, had become part of our own story'. By reclaiming the narrative of Caribbean migration to Britain within the corresponding formation of British Black communities, *Windrush* can now be seen to redefine these developments as critical aspects of the post-war reconstruction of Britain's public identity. Hence, in its fiftieth anniversary, it signified for the first time the possibilities generated by the emergence and consolidation of Black Britain. While it may seem uncharitable to be critical of such an important shift in the public perception of the meaning of Black Britain, celebratory moods cannot postpone indefinitely the idiom of critical thought. Perhaps it is now time to point out that this particular symbolization of the *Windrush* fails to achieve its discursive objectives. Given the thematic of Black Britishness which surrounds the belated appropriation of the *Windrush* as a symbol, there seems to be something uncomfortably familiar left intact. The insertion of a Caribbean migratory commentary does not manage to dislodge the visual regime which established the *Windrush* as the intrusive object of an unreflexive white gaze. The problem is that the assumptions underlying this particular discursive repetition are not sufficiently different from those installed in a race-relations narrative[3] which would have us believe that the development of racism in Britain (like the significance of Black Britain as a formation) simply arises from the impact of post-war migration. In this narrative, whether via the celebrations of the *Windrush* or its condemnation, the proximate, contextual idea of pre-existing, settled, regionalized Black communities simply vanishes. At the same time, the centuries of Britain's racialized involvement with the presence and representations of Black people receives less and less public amplification and acquires very little generational repetition in national discourses. What I am saying here, in relation to the post-war significance of Black Britain, is that the idea of its suddenness or its newness is a deeply misleading invocation because there is a significant residual[4] meaning of Black Britain left unaccounted for. The celebration of the *Windrush* symbol remains unwittingly ensnared at the level of merely *reappropriating* the images of a newsreel that used to unsettle us.

The embrace of the *Windrush* symbol in its post-war perspective has a number of representational difficulties which arise from the extent to which it is entwined, albeit unwittingly and ambivalently, with an oppositionally white British gaze. This leaves the attempt to understand the formation of Black Britishness with at least three contextual questions.

First there is the question concerning the discursive dissemination of Black Britain. Does it involve histories or memories or historiographies that draw on different geographies at different times? If so, how are they connected or entangled? What determines the privileging of particular time-periods or formations of Black settlement and the disregard of others? Second, the question of the particular ethnic elements and racialized representations mobilized in the formation of Black British identities. Currently, the *Windrush* symbolizes a hegemonic concept of Black British identity inscribed in a Caribbean ethnic particularism. It removes from view the significance of Africa and the (West) African presence in Britain, both in the first and second halves of the twentieth century; as well as the role of the politics of Pan-Africanism in the formation of Black British identities. Third, the question of the regional formation of Black Britishness; the possibility of a pre-existing, proto-Black British gaze on post-war Caribbean migration is often overlooked by writers on the post-war period. The construction of the *Windrush* as a national, symbolic event has tended to obscure the extent to which the perspectives of already settled Black communities were regionally significant. It ignores how these perspectives may have contributed to a dialogic basis of settlement, arising directly in relation to the addition of compatriots and solidarities in resourcing the fortitude and aspirations of emergent[5] and residual identities among Black communities. Even a cursory examination of these discursive loose ends should alert us to the fact that there is much at stake in accepting uncritically whatever gets amplified as historically momentous and socially significant in the formation of Black Britain. To understand some of what I have in mind we need to reconsider the meaning of *Windrush* as an originary moment in relation to 1948.

Babylon Makes the Rules: Another Side of 1948

If, as I argue, the symbol of *Windrush* is insufficient by itself to provide an understanding of why *Black* Britain emerges in the post-war period, then we need to consider how it can be approached as a consolidation of its own discontinuous history.[6] That the 1940s represent a major transitional rupture in the representation and formation of Black communities in Britain is not in dispute. What concerns me is how we understand the political and cultural thematics of that transition. For me this means rejecting the symbolic meaning of the *Windrush* as if it were an originary moment. We need to understand the significance of the *Windrush* solely in terms of it symbolizing a precipitative or decisive orientation in the political consolidation and cultural expansion of the British Black population during the second half of the twentieth century. Proceeding in this way requires that we avoid the conventional British race-relations narrative's repression of the long imperial history surrounding 1948. Our understanding of this will become clearer if we juxtapose *Windrush* with an equally significant, albeit less signified, event in 1948.

In August, just two months after the *Windrush* arrived in Tilbury, there was a so-called 'race-riot' in Liverpool. It has been estimated that there were 7–8,000 Black people in the former slave-trading city (Fryer 1984; Murphy 1995). Liverpool had experienced a long history of a discontinuous Black presence since its establishment as the nation's foremost slave-trading port in the eighteenth century (Williams 1944). Although a large number of Black people had arrived in Liverpool from the Caribbean during the early 1940s to help the war effort, particularly in munitions factories, there were already residential areas near the docks in the south end of the city that had been inhabited by mainly West African seafarers since the middle of the nineteenth century (Law and Henfrey 1981). It is worth summarizing the details of the 1948 'anti-Black riots' in Liverpool since they contain various social dimensions indicative of the ambiance and ambivalence of Black Britain, already established prior to the *Windrush*.

Since the end of the Second World (European) War, the National Union of Seamen had mounted a campaign to persuade employers to exclude Black seamen from British ships. The physical attacks on Black people in Liverpool were calculated local attempts to reinforce this exclusion at the source by using violence to dissuade Black seamen from seeking employment in jobs defined as belonging to white seamen. Over a period of three days, white mobs (on one occasion, 300 in number, on another 2,000), laid siege to different hostels and clubs that catered for Black seamen (Fryer 1984; Murphy 1995). This produced defensive counter-attacks by the Black population which in turn prolonged the fighting (Murphy 1995). When the police eventually intervened to restore order, they used the opportunity to inflict violence and arrest mostly Black people (Fryer 1984: 367–71). Black political responses to these events were orchestrated by the London-based League of Coloured people (established in 1931), whose investigation into many allegations of police brutality was reported in its newsletter; while a locally organized Colonial People's Defence Association intervened to arrange the legal defence of the Black people arrested (Ramdin 1987: 384–5). If in this brief outline we see a distinctive scenario of 'racism and reaction' (Hall 1978) that has become recurrently familiar in the post-*Windrush* period, we should note of course that the conditions of its possibility pre-date this.

It might be asked, however, why, apart from its juxtaposition in 1948, does this relatively obscure regional event merit attention alongside the more memorable circumstances surrounding the *Windrush*? In my view it is merely one episode in the twentieth-century history of Black Britain which, if analysed effectively, reveals complexities ignored by the privileging of the discursive logic associated with post-war Caribbean migration. The most remarkable thing to note, of course, is the pre-existence of a Black sea-fearing community. In the early twentieth century these existed not only in Liverpool but also in Cardiff and London. Although recent scholarship has increasingly identified Black sea-faring as highly significant in fashioning the networks and affinities of the Black Atlantic's[7] cultural and political communications (Gilroy 1993a; Bolster 1997; Thornton 1998), this has not yet come to terms with the tradition where it is signified in twentieth-century Britain (see Brown 1998). It is important, therefore, to try to account for the impact and scope of this experience, particularly as the employment of West Africans in the British mercantile trade can be traced back to the eighteenth century (Frost 1999). It has even been claimed that, by this time, nearly a quarter of the seamen in the British navy were Black (Walvin 1973). Whatever credence we give to this speculation, James Walvin suggests that throughout the period both Bristol and London were inextricably identified with the domiciles of 'transient sea-fearing Blacks' and this continued as a constitutive urban element of British society right into the twentieth century. Part of the distinctive configuration of these sea-port communities were the gender and sexual aspects of the their racialized sojourn in Britain, where enduring and ephemeral relationships between Black (West African and Caribbean) seamen and local white women accentuated the 'bi-racial', regional and global entanglements of Black Britain (cf. Brown 1998). Now although these developments were small and firmly located on the social and economic margins of Britain, the question remains, how should they be contextualized? Is it the quantification of the Black presence that determines what meaning we assign to the discursive logic of its inscription in Britain? Or should this logic be constructed from conceptualizing the changing qualitative permanence of that presence? The continuing incidence of Black seamen in Britain seems to transform these ostensibly empirical questions into inescapably conceptual issues.

Keep on Movin': Regionally Black Journeys

By the begining of the twentieth century, the incidence of Black seamen in Britain had dispersed from its eighteenth-century concentration in London to various regional locations as a result of economic changes in the structure of Britain's maritime trade and port facilities. This stimulated a process of internal migration and economically induced settlement for transient Black seamen in search of work. Cities like Liverpool, Cardiff, Bristol and North and South Shields featured prominently. The 1914–1918 World (European) War expanded a British demand for Black sailors to help with the war effort; consequently, the Black population greatly increased its regional demography (Walvin 1973; Frost 1999). With the cessation of the war, many Black seamen were again unemployed and unemployable because they were in direct competition with white seamen for jobs and the 'trade unions insisted on the employment of Englishmen in preference to Negroes' (Walvin 1973: 206). By 1919 there were a number of race-riots in the port cities of Liverpool, Cardiff, Hull, Manchester and London. A twentieth-century logic of racist violence (Hesse 1997) and 'institutionalized racism' (Frost 1999: 77) was inaugurated on the pattern of groups of local whites repeatedly attacking Black residences, motivated by perceived grievances around economic competition in employment, sexual competition over white women, and in effect regional contestations over the urban meaning to be assigned to the colonial demarcations of an increasingly racialized Britishness (Walvin 1973; Fryer 1984; Ramdin 1987).

As Liverpool in 1948 (Murphy 1995) was profoundly implicated in this tradition, it is worth considering what it might signify about Black Britain. Although it is now generally known that the city of Liverpool gained its economic prominence as a major port during the Atlantic transactions of the trade in enslaved Africans, it is rarely acknowledged that by the beginning of the twentieth century, the docklands and sea-faring industry of Liverpool were still booming due to a nineteenth-century shift in the development of Britain's imperial interests. Liverpool had become the location of a vast shipping trade, it was the 'gateway of the British Empire' (Lane 1987: 22), a city that looked outwards and forward towards the Atlantic rather than inwards and backward towards Lancashire. The movement of seamen in and out of the city was a defining characteristic of working-class life in the port areas. The colonial dimension of this shipping enterprise meant that a significant proportion of the transient settlers in the dock areas were Black. As early as the 1830s, Black seamen from West Africa, the Caribbean and the United States had become a familiar sight in Liverpool (Lane 1987: 117). The continuity of this development into the twentieth century became part of the outward-looking formation of Black Liverpool anchored in a pre-*Windrush*, regionalized, urban Black affinity with some of the diasporic lineages of the Atlantic world (Brown 1998). This is just one of the ways in which Black regionalism must be understood as both a precursor to and a correlative of Black Britishness.

Even within the limited context of the twentieth century, it should now be apparent that if *Windrush* 1948 symbolizes developments associated with Black Britain in the second half of the twentieth century and some of their earlier inscriptions, then Liverpool 1948 symbolizes those developments associated with the first half on the twentieth century and their differential continuation beyond that. Putting matters in this temporally discontinuous yet coeval way enables us to think of 1948, despite its arbitrary demarcation, as signifying much more than the singularization of a critically decisive year. What I am suggesting instead is that thinking about Black Britain initially in its twentieth century incarnation is a strategically useful way of assessing the meaning of its culturally national discontinuities. As we shall see, the period is coterminous with the most concentrated and extensive period of Black political activity within the overlapping discourses of the African diaspora, the British Empire, anti-colonialism, decolonization, migration, Black settlement and British nationalism. Because the prevailing narratives of contemporary Black settlement in Britain tend to relegate the earlier part of the twentieth century to the shelf of curiosity studies, while suggesting that matters of real historical interest take place in the middle to late twentieth century, we need to develop ways of thinking that avoid conceptually succumbing to the solipsist lure of the western spectacle,[8] that can attend to formations of the recent past in the receding present, and are capable of recognizing the conceptual terrain in which apparent historical discontinuities are also actual social forms of coevality.

Back to Life, Back to Reality: Pan-Africanism and Post-colonialism

In that history is Africa. Transported in chains and blood to the Americas. *Resurfacing in Europe as demobbed soldiers, migrants, settlers, refugees.* Reconstituted in colonial and racist images which cast Africans of the continent and Africans of the diaspora as inferior, animal, sporty, sexual: 'other'. *Never historically drawn as connected to, indeed of Europe. In this history Africa and its people were never in Europe, only Europe was in Africa.* (Lewis 1992: vii; emphasis added)

As my concern here is to suggest that there are different ways of symbolizing the *enunciation rather than the origin* of Black Britain, it is worth considering how things might look if we were to refer back to the residual meanings of the 1945 Pan-African Congress in Manchester. Although not yet so popularly symbolized as the *Windrush*, the Pan-African Congress held at Chorlton town hall, Manchester, in October 1945, bears as much examination for what it represents about the twentieth century *residual formation*[9] of Black Britain. Unlike the *Windrush* phenomenon, this highly remarkable event was broadly ignored by the British media (Hooker 1967) and has, with a few important histographic exceptions (Fryer 1984; Ramdin 1987; Adi and Sherwood 1995; Sherwood, 1995) been consistently overlooked in otherwise sophisticated theoretical accounts of the political and cultural import of Black Britain (cf. Gilroy 1987; Mercer 1994).

In order to retrieve the importance of Manchester 1945 it is worth recalling that during the 1930s and 1940s, Britain was the main locus of pan-Africanist discourses (in the English-speaking world) and functioned as an activist destination for various anti-colonial luminaries like Kwame Nkrumah, Nnamdi Azikwe, C.L.R. James, George Padmore, Jomo Kenyatta and Amy Jacques Garvey. Of the five major pan-African gatherings (one meeting plus four congresses) held between 1900 and 1930, three had taken place in London (Fryer 1984; Ramdin 1987). By the 1940s there were at least three significant campaigning organizations in Britain with domestic national profiles: the West African Students Union (WASU), established in 1925 by the Nigerian Ladipo Solanke together with the Sierra Leonean H. C. Bankole-Bright; the League of Coloured People (LCP), established in 1931 by the Jamaican Harold Moody; and the International African services Bureau (IASB), established by the Trinidadian George Padmore in 1937 (Adi 1998). In the absence of what might be described as a national discourse of 'race' politics, these London-based organizations could not obscure or ignore the regional diversity and settlement of Britain's Black communities in the port cities (e.g. Cardiff, Liverpool) and elsewhere (e.g. Edinburgh) where a number of distinctive social welfare organizations proliferated, particularly in Cardiff and Liverpool (Ramdin 1987). From this cursory glance at the early twentieth century it needs to be emphasized that Manchester 1945 was hardly an event conceived and designed in the absence of significant, British-inspired developments in pan-Africanist affinities or Black consciousness (Fryer 1984; Ramdin 1987). These distinctive formations were crucial to its organization. As Hakim Adi (1998) has pointed out, in 1944 a Pan-African Federation was inaugurated by various British-based Black organizations and a number of African-based organizations in order to articulate policy proposals that could effectively contest the continued colonial regulation of Africa and the Caribbean in the post-war world. It was 'the first time that so many organizations had joined together in a united front' (Adi 1998: 13). It was out of this collaboration that the initiative emerged to hold the 1945 Pan-African Congress in Manchester.

In asking how Manchester 1945 might be conceptualized as a symbol of Black Britain, it is not my intention to set it up in opposition to what the *Windrush* has come to mean in the poetics of Black Britishness. My concern is to reactivate this residual discourse of diasporic representation so that it too may be embraced, commemorated and rearticulated in defining the political meaning of Black Britain. It was after all the most successful and most representative of all the pan-African congresses, attended by the largest number of delegates, and had among its numbers prominent African leaders of anti-colonial movements. The diasporic compass of the congress was deeply symptomatic of a burgeoning, transnational Black political culture in Britain. We can see this in sessions which covered 'Imperialism in North and West Africa'; 'Oppression in South Africa'; 'The East African Picture'; 'Ethiopia and the Black Republics'; and 'The problem in the Caribbean' (Padmore 1963). However, when we also acknowledge that the first two sessions of the congress (chaired by Amy Jacques Garvey) were devoted to a consideration of 'The Colour Problem in Britain', is there not something profoundly momentous here? Does this not bear some family resemblance to a *political* symbolization of the idea of Black Britain? Consider the Congress's single resolution in this context:

> To ensure equal opportunities for all Colonial and Coloured people in Great Britain, this Congress demands that discrimination on account of race, creed or colour be made a criminal offence by law.
>
> That all employments and occupations shall be opened to all qualified Africans, and that to bar such applicants because of race, creed or colour shall be deemed an offence against the law.
>
> That the Negro Welfare Centres, the League of Coloured Peoples, African Churches Mission of Liverpool and other African organizations (social and religious) which have been doing legitimate welfare work among coloured children, students, seamen and others, shall be given every encouragement and assistance by the responsible Authorities to continue the vital social work in which they are engaged. (Padmore [1963] in Adi and Sherwood 1995)

In framing this resolution under the title 'The Colour Bar in Great Britain', Manchester 1945 posed the politics of Black settlement prefiguratively in post-colonial terms.[10] The idea of the 'colour bar' carried with it all the associations which today we would attribute to the generalized notion of 'institutional racism' (Ture and Hamilton 1992), but with one exception. The colour bar was an unofficial institution of British colonialism, a conventionalized series of racist practices and decision-making which regulated and barred the participation and mobility of colonial subjects within the jurisdiction of British (imperial and national) civilian and military institutions. Yet unlike the idea of institutionalized racism, which is usually understood in Britain today as a racist–nationalist reaction to 'non-white' immigration associated with the post-*Windrush* era (Smith 1989; Solomos 1993), the meaning of the colour bar referenced a longer British colonial history. It spoke to a proactive range of exclusionary and subordinating practices applied to people of colour, not only in the colonies but in the metropolis. By highlighting the colour bar in Britain as a problem within the overall context of British imperialism, Manchester 1945 pointed to the interior colonial formation of British society in which racism was becoming entrenched and detached from the exterior imperial project. If we turn our attention to the resolution on the colour bar itself, it seems extraordinarily prescient. In addressing the criminal law (anti-racist legislation covering social institutions), public policy (equal opportunities in employment) and the voluntary sector (resources for community development initiatives), it defined the social concerns of Black Britain in terms which continue to have an urgent contemporary resonance. It also located Black Britain within the post-war liberal-democratic discourse that was striving to rehabilitate itself as the legitimate and only alternative to a perceived threat of totalitarianism in the western reconstruction of fascist-torn Europe (Hobsbawm 1994; Isaac 1998; Mowzer 1998). Manchester 1945 gave the re-emerging western democratic discourse on rights, equality and peace a double articulation, inscribing both the thematics of post-war and post-colonial scenarios. Yet its political focus had pre-1945 origins which testified to the accumulation of critiques generated by Black political cultures during the first half of the twentieth century. At the same time the resolution's indictment of a racist governance in Britain expressed the same basis upon which the politics of anti-racism and Black self-help strategies have been articulated in the second half of the twentieth century in the so-called post-colonial era.

Nu Colours: A Black Poetics of Post-Colonialism

The relationship between pan-Africanism and post-colonialism[11] has only recently begun to attract important theoretical attention (Serequeberhan 1994; Eze 1997). Here I want to suggest that it is in the constitutive passage of the Black subject through the orientations of pan-Africanism (subsequently and concurrently, Black nationalism, Black feminism etc.) that a poetics of the post-colonial finds its unacknowledged expression. It may help to recall that by the beginning of the twentieth century, facilitated by the 1885 Berlin Conference,[12] the extensive and intensive European colonization of Africa brought the continent firmly within the co-ordinates of the unfree world. With the exceptions of Liberia and Ethiopia, it could no longer be represented unproblematically as the symbolic land of freedom as it had been etched in the nineteenth-century discourse of 'Ethiopianism' (Barratt 1977).[13] Once the twentieth-century impetus of anti-colonialism came to the fore, a discourse of Pan-Africanism emerged outside of and subsequently within Africa that increasingly emphasized Africa as *politically interior* rather than *culturally exterior* to the diaspora. This symbolic move from Africa and the diaspora (i.e. a historically dynamic cultural relationship between a homeland and enforced dispersal) to the African diaspora (i.e. a contemporaneous political analogy between the continuums of colonial dislocation and racialized displacement) signalled its appearance at the beginning of the twentieth century under the imprint of the pan-African congress movement (Geiss 1974; Walters 1993).

The congress movement increasingly framed the discourse in which it was possible to develop pan-Africanism strategically as a political movement on three continents: Western Europe (especially Britain), the Americas (e.g. the Caribbean and United States) and Africa (especially West Africa). Pan-Africanism as a political formation was constituted against the hegemony of western racisms and western imperialism. It expressed relations of equivalence between the identity claims, cultural inheritances and political aspirations of Black people racially subordinated, segregated and exploited within the global, racialized governmental lineages of western jurisdictions. Equally importantly, it was a political movement that understood itself as a direct and radical challenge to the hubristic hegemony and unflinching naturalization of European imperialism on the African continent itself (Magubane 1987; Adeleke 1998). It is usual to consider pan-Africanism strictly as an anti-colonial formation in the Fanonian idiom of a Manichean world violently divided into compartments comprising the colonizer and the colonized, the settler and the native (Fanon 1963). However, proceeding in this way presents the difficulty of trying to explain the currency of pan-Africanist themes (cf. Walters 1993) in the cross-cultural era of formal decolonization, unless we can address the dispersal of its integral post-colonial poetics. Without the latter, the diasporic conceptualization of Black identity in Britain would be impossible. I want to suggest that there are at least four poetics of the post-colonial, symbolized (retrospectively) by Manchester 1945, which underwrite the citations of an agonistic Black Britishness during the latter half of the twentieth century.

The first post-colonial poetic is a *contestatory subjectivity*. According to J. Jorge Klor De Alva, post-coloniality signifies 'not so much subjectivity "after" the colonial experience as a subjectivity of oppositionality to imperializing/colonizing … discourses and practices' (Klor De Alva 1995: 245). This may enable us to think of Manchester 1945's pan-Africanism as inscribed in acts of contestation both within the context of Europe's formal colonization of Africa and outside (i.e. occurring elsewhere and subsequently). Hence, pan-Africanism is a contestatory diasporic formation, a 'regularity in dispersion' (cf. Foucault 1972) which continues to be resourced by 'its questioning of the very norms that establish the inside/outside, oppressor (colonizer)/oppressed (colonized binaries) that are assumed to characterize the colonial condition' (Klor De Alva 1995: 245). In this way we can perhaps understand Manchester 1945 as positioning what would emerge as the *political Black* subject within an interrogation of enduring and reconfigured European/American colonial and racist practices that traverse the African diaspora and have a distinctive configuration in Britain itself.

The second post-colonial poetic evokes what Homi Bhabha (1994) usefully describes as a *contramodernity*. The pan-Africanism of Manchester 1945, sought to link the recent struggle against fascism in Europe with the struggle against imperialism in the African diaspora and the 'non-European' world generally. Through an expanded representation of the meaning of democracy it contravened the racialized principle that the modern idea of human rights arising from opposition to fascistic acts of barbarity and racial genocide could be conceived solely within the Euro-American narcissism of a 'western spectacle' (Hesse 1999b). It served as another reminder that German fascism had brought home to Europe the same imperialist practices that had been imposed in the creation of colonies (cf. Césaire 1972). In other words, fascism was not simply an aberration in the civilized ideals of western political culture, or even the denouement of a systemic debasement of Renaissance and Enlightenment values within the internal drama of European modernity (Adorno and Horkheimer 1969; Bauman 1989). These kinds of indictment constructed an exceptionalism which in turn signified the condemnation of fascism alongside the disavowal of constitutively imperial and hence 'non-European' formations of modernity. Hence, we need to reread the pan-Africanism of Manchester 1945, particularly where it surveys the possibilities of the post-war/post-colonial world, as a discourse which recasts the waste lands of Europe and the antinomies of the West as an ambivalent political location. Consequently, 'the metropolitan histories of the civitas cannot be conceived without evoking the savage colonial antecedents of the ideals of civility' (Bhabha 1994: 175).

A third post-colonial poetics can be named in Stuart Hall's reworking of the idea of *double-inscription*.[14] According to Hall (1996a: 242), the idea of the post-colonial reveals how the culture of colonialism worked in two apparently polarized spaces at the same time – the metropolis and the colony – thereby collapsing an apparent relationship of exteriority between the two, inscribing them both in the unstable, mutually constitutive meanings of imperialism. In this insightful recognition lies the germination of a significant pan-Africanist, post-colonial sensibility. The pan-Africanist critique of the colour bar in Britain, promulgated by Manchester 1945, collapsed the apparent demarcation of inside and outside the colonial system, suggesting that institutional forms of racist exclusion from social, economic and political resources operated across the apparent colonial divide between colonies and metropolis. Not only was the colour bar doubly inscribed transnationally, the colonial etiquette of British culture was translationally as much a part of domestic as foreign policy despite consistent national disavowals. Manchester 1945 insisted on the relation between British racism abroad and British racism at home, thereby resisting and countering the self-serving liberal idea that British nationalism and British imperialism belonged to different discursive universes.

The fourth post-colonial poetics we can associate with Manchester 1945 is perhaps the most important and least remarked upon. It refers to the unremitting, dehumanizing effects and consequences of an unacknowledged but deeply pervasive racialized governmentality. The postulation of a consistent colour bar in Britain points to the interrogation of what I call a *post-colonial racism*. Prior to the dismantling of the formal structures of white supremacy during the hegemony of imperial formations, western countries like Britain, France and the United States were also avowedly liberal and incrementally democratic (cf. Macpherson 1964). In the decolonization processes (between the nineteenth and twentieth centuries) which saw the dismantling of plantation slavery, European metropolitan imperialism, Jim Crow segregation, it was not necessarily racism that was abolished or disestablished, but rather the particular governmental institutions within which its patterns and grammars were embroidered. The end of colonial racism was accompanied by the post-war ratification of the liberal-democratic ideal in the West and the inauguration of a differently regulated racism, pragmatically compatible with western notions of liberty and equality. This racism was not simply an expression of formerly conventionalized ideas of white supremacy and non-white subordination, but was linked to institutional disavowals of the reconfigured continuity of racialized governmentality (Hesse 1999b) as well as the social repression of metropolitan decolonization and western anti-racism.

Post-colonial racism What then is the configuration of post-colonial racism? In my view it is undeniably symptomatic of the ambivalent transformation of western societies from liberal-colonial doubleness to liberal-democratic disavowal. Homi Bhabha has suggested that British colonial discourse, particularly from the nineteenth century, was marked by a 'doubleness' that revealed an 'agonistic uncertainty contained in the incompatibility of empire and nation', thereby putting 'on trial the very discourse of civility within which representative government claims its liberty and empire its ethics' (Bhabha 1994: 96). It was a kind of liberal-colonial doubleness which 'continually puts under erasure the civil state, as the colonial text emerges uncertainly within its narrative of progress' (p. 97). It was both less than what it claimed in colonial enunciations (i.e. concerned not with universal liberty but only with the rights of white Europeans) and more than what it affirmed in liberal enunciations (i.e. not only introducing 'civilization' but underwriting the violations and exploitations of 'non-Europeans'). Maintaining this formation coherently as facing two ways at once rather than as contradictorily 'two-faced', is its *constitutive outside*:[15] its cultural representations of the non-European other as despotic, unsuited to self-government and, by racialized association, infantile, incompetent and therefore fit only to be governed (Bhabha 1994; Mehta 1999).

It is the relation between liberal-colonial doubleness and decolonization during the second half of the twentieth century that transforms this colonial racism unevenly rather than discretely into a post-colonial racism. What Britain experiences as part of its post-colonial reconstruction (e.g. 1948–62) is signified at various social levels by a transition from the politics of 'race' as empire to the politics of 'race as nation' (Hesse 1997: 92–5). The convergence of a number of developments articulate this transition as something distinctive if not necessarily new. It emerges in the aftermath of western liberal-democracy being constructed against fascism and communism (e.g. NATO); worldwide anti-colonial struggles; the dismantling of the British Empire; the construction of the British welfare state; 'race' being declared unscientific by UNESCO; mass migration to Britain under way from the Caribbean, South Asia and West Africa; and urban voices and graffiti in London leading the chorus to 'keep Britain white'. Institutional decolonization was marked as a discrete event rather than a protracted process in which the affirmation of the liberal-democratic ideal and its corresponding distancing from imperialism was accompanied by a racially exclusive institution of a British national identity. It finessed a reinvention of British nationalism which repudiated 'non-white' immigration and pathologized Black and Asian settlement (Hesse 1997). The ostensible decolonization process, its idealization of British civilization and democracy,

which gained ground after the Battle of Britain, and the post-war valorization of its liberal tolerance, were achieved only insofar as it was possible
to conceal the prevailing incompleteness in the decolonization of western
countries. This is what I call *liberal-democratic disavowal*.

Consequently, the persistence of (white) racism points to the limited
nature of decolonization in western nations like Britain. It is imperative
that we reconsider the meaning of decolonization and its effects on the
metropolis itself. It makes sense to claim with Aimé Césaire that the
interrogative discourse of decolonization needs to be extended to the
formative ideals of western humanism and humanities within the metropolis, since its formative racisms have not been 'expatiated' (Césaire 1972).
The incompletion of decolonization in Europe ensured the inauguration
of a post-colonial racism predicated on the disavowal of the constitutive
continuities of imperial culture in the post-war western nation. It also
precluded the possibility of 'a new collective awareness of what had been
involved in the 'division of the world' among so-called 'civilised nations',
which in reality had been the bearers of barbarism' (Balibar 1991: 12).
Unsurprisingly then, especially in the British context, the formalization of
decolonization was conveyed by the government as a form of largesse,
available only once a certain level of maturity had been reached by the
'non-European' (Judd 1996; James 1994).

If racist discourse gained 'new meanings and inflexions in the period of
decolonization' (Lawrence 1982: 66), it was to a large part the result of
cultural work invested in producing a 'historical forgetfulness' (Hall 1978)
as well as 'white amnesia' (Hesse 1997). These cultural repressions reinscribed a limited liberal-democratic recognition of (post-colonial) racism
as the problem of 'race' attendant on the question of post-war migration
(Hall 1978; Lawrence 1982), thereby decontextualizing it from its imperial
gestation, presuming it unrelated to the conventions of western liberal-
democracy and the cultural formation of Britishness, and consequently
projecting it exclusively on to the pathology of extremist right-wing politics
and aberrant, deviant, racist individuals. Where colonial racism as a form
of governmentality had, during the imperial stretch of western history, been
conventionalized rather than conceptualized in metropolitan discourses, in
the era of decolonization and the post-war period, post-colonial racism is
no less a governmentality but is conceptualized and correspondingly revised
as an ahistorical form of *exceptionalism*. Becoming associated with the
presence of the post-war 'non-European' migrant rather than the presence
of unrelinquished European cultural imperialisms, 'racism and discriminatory practices' are seen as 'individual exceptions to an otherwise satisfactory
"rule"' (Hall et al. 1978: 340). In short, post-colonial racism in the second
half of the late twentieth century describes the continuing incidence of an

(un)acknowledged white racism in contemporary western cultures, together with a constitutive disavowal of its antecedents in liberal-colonial doubleness and its liberal-democratic reconfiguration of imperial continuities. Exposing the resistance of this formation to decolonization or simply compromising with it in order to achieve (con)temporary moments of social advancement have long been part of the political dilemmas in the post-1945 genealogies of Black Britishness.

Mind Adventures: A Genealogy of Black Britishness

In my own conversations with groups of young Black women, many have spoken of their identities in essentialist ways, in terms of fixed, natural, immutable characteristics. In contrast, however, definitions of Black identity in the academy and certain forms of popular culture, move away from fixed and unitary conceptions of Blackness, towards conceptualizing it as fragmented and diverse. (Weekes 1997: 113)

I have previously argued that there is a 'constitutive split' in Black identity (Hesse 1999b), which can only be understood diasporically as a temporal oscillation between what Glissant (1989) describes as 'reversion and diversion'. The former specifies the idea of a conceptual return to meanings associated with the historical revalorization of Africa, while the latter articulates a creolized engagement with the contemporary complexities of racialized displacement in the West (Hesse 1999b). However, it can also be argued that either reversion or diversion may be overlaid with 'the tension between essentialist and anti-essentialist ideas in the construction of racial identity' (Weekes 1997: 123). Using this background I want to ask: how should we understand the emergent meanings of Black Britishness? Although very little attention has been given to this as a conceptual formation, there are growing indications that it can no longer evade serious discussion (Mama 1995; Hall 1998). Possible lines of inquiry might involve some or all of the following: 'Black Britain' is an indigenous rather than an immigrant phenomenon (Mullard 1973); 'Britishness' and 'Blackness' have been constructed in racist discourses as mutually exclusive (Gilroy 1987; Mama 1995); Black Britain is intelligible only as part of the African diaspora (Gilroy 1987; Mercer, 1994); Black British identities are gendered co-productions in which the lives, struggles and misrepresentations of Black women are critical to its orientations (Bryan et al. 1985; Mama 1995; Reynolds 1997; Sudbury, 1998); and Black Britishsness is increasingly aspirational and entrepreneurial (Hall 1998). However, while this summary is insightful, the perspectives it invokes do not amount to an overall analytical approach. Perhaps what comes closest to this kind of intervention is the pioneering work of Paul Gilroy (1987; 1993a; 1993b) which examines Black Britain as an agitational, reflexive urban social movement within the horizon of its expressive musical cultures, the latter being defined by an exclusive diasporic indebtedness to the Caribbean and the United States. But this compact formulation says hardly anything about the politically unifying or socially disorganzing impact of conjunctural, gendered, cross-generational, and ethnically diverse post-colonial formations in Black identities. In the following sections I offer something of a corrective to the analytical blind-spots of Gilroy's influential analyses.

Contemporary analyses of Black Britishness need to begin by examining the diasporic meaning of its historical discontinuities. Here we confront an apparent historical series of signifying sequences in which spaces of Black Britishness have recurrently been articulated precisely because there have been constant narrative displacements and interruptions of historiographic continuity. The very sense of historical absence or 'non-history' (Glissant 1989) in Britain, despite the longevity of the Black presence since the sixteenth century, is the radically contingent ground upon which contemporary intimations of Black Britishness construct a relationship to the African diaspora. The meanings of diasporas generally are regulated by ideas concerning the discontinuous relationship between notions of home-lands, incidences of dispersal and conditions of displacement (see Sayyid ch.1, this volume). Diasporas, however, generate by their own specifically internal rules of explication, forms of enunciation and relations of representation which designate their identities and constitutive outsides. This is what I mean by the logic of *diasporicity*. It is a language game[16] that formulates the meaning of its relative markings of distinctiveness as the expressive basis of its culturally relational and political configurations. It conveys the structure of affinities (e.g. in Britain, the Caribbean, West Africa and USA) and cartographic limits (e.g. the Black Atlantic) within which particular diasporas exert representational influences upon populations in particular national formations. The logic of diasporicity enables us to make sense of how the same populations who are identified with these national formations conceptualize and activate their diasporic sensibilities. Inside Black Britishness the play of diasporicity will perhaps become clearer if we reflect on how and why its politico-cultural significations are formed at the interface between the intra-national locutions of its British formations and the transnational meanings of its interpellations by the African diaspora.

Intra-national Black Britishness What does it mean to think of Black Britishness as a form of intra-nationalism? Here I am thinking not so much of regionalism or the local opposed to the global, but of the incidence of social movements of various interrogative persuasions (e.g. ethnic, religious, sexual, class, ecological) which position and contest within the discourse of the nation-state the perspectives from which national investments and disinvestments are made in the imagined community. Intranationalism disorganizes the idea of a tidy, monolithic, uniform, national imaginary. In so far as Black Britishness distinguishes itself from white Britishness (Mama 1995), or Asian Britishness (Sharma et al. 1996), it is a social movement with a differential investment in the national formation. Its intra-nationalisms define and interrogate the terms of its national representation. These can be summarized as four articulations in the transruptive politics of Black (un)settlement.

First, Black Britishness is *discontinuously historicized*. The apparent temporal rupture which separates the late from the early twentieth century in the institution of Black settlement, evidenced by the emergent symbolization of the *Windrush* and the residual symbolization of Manchester 1945, is neither novel nor aberrant. Since the sixteenth century the Black presence in Britain has been invariably subject to social expansion and decline in distinct historical periods, with negligible generational and communal continuity between these periods (Shyllon 1977). It is this interrupted sense of historical dénouement without the coherence of a historical narrative which tends to collapse the referential horizon of Black British subjectivities into the most empirically accessible generational 'experiences' and the illusorily longer histories of other places of diasporic displacement like the United States or the Caribbean. Consequently, critical reformulations of the subjective meaning of Black Britishness negotiate a precarious historiographic pathway of discontinuities in which the constitutive outside of the Black British subject is partly defined by the manner in which its historical formation has been historically uninformed by its own British history.

Second, Black Britishness is *profoundly and disparately regionalized*. The national history of Black communities is lived primarily in terms of locality (cf. Dennis 1988; Keith 1993). Even the ubiquitous serialization of the post-war migration narrative does not transcend its accentuation within the city-bounded histories and memories of London, Birmingham, Cardiff, Liverpool or Leeds (etc.). In appropriating Britishness through regional life-worlds and vernaculars, the cities inhabited by Black communities resemble a geography of disparate identities connected only by diverse investments in imagining a nationally expressive Black Britishness and the mobilization of diasporic affinities.

Third, it is *recurrently politicized* as forms of agency and identification in relation to the complimentary strategic resources of 'communitarian edification' and 'axiological restitution' (Hesse 1999b). I use these terms to highlight the particular logics of *esprit de corps* that animate Black politics. Communitarian edification describes the ideal of empowerment through community formations and values in the development of Black movements for civil liberties, social justice or economic liberation. We can see this logic in a myriad iconic events and campaigns which have exposed the impact, pervasiveness and disavowals of racism in Britain (cf. Solomos 1993). From the so-called race riots in Liverpool in 1948 and Notting Hill in 1958, to the campaigns against the 'sus' laws of the 1970s, the urban uprisings against policing in the 1980s, to the campaign around the racist murder of Stephen Lawrence in the 1990s, the political cultivation of Black identity in Britain bears testimony to a cross-generational critique of and generationally specific challenges to various forms of 'white governmentality' (Hesse 1997). In contrast, axiological restitution refers to the contemporary valorizations of African-derived or inspired values, historical knowledges and cultural identifications, despite the West's skewed representations of anything associated with Africa as inferior, exotic and generally underdeveloped. Axiological restitution subsists here as a social discourse that continually interrupts the reduction of the meaning of Black identities to the semantic requirements of Britishess. Always sensitive and resistant to its popularization being debased by commericalization, it reiterates the contemporary relevance (contested, affirmed, transformed, etc.) of cultural materials from Africa and the Caribbean in the creative and public endeavours of British Black British sensibilites. Whether evidenced in fine art (Sonya Boyce, Chris Ofili), literature (Joan Riley, Ben Okri), popular music (Courtney Pine, Caron Wheeler), stand-up comedy (Curtis Walker, Gina Yashare), newspapers (the *Voice*, the *Nation*) or the annual Notting Hill carnival, its 'regularity in dispersion' (Foucault 1972) orchestrates its compositions as a repeatable politics in the cult of memory (Hesse, 1993).

Fourth, Black Britishness is *dialogically differential* around various conceptions of Black subjectivity, increasingly dissected by critical investments in gender, ethnic, sexual, class and religious differences. Certainly, since the 1980s, these dialogical differences have become more explicitly valorized, through both affirmation and contestation, introducing far greater complexity into the meaning of a Black British constituency (Mercer 1994), as well as facilitating the demise, at least theoretically, of the essential Black subject (Hall 1988). The configurable impact of Black feminism here is perhaps of greatest importance in resisting gender-exclusive formulations of Black cultures as masculine preserves, while at the same time articulating the specificity of Black female agency in community organizing, cultural work and intellectual interventions within the transformative context of an inclusive Black identity (Mirza 1996; Sudbury 1998). This, taken together with what might be described as *familial ethnicities*, derived from and preserved in migratory identification with kinship relations in particular African or Caribbean nations or in terms of what is conventionally referred to as 'mixed race' or 'biracial identity' and less conventionally 'metis(se)' identities' (Ifekwunigwe 1999), points to the increasingly dialogical locations from which locutions of identity are enacted as part of a cross-cultural formation of Black Britishness.

Transnational Black Britishness Despite the dynamic cultural expressivity of these intra-national formations, they remain only one half of the transruptive story. Black Britishness in a global world also has to be understood as a form of transnationalism. Aihwa Ong describes transnationalism as an intensification of the social processes constituting 'conditions of cultural interconnectedness and mobility across space' (Ong 1999: 4). While the diaspora connotations are obvious, there is also a complex chain of associative formations in the changing logic between Black people, the British nation-state and the circuits of capital. During the late twentieth century it can be seen in the protracted incompleteness of decolonization and the globalization of the western identity (Hall 1991; Said 1993; Sayyid 1997); the discontinuous racisms and racialized economies confronting pre-1945 and post-1945 Black settlements (Walvin 1973); the Europeanization of racist immigration and nationality legislation (Miles 1993; Brah 1996); and the commodified expansion of a transatlantic Black visibility in the expanded public sphere of globalization (Gilroy 1993a). In relation to that regulative experience, the transnational encapsulates the stretching of a Black British public's interpretive, diasporic repertoires beyond the parochial landscape and limited imagined community of Britain. We can specify the locus of this transnationalism as three differently transruptive modes of diasporic identity.

First, in terms of *the migratory orbit of familial ethnicities*. The Black population in Britain remains diversely related through family ties, interests, communications and travel to Black populations elsewhere in the world, primarily the Caribbean and Africa and to a much lesser extent Canada and the United States. I refer to this as an orbit of migration. It is intended to capture the sense in which part of the cultural marking of Black British identities, which weaves its way into the social dynamics of British life, is recruited from the communal legacies and familial associations of 'migratory subjectivities' (Boyce Davies 1994). These are regularly animated and ethnicized by communication or involvement with the diasporic locations of economic investments, cultural belongings and political loyalties. The transnational formation of the migratory orbit translates Black British identities in a 'discontinuous intertextual temporality of cultural difference' (Bhabha 1994: 38). In other words, the transnational meaning of Black

Britishness is constantly renegotiated in comparative oscillation between minority status (in Britain) and majority status (in the Caribbean or Africa), as well as in relation to similarities and differences perceived in the formation of Black communities in the United States and Canada.

Second, as *antiphonal forms of commodification* in popular culture. Whether via music, film, literature, sport, fashion or vernacular, Black aesthetics are visibly urbanized around the specularization of Black youth-styles in communication with each other across the Black Atlantic (Gilroy 1993a). This is particularly expressed in a gendered affinity and fascination with Black American cultures of hip-hop and R&B, alongside which the Black accentuation of British alternative sounds and styles assert themselves with increasing confidence (Back 1995). Although always running in subversion and combination with this antiphonal formation, contesting or transforming its hegemonic inflexions, are the less assimilatory and more ostentatiously gendered Jamaican forms of Ragga expressiveness (see Noble ch. 7, this volume). As elsewhere, British Black youth in their fashioning of a culturally popular, stylistic presence on the urban retina, in the street, clubs, schools and workplaces, have stimulated a racialized rearticulation in the transmission of images, sounds and advertising across the urban British landscape (Hall 1998).

Finally, diasporic identities in Black Britain take the form of political, cultural and intellectual *relations of elective affinities* (Gilroy 1993a; Hesse 1999b). The conceptual meanings ingested within the imprimatur of Black British discourses have many sources and sites of interlocution, particularly outside the British context and beyond the British state's network of international allies and affiliates. What endures here are variously contested concerns and interests in: the histories and futures of Africa and the Caribbean; the diasporic impact of racialized modernity on peoples of African descent; and the discursive meaning and social formation of Black Britain. These articulations continually inscribe the horizon within which diasporic reflexivities are enacted. At the end of the twentieth century there is, however, nothing particularly systemic about the British reactivation of diasporically Black identities, although it is strategic. For example, in intellectual discourses Black Britishness draws eclectically and cross-culturally from the themes of critical thought aligned with Black social movements (e.g. pan-Africanism, Black power, Black feminism, Rastafari) and also experiments with their inflections through 'other' interventions subversive of western naturalisms (e.g. anti-racism, multiculturalism, (post) Marxism, feminism, psychoanalysis, post-colonialism, post-structuralism, postmodernism). All of which, circulating within various locations and locutions of the African diaspora (e.g. United States, France, the Caribbean, West Africa, South Africa), reveal just one of the ways in which Black

Britishness is contextualized by the post-colonial logic of its own diasporicity.

Conclusion

Sometimes it's not only what you say that matters, but to whom you say it. Since beginning my sojourn as an academic it has been impossible to ignore the dearth of British intellectual spaces where the sorts of issues I have been raising here can be formally discussed, researched and taught. At the same time there is an expanding generation of students whose interests and passions in these areas are simply overlooked. Consequently, what I have attempted to provide in this chapter is a strategic indication of some theoretical ideas that could assist in developing an approach to Black British studies. There is much that remains to be said about the post-colonial formation of Black Britishness, particularly its implications for how we think about a more inclusive agenda of British research in cultural, social, political and historical studies. Unfortunately, questions raised by the African diaspora in Britain, and Europe generally, are usually confined to marginalia in the British academy. It takes a profound effort of the intellectual imagination to think within and against a social scientifc discourse that conventionally universalizes elaborations of Euro-American global structuration in modernity, as if at any time in the last five hundred years it was not also implicated in African diasporic formations. One of the profoundest, initial challenges of Black British thought is consistently to question this disavowal. Of course, none of this ever occurred to me when I was a student struggling and growing with the meaning of my own Black British identity.

Notes

A version of this chapter was given at a seminar organized by the Center for German and European Studies, University of California, Berkeley, March 1999. I am grateful for the comments and feedback from Donald Moore and Gia White on that occasion. Also to Paula Williams for an initial response and to S. Sayyid for that final critical perusal.

1. Throughout the year up to June, there were many public events staged, including a high-profile television series shown on BBC 2, *Windrush*, based on the Phillips brothers' book.

2. Although a number of other publications appeared, I have made particular reference to this book because it summarizes the dominant sentiments popularized about the *Windrush* during the celebrations. But see Sewell (1998).

3. It is important to recognize that the very notion of 'race-relations' perpetuates a colonial idiom, the Manichean divide that Fanon spoke of; it is the language of an assumed 'natural' social segregation, in which people 'naturally' live in accordance with

the dictates of their 'race'. Of course, to tell the story of post-war migration in these terms is to disavow the history of white British racism and its constitutively imperial repertoires. See my Introduction (this volume) where I discuss this in more detail.

4. The 'residual' (Williams 1977) refers to meanings accreted from the colonial past which accrue influentially in the so-called post-colonial present. I discuss the wider conceptual meaning of the 'residual' in my Introduction to this volume.

5. By using 'emergent' (Williams 1977) here, I am thinking of social identities and cultural repertoires which emerge directly in relation to the period of decolonization and the challenges represented by racism and its disavowal in the post-colonial period (see note 8 below). I discuss the wider conceptual meaning of the 'emergent' in my Introduction to this volume.

6. Modern Black British history has conventionally been divided into the following four periods: 1555 to the beginning of the seventeenth century; the eighteenth century; the late nineteenth century to the early twentieth century; post-1945, the *Windrush* era (Shyllon 1977; Fryer 1984; Ramdin 1987). What is noticeable about this or any other conceivable periodization is its interrupted, discontinuous arrangement.

7. While Gilroy (1993a) has been particularly influential in developing the idea of the 'Black Atlantic' as a concept of modernity, it is noticeable that he fails to consider a much earlier innovation of the same nomenclature in the work of Thompson (1983) where the question of visual art and African aesthetics is given exclusive attention as part of a disseminated tradition that links the cultural repertoires of West Africa and the African-Americas.

8. I have discussed the meaning of the 'western spectacle' in detail elsewhere (see Hesse 1999b). Here I am using it to draw attention to the conceptual lens in theoretical and popular discourses which focuses on the world as naturally divided into exalted western and debased 'non-western' dimensions, distinguishes western nations as normatively white and aberrantly 'non-white' and erases from explicit portrayal the imperial and racist constitution of these formations. Hence we arrive at the naturalized demarcation of 'race-relations' arising, as it were, outside of history.

9. I am suggesting that the issues confronting Black communities arising from the early twentieth century did not simply disappear in the post-1945 period but became reconfigured and amplified in the trajectory of its different political conjuncture. See Adi (1998) and Bush (1999) for an indication of these residual similarities.

10. This draws upon the idea of the post-colonial I discuss below, where I argue that it is a perspective that allows us to interrogate the terms of a decolonization process that fails to address the persistence of racism in the metropolis. It identifies racism as deeply symptomatic of the incomplete decolonization of the imperial dimensions of British culture and politics.

11. It is beyond the scope of this chapter to analyse this in detail. I confine myself here to expressing the thematics of post-colonialism in the critical idiom of Pan-Africanism in order to emphasize their interconnectedness.

12. Between December 1884 and January 1885 the Berlin conference was convened to formalize arrangements between European nations competing in the military colonization of Africa. It was attended by all the western powers with the exceptions of the United States and Switzerland. There were, of course, no Africans present. It launched what became described by historians as the 'Scramble for Africa'. See Boahen (1987).

13 Ethiopianism became prominent in North America, parts of the Caribbean and South Africa during the nineteenth century as an alternative Christian church movement

which venerated the idea of Africa and the Christian antiquity of Ethiopia. See Barrett (1977).

14. For the initial theoretical exposition see Derrida (1981).

15. The Derridian notion of 'constitutive outside' describes the relational elements of meaning against which a particular formation radically distinguishes its identity, but which in remaining external to that formation are at the same time a necessary condition of its identity as well as a potential threat to its coherence.

16. Wittgenstein's concept of 'language games' refers to the boundedness of linguistic and non-linguistic activity in the context of socially constituted experiences or 'forms of life'. In other words, a language game's forms of enunciation and connectedness with relations of representation and activity are unique and internal to the context that engenders them. There is no essence to a language game, only contextual rules and contingent articulations. See Fogelin (1995) and McGinn (1998).

Part II

Cultural Entanglements

(Dis)Entangling the 'Asian Gang': Ethnicity, Identity, Masculinity

Claire Alexander

The term 'Asian' marked as an ethno-cultural category in both popular and academic discourses has so far been confined to the simplistic describing and subsuming of specific, national, ethnic and religious identities. Those accounts that have attempted to explore the category 'Asian' in more political terms have only served to reassert an essentialist and culturalist under-standing of Asian identity formation. (Sharma et al. 1996: 33)

My identity and my history are defined by myself – beyond politics, beyond nationality, beyond religion and Beyond Skin. (Nitin Sawhney 1999)

On 25 April 1997, a group of Sikh young men from Southall arrived in the Chalvey area of Slough. According to a newspaper report in *Eastern Eye* (2 May 1997),[1] the 'gang of 60 youths ran amok', targeting Muslim homes, shops and cars, and causing thousands of pounds worth of damage. The report continues that the assault was thought to be a response to recent attacks on the Sikh community in Slough, and was followed by a swift revenge attack by Muslim youths from the area on a local Sikh shop. Whatever the immediate motivations and subsequent responses, the wider ramifications of these events are flagged starkly in the article's headline: 'Gang Warfare'. With the heading 'Sixty armed youths go on the rampage in orgy of violence', images of social breakdown and incipient anarchy are threaded throughout the report: there are growing 'fears of a violent gang war', 'gang-related incidents', a 'frightening attack' by 'armed' youths 'believed to be from a known gang in Southall', running 'riot', smashing cars and windows with sticks and stoning the police and passers-by.

What is of particular significance to the present chapter is the conflation of common-sense notions of ethnicity, gender and generation in this article, and its relation to wider emergent concerns about Asian youth identifica-tions. Although the article echoes 'community leaders' in overtly eschewing 'ethnicity' as a motivation for the conflict, ethno-religious labels are used uncritically throughout as the sole definer of collective identities and naturalized in the appeal to 'community'. The chairman of the Slough Sikh Union, Rajinder Sandhu, is thus quoted, 'We want to make it clear that these problems are not religious based. Both *communities* are living peacefully and respect each other's values ... These are *gang*-related incidents which are giving a bad name to the *communities*' (*Eastern Eye*, 2 May 1997, emphasis added).

There is, however, an obvious and significant tension in this picture of multicultural harmony, which is implicit in the assertion of an ethnically defined and reified notion of community 'difference', and which in turn provides the symbolic repertoire of the conflict rehearsed in the article – these are 'Sikh' youths attacking a 'Muslim'[2] area, in response to earlier attacks on Sikh homes 'on the eve of Vaisakhi'.[3] Within this logic, an attack on a local Sikh shop by the young Sikh men can be understood only as a 'mistake' – an individuated error – but becomes transformed into a marker for a collective 'Sikh' identity during a 'revenge attack' by Muslim youths the following day.

'Ethnicity' thus resurfaces throughout the article as the implicitly inescapable rationale for the conflict. There is, however, a crucial reconfiguration of this understanding: this is noticeably a *male* identity, structured through violence; or, as DI Steve Neale of Slough police asserted in the same article: 'It comes back to a hard core of young men intent on kicking lumps out of each other.' More than this, then, it is about *young* men, who are at once positioned as both the representatives of a collective ethnicity and as its periphery, both part of and apart from 'the community'.[4] This constellation crystallizes in the symbol of 'the gang', with its incumbent notions of conflict, deviance and youth subculture. The image of an ethnically or racially defined 'gang' additionally evokes images of tribalism, social breakdown and, above all, of a crisis in masculinity, manifested in acts of collective violence: in 'gang warfare'.

The present chapter has two major concerns: first, to trace the emergence of 'the Asian gang' in the public imagination and to interrogate the racialized notions of gendered identities this encompasses. It argues that Asian identities are increasingly reinvented through new structures of generation and gender, positioning young Asian men increasingly in the 'public' domain, with its implications of social surveillance and control. This has led to the reification of essentialized and problematized identities centred on notions of a racialized crisis of masculinity among Asian youth. In particular, the chapter argues that these representations have drawn on, and translated, dominant discourses (both popular and academic) of black masculinity, constructed through images of deviance and violence, to legitimate this reinvention – a conflation of assumed raced, gendered and generational deficiencies which constitute a 'triple pathology'[5] of young black and Asian men and place them in the public imagination as fully-formed 'folk devils',[6] with all the ideological authenticity of 'common-sense' knowledge. Second, the chapter contends that while dominant representations of 'the Asian gang' have imaged (or, indeed, imagined) young Asian men transfixed in a moment of crisis, in reality, such moments of confrontation and conflict encapsulate a complex matrix of identifications in which diverse understandings of ethnicity, gender, age, family, territory and community are enacted, and often 'entangled' (see Hesse, Introduction, this volume). The present chapter is primarily concerned with the inter-action of 'race' and gender categorizations in the invention of 'the Asian gang'. It argues that while gendered identifications are rendered invisible in this discourse, notions of racialized masculinities constitute a crucial ideological framework within which Asian youth identifications take shape and are ultimately enmeshed.

The chapter thus explores the tension between: *discrepant* masculinities, that is, the notion of subordinated racialized gender formations which are marginalised in dominant discourses and which are constructed both in opposition to white masculine norms and used to reconstitute these norms; and *transruptions*, the performance of alternative masculine identifications which contest and unsettle these definitions. 'Entanglement' here, then, refers at once to the interrelationship of these representations of Asian youth masculinities with their more concrete manifestations, and to the shifting and ambiguous negotiations which make up these apparently concrete events. Rather than a simple picture of identities forged in the intersection of multiple pathologies, what emerges in this arena is a more contextual and performative set of identifications, in which there are 'no guarantees' (Hall 1992), in nature, society or, indeed, in 'art' (Alexander 1996).

The chapter falls into three main sections: first, a brief overview of the emergence of 'the Asian gang' in the media. This examines the notions of racial/ethnic difference and incommensurability, generational conflict and gender dysfunction which form the crux of these representations and argues for understanding the racialization of Asian youth identities that these processes enact. Second, a consideration of the theorization of black masculinity, exploring the marginalization of black male experience and subjectivity and the demonization of black men in academic discourse. Finally, the chapter hopes to unpack and contest these common-sense representations through an exploration of gendered and ethnic identifica-tions as they were enacted during one incident which occurred in my recent fieldwork with young Bengali men in London.[7]

The New Asian Folk-devil: the Rise and Rise of the 'Asian Gang'

The article in *Eastern Eye* reflects a growing concern in the British media, and more generally, with the 'problem' of Asian youth – and more specifically with the growth of a 'gang' culture among young Asian men. An article in the London *Evening Standard* six months earlier (13 November 1996) captures the arrival of this new folk-devil, 'Asian teenage gangs terrorising London'. As with the *Eastern Eye* article, the headline says it all: the combination of a racialized ethnicity, generation and gender markers in the evocation of a new threat to the social order – 'foreign' young men 'terrorizing' a landscape which they are within but do not fully inhabit. The article rehearses all the markers of racial disaffection, social marginalization, cultural and generational conflict which have become inseparable from the invention of 'gang' subculture – these are youths wielding weapons, alienated from their families, their communities and the wider society, locked into a cycle of inevitable but meaningless violence, low self-esteem and self-destruction. Headteacher Michael Marland[8] thus warns of 'a new underclass of illiterates, who have acquired a habit of violence', creating what is described as 'almost apocalyptic vision of unrest' (*Evening Standard*, 13 November 1996).

It is significant that these images of 'nihilistic violence' re-create the same well-established tropes of racial alienation and social breakdown which created, and continue to create, moral panics over so-called 'Rastafarian drug dealers', 'black rioters', 'muggers' and 'Yardies' from the 1970s onwards (Hall 1978; CCCS Collective 1982; Gilroy 1987; Alexander 1996). It is revealing that this recent reinvention of the black folk-devil also wields the same deeply gendered markers of a racialized masculinity, centred on criminality, violence and exaggerated machismo, to create a new cultural formation. Ironically, until comparatively recently these markers were used as a form of distinction between the African-Caribbean and Asian communities. Where the former were characterized by tales of culture conflict, generation gap, lack of parental control, alienation and despair, Britain's Asian communities were held to be, by contrast, holistic, coherent and largely unproblematic entities – at least as far as the rest of British society was concerned (Benson 1996). Concerns about Asian cultures were thus focused on the 'private' domestic sphere of family life and particularly on the 'issue' of arranged marriages for Asian women[9] (CCCS Collective 1982: 123), as opposed to the more 'public' threat posed by young black (African-Caribbean) men. Increasingly, as youth have emerged into the perceptual and visual forefront of concerns over Britain's Asian (and notably Muslim) communities, in the wake of the *Satanic Verses* furore, the Gulf War demonstrations and the Bradford 'riots', there has been a shift in focus away from the problems of young Asian women[10] towards the activities of young Asian men – the youth in the streets (Keith 1995).

This complex intersection of age, 'race' and gender forms the perceptual baseline for the rise of the Asian 'gang'. It is worth noting here two additional constellations implicit in what follows: first, the inextricable linkages between 'race', ethnicity and religion, in which religion and ethnicity are seen as interchangeable labels and both are viewed through the essentializing lens of 'race', which privileges a unitary and almost primordial core identity; second, the interweaving of class and notably 'underclass' deprivation with notions of raced identities, whereby 'race' acts as an emblem of socio-economic position (cf. Alexander 1996: 92). This is particularly true of Britain's Muslim communities, where theories of the Pakistani and Bangladeshi 'underclass' and 'crime timebomb' (*Independent*, 22 July 1995) abound, layering notions of cultural and religious primitivism with economic marginalization and racial alienation. This 'kaleidoscope' (Brah 1996) of images crystallizes in the symbol of the 'ghetto' – an *Independent* article in 1992 thus captures the emergence of this new configuration:

> The East End is fast becoming a neighbourhood of ghettos, a breeding ground of intolerance and violent frustrations. Racial violence has been increasing for several years, but the Asian gangs are a new phenomenon, and the increasing frequency of their confrontations is a sign, many fear, of things to come. (*Independent*, 20 April 1992)

The links between and conflation of 'race', violence, the ghetto, the underclass, poverty, tribalism and criminality are made explicitly here, captured in the prophetic spectre of the 'Asian gangs': 'Every estate has its gang … They fight to protect not only their territory but their rights to steal.'

Of particular significance to the present chapter is the incorporation of these multiple images and common-sense understandings into the projection of a culturally specific, but deeply racially encoded, hyper-masculinity which, as argued below, draws on a well established popular and academic discourse of black male[11] crisis to legitimate its new imaginings. In a revealing article, written shortly after the death of Richard Everitt[12] in Camden in 1994, a *Sunday Times* feature article reports on a new Asian gang subculture modelled on African-American examples:

> The gangs, predominantly youngsters from Bangladeshi families, take their inspiration from Afro-American [sic] culture. Mimicking gangs in L.A., they wear hooded jackets and baggy jeans and listen to rap and ragga music. An increase in drug taking and dealing among young Asians has happened in tandem. (*Sunday Times*, 21 August 1994)

It is noticeable that this extract makes no overt reference to gender, which is subsumed into a raced identity that is made to stand for it. Markers of a hyper-masculinized black identity, which is also inextricably linked to issues of 'youth', are strongly woven throughout – references to rap and ragga music, both constructed as 'macho' and misogynist (at least superficially, but see ch. 7, this volume), drug use and the undifferentiated but implicitly masculine 'Afro-American culture'[13] evoke a long-standing tradition of black alienation and threat. The same argument can be made in relation to the category 'youth', which is uncritically posited as a male subculture and feeds easily into notions of cultural dysfunction and identity conflict.[14]

What the combination of 'race', generation and gender most potently captures is a sense of crisis. This sense is acutely precipitated through a process of 'othering' – of groups divided by age from their parental cultures and by 'culture' from the rest of society. This 'between two cultures' (Watson 1977) identity crisis among Asian youth constitutes the dominant discourse in the invention of the Asian gang, notably in the wake of the Everitt murder in August 1994 and the 'riots' in Bradford the following summer. Both events were understood and presented in the media as a compelling mixture of culture clash, inter-generational conflict and social breakdown – a portrait of young men caught between a rigid and oppressive culture at home and a hostile ghettoized subculture of poverty outside. What emerges in this space – or cultural void – is a youth sub-culture characterized by violence, criminality and 'nihilism'; what a *Daily Mail* article captioned on 16 August 1994 as 'Youths [who] combine the worst of both worlds'. In a letter to the *Observer* newspaper after the Everitt murder, Jonathan Stanley, an officer in Camden's Race Equality Unit, fleshes out this portrait:

> The first generation of Bengalis born in the area are now reaching adulthood. Their formative influences largely coincided with those which shaped the values of their white peers; television, school, poor quality housing , inner-city streets, long-term unemployment. It is unsurprising that they are prepared to react to violence in the same way as their white counterparts. (*Observer*, 19 August 1994)

This tension between, and conflation of, 'culture clash' and 'culture of poverty', between 'race' and 'class', the Asian alien on the one hand and marauding youth gangs on the other, marks out the creation of the new Asian folk-devil. Throwing in the spectre of religious fundamentalism for additional authenticity, Yasmin Alibhai-Brown thus reports of the Bradford 'riots':

The result is unexplored territory for young Asians – adrift from the values of their elders, immersed in an Islam which is essentially a reaction, out of step with the liberal values of secular society and yet enamoured of its amoral materialism, while being denied the means to fulfil the modern dream. (*Independent*, 13 June 1995)

Within the parameters of such 'common-sense' constructions (CCCS Collective 1982), it is a comparatively short conceptual step to the representation of 'nihilistic ... violence' and 'vicious schoolboy tribal wars' of the *Evening Standard* article referred to earlier. Where Alibhai-Brown's article rehearses notions of cultural oppression and anachronism, of a reactive and reactionary religious affiliation[15] and of economic failure, the later article replays images of uncontrolled, unemployed and unemployable young men, who live in overcrowded and substandard housing, whose command of English is poor, but whose attraction to the 'freedoms' of 'Western' youth subcultural styles is at once overwhelming and unsustainable, both economically and culturally. The article continues: 'The evidence is clear that Bangladeshi youth are turning violently against each other – almost as if their prowess in a brawl and their collective strength offer the only prospect of status and self-esteem' (*Evening Standard*, 13 November 1996).

This reinvention of Asian identities as 'gangs' thus brings together constructions of gender, generation and 'cultural difference', each acting as a sufficient explanatory palliative for, and emblem of, the other (and, indeed, 'The Other') – at once substituting within and reinforcing a naturalized pathology. 'Ethnicity' here serves as a marker of essentialized and incompatible cultural groupings which are further imbued with the certainties of attributed 'race'. Although, as Benson (1996) has argued, Asian communities in Britain have been traditionally transfixed in the anthropological gaze as bounded, static, culture-rich 'ethnic' collectivities, this emergent focus on Asian gangs marks an explicit racialization (or re-racialization) of young Asian men which returns them, almost full circle, to the position occupied for almost three decades by African-Caribbean youth. It is ironic, in the light of the assertion and celebration of cultural 'difference', the disavowal by some Asians of the label 'black' and the increasing fragmentation of Asian and African-Caribbean experience and political consciousness (Modood 1992), that young Asian – and particularly Muslim – men should be positioned in the same ideological space as their African-Caribbean counterparts. Even more so, if one considers the ways in which Asian youth protest and concerns throughout the 1970s and 1980s were earlier subsumed into the political category 'black' and then largely forgotten (Solomos 1993). This new visibility, then, reconfigures earlier racialized discourses about young black men – usually imagined as African-Caribbean, but also enveloping young Asian men – in a more culturally specific format, but using the same symbolic markers and the same discourses of dysfunction and incipient conflict that Benson (1996) sees as the marker of 'race'-relations studies in Britain. It is important to note that the same arguments cannot be made about young Asian and African-Caribbean women, who are still constructed as ideological opposites.

This gendered racialization is crucial to the invention of the idea of 'the gang', both in the media and in academic discourse. In his work on gang masculinities in America, Hagedorn notes that gender has largely been ignored in 'gang' research because of its assumed omnipresence: 'gender, like water for fish, is often taken for granted in gang research' (Hagedorn 1998: 154). What Hagedorn overlooks, however, is the increasing definition of 'gang' identification in terms of 'race'; indeed, in his own work on 'Frat Boys, Bossmen, Studs and Gentlemen', 'race' is so ubiquitous that he neglects to mention it, despite the fact that all the young men he interviews are of African-American or Hispanic origin. 'Race' is, however, encoded throughout the piece in references to 'inner-city males', 'the ghetto', 'street culture', 'the underclass', 'lower class' and, of course, the label 'gang members' itself.

Like the term 'mugging' (Hall et al. 1978) before it, then, the label of 'the gang' in its American formulation is deeply gendered and raced – it can be argued that the contemporary understanding of gangs in Britain has similarly drawn on its transatlantic counterpart, along with its associated meanings and images. In *Gender and Power* (1987), Connell thus notes that 'concentrations of adult young men are the most intimidating and dangerous' (Connell 1987: 133), continuing that this is particularly (or perhaps exclusively) the case in areas of 'high unemployment and ethnic exclusion'; it is significant that Connell encodes this in the gendered and raced symbol of 'the street'. In the later *Masculinities* (1995), he elaborates: 'Youth *gang* violence of *inner-city streets* is a striking example of the assertion of *marginalised masculinities* against other men' (Connell 1995: 82, emphasis added).

The construction of racialized masculinities in terms of marginality and deviance will be considered in greater detail below. What is of significance here, however, is the correlation of marginality with 'race' and the ways in which a series of common-sense images about discrepant masculinities are formulated in relation to 'gang' identification. The overlap between such academic discourses and media representations traced above is striking, and is echoed in recent years in the moral panics about Triad gang activity in the wake of the murder of headmaster Philip Lawrence in December 1995.[16] Most importantly for the present argument, however, is the way in which these racially encoded masculinities – what I choose to refer to here as 'black masculinities' – draw on established notions of deviance which position young black men implacably outside, and in opposition to, dominant norms of raced and gendered identities. This positionality characterizes the invention of 'the Asian gang', imaging these new identities as young, male and 'black'. Black male identities are, moreover, constructed by definition as being 'in crisis' – violence, disorder and criminality are thus understood as a natural, and naturalized, response to a marginality which is both assumed and unscrutinized. At the heart of this 'crisis' is a notion of a masculinity which is inevitably flawed and eternally failing, of a manhood which is at once a biological imperative and a social impossibility. At the same time as 'race' comes to stand for masculinity, it also denies its fulfilment – it becomes a symbol of its own atrophy. More than this, however, the discrepant construction of black masculinity effectively silences alternative interpretations, occupying and espousing a position of 'Truth'; black masculinity becomes, then, 'invisible'.

Making Black Masculinity Visible

The title of a 1982 collection of black feminist writing unintentionally reveals the present dilemma of black masculinity: 'All the Women are White, all the Blacks are Men, but Some of us are Brave'. What this protest against the invisibility of black women within academic discourse points to is the homogenization of categories of race and gender – the essentializing and normalizing processes by which the assumed experiences of a dominant section come to stand for, and subsume, 'other', alternative or potentially *transruptive*, experiences and identifications. What is interesting in terms of the present argument is the way in which making visible these processes for black women also places these norms under a wider, more silent scrutiny. If black women constitute the stated absence within this framework, what is also brought into question is the components of the framework itself. Re-placing black women within the equation, significantly, does not alter this more fundamental dislocation which places constructions of whiteness and blackness, masculinity and femininity in the foreground and under interrogation. The add-black-women-and-stir approach does not sufficiently interrogate the norms against which black feminism defines itself, and which it, perhaps unknowingly, translates; it does not address constructions of whiteness, nor does it critique the imagination of masculinity. It thus essentializes femininity in its whiteness and blackness in its masculinity, asserting the alterity of black women's experience without challenging and dislocating these imagined absolutes from within. 'Whiteness' and 'masculinity' tellingly go unchallenged in this formulation; white masculinity, it should be noted, constitutes the overarching and supremely invisible norm against which these other elements are configured, and defined as 'other'.

The preceding comments are not intended, and should not be read, as an attack on black feminism. They are, rather, an attempt to locate black masculinity in relation to wider debates and, in particular, to consider the processes whereby questions of black masculinity have been either taken for granted or largely ignored. Where black feminism has placed 'race' and gender blindness at the centre of debates on identity and politics, its alternative formulations – white feminism, white masculinity and, of course, black masculinity – have remained unscrutinized, ironically marginalized in their assumed dominance. If, indeed, all the blacks are men, then this actually tells us very little about their positionality, their subjectivities or the processes through which masculine identifications are created, sustained or transformed (cf. hooks 1992; Williams 1995).

There exists, then, a curious inversion of 'race' and gender blindness whereby black men are rendered effectively silent and invisible within discourse; without substance or life, more a cipher than a presence.[17] It is interesting to note that in even comparatively recent works, notably in Britain, the 'race'/gender intersection is conceptualized around black women exclusively: Anthias and Yuval-Davis' *Racialized Boundaries* (1992) for example, which asks 'In what ways do questions of race connect with questions of gender?', fails to raise the issue of black masculinity even in passing, while in Heidi Mirza's (1997) otherwise revealing collection of black British feminist thought, masculinity does not merit a consideration by any author. Black masculinity then remains, by default, subsumed into an undifferentiated (white) patriarchal masculinity, which ignores the complex struggles, alliances and tensions around black gender relations.[18]

There are a number of elisions which occur in relation to conceptualizations of black masculinity, that contribute to this silencing. First, the continuing conflation of gender with women, which defines masculinity as a homogeneous and essentialized norm, almost outside this discourse; second, the slippage between masculinity and men, in which the apparent visibility and dominance of men as a collective entity substitutes for critical analysis, naturalizing male identities at the expense of questions of difference, differentiation and subjectivity; third, and particularly in relation to black masculinities, the equation of male hyper-visibility with a position of power and dominance. In this latter case the focus on black men, and particularly black youth, has obscured the processes by which specific configurations of black male identities, such as those centred on violence and criminality mentioned earlier, have been placed in the public domain, at the expense and suppression of alternative formulations. As Patricia

Hill Collins (1991) has noted in relation to black women, a focus on single parenthood or welfare dependency has placed a spotlight on the black family which renders black experience visible, or hyper-visible, in very specific, racially coded and politically motivated ways; ways which distort and obscure a wider, more complex understanding. The same process can be seen in relation to the 'Asian gang', in which a focus on 'race'/ethnicity serves as a palliative for explanation (see Alexander 1998). Hyper-visibility, then, constitutes a mirage disguising a more profound 'invisibility' (West 1990).[19]

The 'invisibility' of men has been challenged in the past decade with an increasing interest in, and focus on, issues of masculinity. Interestingly, this shift in focus can be linked less directly to the influence of feminist theory in deconstructing gender categories than a wider process of perceived social, economic and political change. Rutherford notes in the Introduction to *Male Order*, significantly titled 'Men in Trouble': 'The decline of traditional male roles, job insecurity, the boredom, poverty and sense of worthlessness created by redundancy, unemployment and meaningless, badly paid work have placed many men on the threshold of an inner feeling of emptiness, whose dreams, wishes and desires appear to be entirely lost' (Rutherford, in Chapman and Rutherford 1988: 9).

The incipient collapse of an imagined patriarchal authority, most notably in relation to the family, has given birth to both the redefinition of masculinity (through, for example, the men's movement in the USA) and its retrenchment (through an aggressive hyper-masculinity) – what could be broadly characterized as a tension between the *New Man* and the *New Lad*. For young men, in particular, it appears that masculinity can only be understood and performed as crisis. Rutherford thus writes: 'Male redundancy has created cultures of prolonged adolescence in which young male identities remain locked into the locality of estate, shops and school ... Violence, criminality, drug taking and alcohol consumption become the means to gaining prestige for a masculine identity bereft of any social value' (Rutherford 1988: 7).

The echoes here with the invention of 'the Asian gang' are tangible and significant: the growth of a pathologized male youth subculture premised on social and economic deprivation and personal crisis leading to tribalism and violence.[20] Add to this the naturalizing spectre of 'race'/ethnicity and what emerges is young black men *doubly*, or perhaps *triply*, in trouble. This emergent sense of masculinity in crisis has served to make visible positions and processes which were hitherto too easily assumed and conveniently ignored. Solomon-Godeau thus writes of: 'a destabilisation of the notion of masculinity such that it forfeits its previous transparency, its taken-for-grantedness, its normalcy. It is doubtless this loss of transparency that underpins the now-frequent invocations of a "crisis" in masculinity or, at the very least, a perceived problem in its representations' (Solomon-Godeau 1995: 70). In other words, the demystifying process of making (white) masculinity visible has simultaneously revealed its inherent variations and contradictions so that masculinity has not so much been transformed as unmasked.

Challenging the notion of a uniform, pre-crisis masculinity, work has now increasingly focused on its more inflected, multiple and shifting manifestations; its constructedness, its conflicts, its ongoing struggle for hegemony, its implication in processes of personal and institutional power (Berger et al. 1995: 3). The relationship of black men to this proliferation of masculinities, however, remains an ambivalent one. The acknowledgement that masculinity is a discursive and interdependent construct, always in production and thus always, potentially, in crisis (Solomon-Godeau 1995) has, curiously, tended to overlook the creation of Black masculinities; the Introduction to *Representing Black Men* (Blount and Cunningham 1996) thus notes that the construction of black manhood in the social sciences has rarely been informed by critical theory and thus continues to occupy a position of 'Knowledge' or 'truth-giving', while, conversely, African-American men as explicitly gendered beings are seldom used within contemporary theory to interrogate constructions of gender and sexuality. Connell, for example, in his influential work *Gender and Power* (1987) defines sexuality as the main division of gendered identities, arguing, 'The most important feature of contemporary hegemonic masculinity is that it is heterosexual ... and a key form of subordinated masculinity is homosexual (Connell 1987: 186).

'Ethnicity' is referred to only in passing and only in terms of a benign 'cultural difference'[21] while 'race' is significantly absent, even in its black feminist formations. In an unconsciously ironic performance of self-fulfilling amnesia, Connell notes: 'achieving hegemony may consist precisely in preventing alternatives gaining cultural definition and recognition as alternatives, confining them to *ghettos*, to privacy, to unconsciousness (Connell 1987: 186; emphasis added). In his later *Masculinities* (1995), Connell considers black male identities, only to construct them through the white hegemonic gaze as 'symbols' through which white gender categories are imagined and performed. He notes: 'hegemonic masculinity among whites sustains the institutional oppression and physical terror that have framed the making of masculinity in black communities' (p. 80). Black masculinities are thus both marginalized and authorized by white masculinity – constructed, legitimated and transfixed by the white hegemonic imagination.

As bell hooks has argued, black masculinity has always been defined as 'lacking' in relation to dominant patriarchal norms, 'tormented by their inability to fulfil the phallocentric masculine ideal' (hooks 1992: 89), measured against a notion of manhood which their 'race' denies them. Black masculinity, then, is constructed as 'in conflict with the normative definition of masculinity' (Staples, cited in hooks 1992: 96), but as a failing rather than an alternative formulation. Staples continues: 'the black male has always had to confront the contradiction between this normative expectation attached to being male in this society and proscription on his behaviour and achievement of goals' (p. 97). Unable to fulfil their patriarchal responsibilities as providers, heads of household and authority figures, this argument continues, black men turn to a highly visible and exaggerated masculinity centred on hyper-sexuality and violence to compensate, creating a deviant male role, at variance with – and most importantly *apart from* – the mainstream model.

Most accounts of black male identities have thus sought either to reinforce this image of the 'deviant', notably in relation to *young* black men (cf. Pryce 1979; Cashmore and Troyna 1982) or to argue against it and for the fulfilment of the patriarchal ideal (Liebow 1967; Duneier 1992). Either way the norm remains intact – an object of aspiration or negation, but always the authoritative defining presence, the measure of black manhood. The defining characteristic of such portrayals is the denial of agency to black men. Black men, by virtue of their 'race' are thus denied access to 'real' power (hooks 1992) and are thereby reduced to their blackness, which at once stands for, and transfixes, their masculinity and all other identifications.

This spectre of 'race' continues to haunt recent approaches to deconstructing masculinities, in the same way as it has created stumbling blocks for the reinvention of ethnicity theory. In her work on white ethnicities in America, Waters (1990) argues that the existence of racial inequalities denies African-Americans the ability to construct and invent their identities in the same way as white groups. This denial of black agency is similarly reflected in the construction of black masculinities as subordinated, marginalized, discrepant; as the reflection of the dominant white imagination – undifferentiated, unidimensional, unalterable. Perhaps more accurately, then, the intersection of 'race' and gender has served as a means to authenticate and reinscribe the position of black men as the ultimate Other, the norm, the 'real' – what Messerschmidt (1998) has termed 'Doing White Supremacist Masculinity'. Ironically, the problematization of masculinity has served to reify black masculinity in its crisis, so that it becomes the new certainty around which all else revolves, or dissolves.[22] Masculinity in its blackness then serves to naturalize and essentialize male identifications, censoring and suppressing more complex representations (hooks 1992). As bell hooks has argued: 'Erasing the realities of black men who have diverse understandings of masculinity ... puts in place of this lived complexity a flat, one-dimensional representation' (hooks 1992: 90).

Black masculinity thus undergoes a double naturalization, through 'race' and through gender, which at once transfixes it in the invocation of a publicly visioned hyper-sexuality (Mercer 1994; Hall 1997), while simultaneously erasing its ambivalences and threatened alterities. As Kobena Mercer and Isaac Julien have argued, however, black masculinity can be understood only as part of wider and more complex dialectics of power, in which blackness constitutes a 'subordinated masculinity' (Mercer and Julien 1988: 12), made visible, surveyed and policed in specific ways. Black masculinity thus represents 'a highly contradictory formation' (Mercer and Julien 1988), constructed as both emasculated and 'macho' (Wallace 1979), objectified as threat, demonized and desired (Young 1995; Hall 1997). Mercer and Julien write: 'There is a struggle over the definition, understanding and construction of meanings around black masculinity, within the dominant regime of truth' (Mercer and Julien 1988: 137).

If there are ambivalences inherent in the dominant construction of black masculinity, this is even more the case in the ways in which black male experience is understood and lived through subjectively and experientially (Alexander 1996). Mercer and Julien have observed that black masculinity has at once internalized, lived through and supplanted dominant constructions of black male identities – challenged, subverted, claimed, inhabited and discarded them, not always with success, sometimes with negative consequences[23] and often without notice, silently levering open space, however temporary or illusory (Alexander 1996).

Recognizing the performative nature of masculinity and the constructions of 'race' demands both a recognition of the plurality of black male subjectivities (hooks 1992) and, perhaps more importantly, a reconceptualization of the connection between categories of 'race' and gender. The place of black masculinities within this reconfiguration is crucial in disrupting the silent reinvention of white masculinities around the black male 'Other', and the too simplistic notion of the dominant, often invisible, enemy in some strands of black gender theory (cf. Wallace 1979). Such connections are more contingent, fluid and potentially transgressive than conventional race/gender theorizations allow. More than this, it is important to recognize the way in which black male subjectivities not only enact but also dislocate dominant discourses about the place of the black 'Other'; the debate is thus not only about 'alternatives', but about 'discrepancies' – the performance of alterity which threatens to break through such discourses and translate them. It is also crucial to account for the complex and interwoven layers of black male subjectivities which differentiate, dislocate and transform identifications internal to an imagined collective black male identity.[24] The challenge facing black masculinity, then, is to move beyond convenient binary categorizations – white/black, male/female, inside/outside, dominant/subaltern, plural/single, straight/gay – to confront a more complex and conflicted reality.

Representing Black Masculinities: (Un)Race-ing and Gendering the 'Asian Gang'

The position of Asian masculinities within the previous discussion perhaps remains a controversial one. Modood (1992), among others, has vehemently argued for the inapplicability of the inclusive term 'black' for Asian communities and has rejected it in favour of what he claims as a more culturally sensitive and pluralistic model. It can certainly be argued that Asian sexualities have been conceptualized differently from, and perhaps even in opposition to, African and African-Caribbean representations in the white imagination. Where the latter are constructed as aggressive, violent and hyper-masculinized (CCCS 1982: 134), Asians are portrayed as passive, weak and hyper-feminized (CCCS 1982: 134; Said 1978). Mercer and Julien characterize this orientalist image thus: 'The Oriental has no capacity for violence; he is mute, passive, charming, inscrutable' (Mercer and Julien 1988: 108).

Such images have their foundation in orientalist discourse, which has constructed Asia as female, weak and sensual (Said 1978: 203). As Said has argued, if only in passing, the elision of 'the East's' difference with weakness and with femininity in the imagination of the dominant penetrative and all-conquering imperialist masculinity (p. 206) has served to construct, oppose and subordinate the Asian/Oriental woman to the white man. Asian masculinity (and white femininity) have no independent space within this opposition, subsumed into a feminized Orient, 'its eccentricity, its backwardness, its silent indifference, its feminine penetrability, its supine malleability' (p. 206). Interestingly, Said's work itself reflects this silencing – although the focus of Orientalism is visioned unreflexively as 'male'; Asian men and masculinity are constructed as absences in discourse – unrealized and shadowy figures, ungendered (but, significantly, *raced*) objects rather than gendered subjects.

What orientalist discourse shares with the construction of African, African-American and African-Caribbean identities is the racialization of its subjects, along with its hyper-sexualization of black women and its erasure of black manhood. What these superficially opposing set of representations rely on is the same reductive stereotyping based on the conflation of assumed biological/cultural markers (Hall 1997). They share the same denial of agency, the same objectification, the same very specific hyper-visualization, the same silencing. It is then hardly surprising if these seemingly opposed representations prove easily substitutable for each other – think, for example, of the critiques of Robert Mapplethorpe's photography (Hall 1997; Mercer 1994). The perception of 'race' as threat, most notably in its association with violent masculinity, is likewise built into orientalist discourse along with its denial. Said, for example, notes the re-imagination of, significantly, Muslim identities as threat in the post-war period (Said 1978: 284), and especially after the Arab–Israeli war of 1973. Interestingly, this shift is accompanied by the re-imaging of the Orient as male, as public, as collective and as overtly, actively sexualized (p. 287).

The same processes are at work in the invention of 'the Asian gang', which achieves its most vivid imaging in the wake of the demonization and pathologization of Britain's Muslim communities, notably from the late 1980s. It is particularly ironic that the champion of 'ethnic diversity', Tariq Modood, should reinscribe the equation of discrimination, religion, socio-economic and cultural disadvantage in the criminalization of Muslim youth identities. In the 1997 PSI survey, tellingly subtitled 'Diversity and Disadvantage', Modood thus writes of an 'anxiety about a possible trend of criminalisation among young Pakistanis and Bangladeshis, *which in some ways parallels the experience of Caribbean male youth*' (Modood et al. 1997: 147; emphasis added). I have written elsewhere (Alexander 1998) about the increasing conflation of Muslim communities with disadvantage and their opposition to the relative success of non-Muslim South Asian communities – what Modood terms the division between the 'achievers' and the 'believers' (Modood 1992) – but what is of particular relevance here is the racialization of Muslim youth identities: first, in the reification of 'Muslim' itself as a category which increasingly supersedes and envelops other identifications; second, in the representation of these identities in terms of 'political alienation', 'prejudice' and criminality;[25] and lastly in the explicit equation of Muslim and African-Caribbean young men. Modood's position then shares the same framework of assumptions, the same predictive knowledge, the same position of unscrutinized 'Truth' as those media images outlined above: most importantly, it makes the same unequivocal correlation between 'race' (whether coded as religious or 'ethnic' difference), masculinity and crisis.

My concern here, then, is two-fold: first, to make explicit the essentializing processes of racialization in the invention of 'the Asian gang' – to 'race' it, and, having done so, to 'un-race' it by introducing the possibility of agency, change and subjectivity; second, to render visible the gendered dynamics of these constructions and to consider some of the complexities of masculine identifications that are thereby revealed. The aim, then, is to move away from the black-masculinity-in-crisis thesis towards a more contextual, fluid and perhaps subjective account, one that opens space for re-imagination, contestation and transformation; an account that allows for the entangled performance of masculine identifications, that moves from the inscription of *discrepancy* towards the potentiality of *transruption*.

Critically Researching Young Asian Men

The remainder of this chapter is concerned with tracing some of these images, their performance and their disruptions, in relation to a group of young Bangladeshi men, aged fourteen to twenty-one, living in London. The young men who form the subjects of this analysis are all members of a statutory youth project, the SAYO Project, for young Asian men, where I have been working and researching for the past three and a half years. The project is based in More ward, an area of a south London borough in which 35 per cent of the population are of Bangladeshi origin. The majority of these families live on the local Stoneleigh estate (comprising 18 per cent of the estate's population)[26] where there is estimated to be 60 per cent unemployment among Bengali males. A report for a single re-generation Budget in 1996 thus stated: 'the ward has particular problems in relation to unemployment, education performance, crime and racist behaviour.'

Of particular relevance to this chapter are the images associated with the area, and with this group of young men. It is recognized as a 'problem' estate, particularly in relation to 'youth crime' (for example, drug offences, motor vehicle crime, vandalism, and general anti-social behaviour), and the young men who visually dominate its landscape have similarly been regarded and labelled as a 'problem' group and, increasingly, as a definable 'gang', subject to what feels like constant surveillance and control by school and police, and targeted by local training initiatives concerned with the reduction of youth crime or, more accurately, 'young people at risk'. The complexities of this process, its history, realities, fictions and interactions are too vast to deal with in this chapter, but these images are significant here in the ways in which they draw on the common-sense notions of economic and social deprivation and cultural dysfunction that underpin the representation of Asian (Muslim) youth, to create a series of labels, categories and understandings that are, in turn, used to 'explain' events, encounters and, particularly, situations of conflict. As I have argued else-where (Alexander 1998), this process privileges an essentialized 'ethnicity' and renders alternative explanations at once unnecessary and impossible, asserting a primacy of racialized meaning which decontextualizes incidents, projecting a homogeneity among events with often very disparate motiva-tions, understandings, histories and responses. Making explicit and distinct the significance of alternative, and often entangled, formulations – around territory, age, local history, family, friendship peer group and personality – which distinguish each encounter, serves to dislocate the certainties of a too simplistic and far-too-convenient reliance on racial–ethnic identity, allowing for agency, for rearticulation and, perhaps most importantly, for action. Making gender visible, in particular, provides new insights into the dynamics of these encounters, not by silently asserting the inevitabilities of 'race', crisis and violence, but by recognizing the creativity and potentiality of identifications structured through multiple and shifting notions of masculinity, of brotherhood, of responsibility and of family.

In the spring of 1997, a fight took place in a north London further education college. The conflict involved a small number of the young men I work with, now aged sixteen, who were attending the college to study for A-levels, and a larger number of local young Bengali men of around the same age, some from the college, others who showed up for additional support. The fight began during the day, when some of the young men began to insult and push one of the 'outsiders' (as they saw it), Jamal, because they apparently felt that he thought too much of himself. The local young men waited for Jamal after college and a group of about twelve people attacked him, then turned on his friends, Hanif, Sayeed, Liton and Ismat, as they came to his aid. Jamal escaped serious injury only by flagging down a passing car. The others made their escape by bus and returned to the Stoneleigh estate, where they contacted Hanif's older brother Shahin and his friends. Fortunately, none of the young men was seriously injured in this encounter, sustaining bruises, a gashed lip, a cut eye and a chipped tooth.

On one level, this incident can easily be read as an example of inter- or intra-ethnic violence of the kind described in the *Evening Standard* article: a seemingly meaningless clash of territorially exclusive and ethnically defined groups over a tenuous or imagined affront, designed to assert collective control over an 'invading' and potentially threatening entity. Though both groups were of Asian, indeed, Bengali, origin this 'sameness' became transformed into a symbol of antagonism between the two groups, an identity fractured through locality; one group from north London, one from south London, both areas with something of a 'reputation' for strength, solidarity and fighting ability. The equation of a highly localized ethnic group identity with this form of conflict feeds very easily into notions of a racialized hyper-masculinity focused on violence referred to earlier which underpins the myth of the 'Asian gang'. The role of alternative formulations of gendered identities, centred around age, family, friendship, peer group and local ties, however, dislocates any such neat analysis, cutting across these imagined distinctions and disrupting pathologized notions of ethnic or male crisis. These linkages and reformulations of individual and collective identifications became clearly apparent in the aftermath of the attack.

One of the crucial configurations through which this event is to be understood is that of age. This goes beyond the catch-all categorization 'youth' to constitute a relatively narrowly defined age-set, aged sixteen to seventeen. It should be noted that all the young men involved in the incident were of the same age; this is partly a function of the setting – a further education college – which is also significant in terms of locality. The young men from both areas can thus be seen to constitute a self-defined peer group, though formed here through conflict. This is particularly significant in relation to events after the attack, where informal mediation was facilitated through the establishment of an imagined community centred on shared status within a hierarchy of age and family position. This worked on two distinct levels: first, from within peer group boundaries, through the intervention of Majid, a contemporary of the north London young men, who had grown up with them, and some of whose friends had been involved in the attack. Majid had also been working on the Stoneleigh estate over the summer as a volunteer playworker and had come to know Jamal and his friends well during that time. He was thus able to occupy a position of trust with both sides and to act not only as a mediator but as an emblem of the moral error of the attack. To attack Jamal, who was a friend of Majid's, was thus seen to be an attack on Majid himself, and therefore an attack on one's own. Majid was able to use his position to open dialogue between the two groupings, and to set up a meeting during which an apology was to be delivered to Jamal and the others. His position was further strengthened through his 'family' ties with Yasmin, the youthworker for the SAYO project, who had grown up in the same north London area, knew many of the attacker's older brothers and was placed in the mission of *apa* (older sister) to both sets of young men, with all the linkages of respect, authority and protection that this carries.[27]

At the same time as Majid's intervention, dialogue was also opened between the two areas at another level. This was initiated by Shahin, Hanif's older brother, and was premised on the status accorded to older males within the Bengali community. Although only three years separate Shahin from Hanif, his role as *bhaya* (older brother) to Hanif and, beyond this, to Hanif's friends and, indeed, all younger members of the local community, male and female, gave him a role and duty as protector and retributor on behalf of all the young men involved in the incident. Gathering a number of his peer group together in their position as 'elders' of their south London community, Shahin travelled to north London to meet with the elder brothers of the attacking group to discuss the events and, it was hoped, to prevent any escalation. This intervention also functioned on two levels: first, within Shahin's peer group, which was mediated through long-established ties with the north London area formed in clubs, colleges, community events, through friendship and family connections, however tenuous, and through shared struggles against other groupings. For example, when Shahin himself had been attacked two years previously at his college in west London with a young man from the same North London area, both groups had met to discuss the plans for action (Alexander 1998). Second, in his role as *bhaya* and as a contemporary and friend of the north London grouping's elder brothers, Shahin was also able to occupy a position of authority over the younger culprits. He was thus able to demand that the younger members respected him as their elder brother and thus cease any further hostilities towards Hanif, Jamal and the others, establishing a fictive kin association – a bond of brotherhood – through which hostilities could be appeased without obvious loss of credibility on either side.

This dual relationship, of peer group and of brotherhood, served thus to mediate the notion of absolute boundaries within this encounter. It should be noted that the language of brotherhood did not operate within each peer group – the young men were 'friends' rather than 'brothers' – but functioned across peer groups segmented by age to create bonds of authority and obligation. These bonds, between Hanif and Shahin, Shahin and Hanif's friends, and between Shahin and the attacking group, served to impose surprisingly strong notions of respect which could be manipulated, in this case at least, to cease further hostilities. Interestingly, these 'brother' ties also create an authority which is both rooted in, and ultimately sanctioned by, the peer group loyalties, however temporary and transient. Thus, Shahin's role as 'brother' was legitimated by his ties as 'friend' with the north London older brothers, a position which carried with it a set of obligations on the latter to ensure their younger brothers did not step out of line in the future. Failure on this account could be read as a sign of disrespect to Shahin and his friends, and would almost certainly lead to further confrontations, but now at this 'higher' level, between the older brothers. It is important to note that, either way, matters no longer rested with the initial protagonists of the incident.

Indeed, it can be argued further that this intervention by the 'elders' made it effectively impossible for action to be taken by either of the original peer group antagonists, since this would constitute a 'disrespecting' of the older group. It is significant, then, that although Jamal's immediate support after the attack was drawn from his own peer group – or, more accurately, his friendship circle – the subsequent events excluded the enactment of these ties. The original victims and their wider circle of friends from the

Stoneleigh estate (who, incidentally, were the core members of the so-called 'gang' which featured in the article referred to earlier), were not consulted or involved in the following negotiations; both they and their north London counterparts were rather the subjects of legislation than the vanguards of action. It is interesting to contrast this, if only in passing, with the series of encounters which formed the basis for the local press report, in which these conflicts remained confined to a more clearly defined locale and inclusive friendship group, and did not involve the elder members of the community in any structured format.

It is also worth comparing the structuring of response in these incidents to another attack, this time on Enam, who forms part of Jamal's peer group, which took place a couple of months prior to the attack on Jamal. Enam was attacked in east London by a group of young men, this time over longer-standing frictions between the two areas which had erupted several times previously. In this case there was no immediate response and it was only two months later that several individuals from the Stoneleigh estate sought out the attackers to exact their revenge. The young men involved here formed a very small subset of Enam's peer group and involved no elders. This reflected two important variables which challenge any straightforward notion of collective action or response: first, that frictions within the peer group, particularly over the position of Enam himself, meant that many of his former friends felt no inclination to get involved. This illuminated the recent dispersal of the previously tightly bonded group identity around issues of personality and also personal aspirations after the young men left school and went in separate directions. Second, the absence of involvement by any 'elders' reflected Enam's comparative isolation within this male youth community. Enam has no older brother to turn to (his *bhaya* being married and living outside the area, and therefore on both accounts no longer forming part of this public peer group 'community' in the same way), and is therefore at once freer from the obligations enacted by these fraternal roles and expectations, and less protected by them. This again suggests the congruence of fraternal roles with friendship ties; had Enam been closer to Hanif, for example, and thus enacted the role of younger brother to Shahin and his friends, he, like Jamal, would have been able to draw on the support of the older group in his defence. By choosing to opt out of this status hierarchy, Enam also forfeited this protection.

If the interaction of these two groups in the Jamal incident was mediated and transformed by age, peer group and fraternal imaginings, the same can also be seen in the intersection of group and territorial boundaries. As mentioned earlier, the conflict arose partly as a function of the setting – a college with strong links to a local, predominantly Bengali community. The young men from the Stoneleigh estate travelled into this community as 'outsiders', having comparatively little, or no, established contacts or points of reference with the local community. This was due mainly to the transition from a highly localized school environment to a new and more distant establishment which brought them into contact, and potential conflict, with new people and new groups. It is interesting to contrast this with the more fluid connections linking the older members of both communities, which had grown through years of institutional and informal contact. One of Shahin's friends, Humzah, for example, had grown up in the same north London area before moving to the Stoneleigh estate, still has relatives there and had long-standing ties with its members, while, as mentioned earlier, Shahin himself was a well-known figure in the area. The position of Majid as mediator points to the development of these personal, informal links in the early stages, as does a reported comment from one of the attackers that 'had he known Hanif was Shahin's brother he would never have got involved'. The significance of personal ties, contacts and reputations should not be overlooked in this encounter, notably in transgressing imagined group and territorial identities and in establishing new, more inclusive collective identifications. It is worth bearing in mind, however, that if Enam's earlier attack had taken place on 'home' ground, on the estate itself, that many more young men would have been involved in reprisals, since this could have been read as an infringement of their territorially defined collective identity and hence their 'reputation'. Indeed, a couple of months after the attack on Jamal, there were a series of skirmishes on the Stoneleigh estate, initially involving the members of the SAYO project and some African-Caribbean young men from a neighbouring area, Clifton. The events have a longer history than it is possible to explain here, but it is significant that when the young men from Clifton returned to the Stoneleigh estate to exact revenge, they attacked first a young white boy, Jamie, and then Khalid, a young Bengali man, who had nothing to do with the initial conflict. In this case, then, the attacks (and subsequent reprisals) were premised first and foremost on a territorial basis, irrespective of ethnicity, peer group, age or personal involvement. When a mass confrontation was planned between the two groups, over sixty young men from the Stoneleigh estate and its surrounds, of all ages, diverse ethnic/racial groups and disparate peer groups collected in the youth club building in preparation for the fight, which, as in many cases, never took place. It was, nevertheless, an astonishing demonstration of mutual support and collective strength which muted other antagonisms and divisions in defence of what was, for that moment at least, 'their own'.

There is a postscript to these events, which for me puts some of these representations and the challenges to them into perspective. Dropping

Jamal home from the youth club several weeks later, we were talking about the fight in college and what happened afterwards. I asked him about the meeting that was supposed to take place with both groups of young men for the delivery of an informal apology. Jamal shrugged and told me that the meeting never took place, but continued, tellingly, 'I'm not really that bothered about it. I just want to do my studying and live my life peacefully.'

Conclusion

What Jamal's comment brings home to me most clearly is the very different perspective on 'the Asian gang' that emerges from a more personal and subjective approach – one that is unaware of overarching theorizations of identity crisis, cultural dysfunction, low self-esteem attributions of economic and social emasculation, and that is concerned less with the performance of 'black macho' than with getting his A-levels done. The focus throughout the chapter, then, has been on disentangling 'the Asian gang' on two levels: first, by examining the ways in which media representations of Asian youth identities have drawn on, and reinvented, a tradition of racialized images which position young black men as being outside the (white) norm and constructed in opposition to it; and second, by considering the range of positionalities that these representations render invisible, but which are none the less performed on a day-to-day basis. While in no way claiming 'insider' status, this chapter has attempted to make visible and unravel some of the complexities of what can be (mis)read as apparently simple encounters – the shifting and entangled definitions of ethnicity, gender, family, community, peer group, age and territory – and through doing so, to challenge the myth of 'the Asian gang'.

The invention of 'the Asian gang' must then be viewed as a product of complex processes of racialization and hyper-masculinization, in which theories of black-masculinity-in crisis reify common-sense beliefs in black male threat and legitimate emergent forms of social stigmatization and control. Making black masculinities visible reveals the complex, shifting and multifarious performance of racial/ethnic and gendered identities which disrupts this process of naturalization, and challenges dominant discourses. More than this, however, the chapter has been concerned with the tension between these images and their performance, which contests a straightforward representation/reality dichotomy to explore the entanglements it contains. It has argued that while monolithic categorizations of 'race' and gender are reinvented and reinscribed, they are simultaneously contested and dislocated through cross-cutting formations which cannot be entirely contained or erased. Essentialized notions of 'blackness' or 'Asianness' or unscrutinized theories of 'patriarchy' or 'masculinity' are imploded through the intervention of alternative or transruptive discourses – the potential for a more than transitory transformation remains, however, uncertain.

Notes

I am grateful to Barnor Hesse for his encouragement and critical insights in the preparation of this chapter, and to the young men of the SAYO project for allowing me into their lives for the past five years.

1. *Eastern Eye* is a weekly tabloid-style newspaper delivering 'the Asian perspective' to Britain's South Asian communities.

2. It is significant, in the light of later arguments, that the young men from Slough are labelled 'Muslim' rather than 'Pakistani', although the 'Muslim community' is represented in the article by the Pakistan Welfare Association, whose chair appeals to 'the whole Pakistani community'.

3. A Sikh religious festival marking the birth of the Khalsa.

4. This ambiguous positionality is apparent in the quote from Rajinder Sandhu (above), which places 'gangs' both in opposition to, and yet as representative of, 'the community'.

5. 'Class' is an additional axis of pathologization, but is generally subsumed into broad categories of 'race' and of masculinity, especially in the formulation of the 'masculinity-in-crisis' thesis explored later in the chapter.

6. Cf. S. Cohen 1980.

7. I have been working with the members of a youth project for young Asian men in south London as both researcher and volunteer youth worker for the past three and a half years. The ethnography based on the research is currently being written.

8. Michael Marland is headmaster of North Westminster Community School in Camden, north London, and was a member of a school's working party on crime prevention for the government.

9. Young Asian men were largely absent from this discourse, the invisible assumed beneficiaries of a rigid and enveloping patriarchal order.

10. Although, of course, young Asian women still provide a potent and popular symbol of community dysfunction and a generational 'between two cultures' identity crisis, especially around issues of marriage and sexuality.

11. Traditionally, the focus of this discourse is African-Caribbean and African-American men.

12. Richard Everitt was a white teenager stabbed to death by a group of young Asian men. Badrul Miah, who was gaoled for life for the murder, was described in court and the papers as a 'gang leader' and as 'leader of a 10 strong Asian mob' (*Independent*, 1 November 1995).

13. It is interesting that the article refers explicitly only to African-American culture, although the cultural markers refer implicitly (and intentionally?) also to Caribbean and black British cultural expression.

14. It is revealing that work on youth subcultures has its origins in the sociology of deviance, which has argued for the same notions of identity crisis, lack of self-esteem in peer group (especially 'gang') formation (cf. Alexander 1996: ch. 5 for a fuller discussion).

16. The same arguments are significantly also to be found in the understanding of Rastafarian identifications (cf. Cashmore and Troyna 1982; Pryce 1979).

16. Philip Lawrence was stabbed to death outside his school in December 1995. The attack was carried out by a supposed Triad youth gang, headed by teenager Learco Chindamo. Media coverage drew attention to the race-specific nature of the gangs, with references to their 'immigrant' origins (*Guardian*, 11 December 1995), the racially exclusive membership (mainly Chinese and Vietnamese, but also Asian and black) and motivation, and how 'race is often a factor' (*Guardian*, 18 October 1996)

17. There are, of course, literary explorations of black masculine identities from the work of Richard Wright and James Baldwin through to Iceberg Slim or, in Britain, Patrick Augustus. A recent interesting collection, *Brotherman*, published in 1995, collects together a range of writings by African-American men. See Boyd and Allen (1995).

18. It is possible that this absence marks out a peculiarly British trajectory of black feminist thought, which has tended to underplay gender relations in black communities, in contrast to the more explicitly fraught debates waged in America, and has engaged more single-mindedly with white feminism.

19. West defines 'invisibility' as 'the relative lack of black power to present themselves and others as complex human beings and thereby to contest the bombardment of negative, degrading stereotypes put forward by white supremacist ideologies' (West 1990).

20. Note the silent markers of 'class' within this formulation – these are young men from 'estates' whose lives are defined through drugs, alcohol and crime; again, these images of the 'underclass' are particularly salient to the construction of 'the Asian gang'.

21. Connell does note that colonialism disrupts conventional forms of masculinity, which again reinforces the notion that black masculinities are inherently damaged.

22. Messerschmidt (1998) argues that the growth of lynching in the Reconstruction period can be understood as the construction of new sexual-racial hierarchies in a period of crisis for white men. White masculinity then, constructs and is constructed through subordinated masculinities, enacted and legitimated, in this case, through violence against black male bodies.

23. I am thinking here about controversies over, for example, misogyny in rap music (the 2 Live Crew affair) and homophobia in ragga music (especially Buju Banton).

24. It is, I think, significant that the main challenges to the construction of black masculinity has come from black gay men; for example, Kendall Thomas, Isaac Julien and Kobena Mercer and, of course, from James Baldwin.

25. This set of images is particularly ironic given Modood's assertion that one primary reason for the rejection of the term 'black' by Asian groups was its negative connotations.

26. These figures are from a 1996 single regeneration budget bid for More ward. It should be noted that all area, street and personal names have been changed.

27. It is important to note that age and family position rather than gender form the salient factors in Yasmin's status, disrupting stereotypical notions of Asian family structures as being rigidly patriarchal; there were, however, gendered limitations on Yasmin's role in the mediation process, which was accordingly more backstage than frontline.

Ragga Music: Dis/Respecting Black Women and Dis/Reputable Sexualities

Denise Noble

> We take the girls dem out the darkness,
> And put the girls dem in the light,
> That's why the girls love to hear, Shabba voice 'pon mic'
> (Shabba Ranks, 'A Wi De Girls Dem Love', 1990)

Through the blues, black women were able to autonomously work out – as audiences and performers – a working class model of womanhood ... it revealed that black women and men, the blues audience, could respond to the vastly different circumstances of the post slavery era with notions of gender and sexuality that were, to an extent, ideologically independent of the middle class cult of 'true womanhood'. In this sense ... the blues was a privileged site in which women were free to assert themselves as sexual beings. (Angela Davies 1998: 46)

In thinking about my own enjoyment of Ragga music as a Black British woman, I have been intrigued by my own contradictory responses. For as much as I have 'disapproved' of some of the overtly sexist and porno-graphic lyrics of some songs, I have also found myself basking in their celebration of Black womanhood. Furthermore, this very public display and celebration of Black sexuality, and particularly Black female sexuality, struck me as very different from other forms with which I had been familiar which represented Black women's sexuality in my immediate experience of Black culture; an experience that is geographically located in London, but traversed by my familial connections with Jamaica and the USA, travels in Europe and a diasporic consciousness of Blackness that shapes my sense of myself as a Black British woman.

The central focus of the contention between those in favour of Ragga and those against is whether it celebrates or disrespects Black women. In Britain, many of us are preoccupied with whether Black women are represented in the public domain in ways that are likely to reinforce racist perceptions of us as objects of ridicule, pity or disrespect. When, in 1996, I gave a presentation of my work at the British Sociological Association's annual conference in Reading,[1] several of the other Black women there expressed their discomfort with some of my ideas. One woman remarked that, although she had liked my argument, she had felt embarrassed about my frank discussion of Black women's bodies and sexuality in front of white people. This view was typical of an ambivalence expressed by many Black women with whom I have discussed Ragga. Mostly they have expressed a tension between an openness to Ragga's celebration of Black women, and an unease and concern about what many regard as Ragga's reinforcement of racist stereotypes of Black women as sexually licentious; stereotypes that these high-achieving, mostly 'thirty-something' Black women regarded as potentially damaging to how we would be viewed and more importantly might be treated, not only by Black men, but by the wider British audiences of Black popular culture.

I share in this ambivalence, and it is my interest in my own and other women's contradictory responses that I have sought to understand and analyse. Although I have been proud of the display it has enabled of an often outrageously sexy, rude and unashamed enjoyment of Black female sexuality, I have also felt uneasy about how these might be translated into everyday perceptions of Black women outside the dance-hall, especially by those whose only engagement with it, or for that matter, us, comes from *Top of the Pops* or MTV. But even more than this, I wanted to understand what Ragga, and Black female audience response to it, might indicate about Black British women's concerns, feelings and aspirations, and the implications of these for the development of Black British feminism. My analysis of Ragga, then, begins from my own participation in Black cultural life and my own enjoyment of Ragga as a valuable and positive opportunity to raise questions about eroticism and sexuality in Black life, in a way that very few other forms of Black culture in Britain previously have

Ragga Dance-hall Culture

Ragga music emerged in the 1980s from a range of musical styles in reggae music. Ragga is an abbreviation of ragamuffin, a word that emerged in the 1980s, within the lyrics of male DJs, as a self-referential term. To call oneself a ragamuffin was to state an attitude similar to the use of the Jamaican term 'rude boy' or 'rudie' in the 1960s and early 1970s. A ragamuffin is located in ghetto culture, and has a 'bad' attitude towards authority and mainstream conventions. The positive reappropriation of the ragamuffin image was a subversive rearticulation of pride in an identity which had been devalued within legislative mainstream 'Jamaican' Creole culture as well as the hegemonically afrocentric cultures of the ghetto. Instead of a term of abuse, to be called 'ragamuffin' (and, subsequently, 'Ragga') became a badge of pride, indicating belonging to a set of marginalized and devalued practices and values. Both versions of culture – creolized and Afrocentric – are concerned with the maintenance of the values and forms of Black cultural life which will enhance communal growth and racial advancement, regarded as an important function of Black culture. Ragga, on the other hand, is viewed by many, in its preoccupation with sex, as a meaningless distraction, as crude rather than culturally uplifting to Black people, as mere 'slackness'.[2]

As in many other forms of Black popular music, the main producers of Ragga have tended to be male, expressing through the lyrics and the DJ sound systems – exemplary forms of musical production and distribution – a strongly urbanized working-class male culture. Yet through the 1990s women have gradually gained significant influence and power to shape the nature and content of Ragga dance-hall culture. Since its gradual rise in the mid-1980s, the Ragga dance-hall has become less and less an un-contested Black male working-class space. There has been a shift in focus from the male 'ragamuffin' DJ/audience as the predominant sign of Ragga identity in the mid– to late-1980s, to a greater presence and recognition of the female Ragga devotee or 'queen'. There seem to be two key developments through which we can trace this movement: first, a shift within the lyrics from an exclusionary male to male discussion about women, to a greater emphasis upon a male to female dialogue. In Ragga lyrics the male DJs for the most part are speaking directly to the female audience. This shift acknowledges both the presence and power of women in the dance-hall, which comes mostly from their position of being consumers of Ragga music rather than producers. The prime exponents of Ragga lyrics are male, with only a few female DJs gaining diasporic attention in the 1990s (namely Lady Saw and Patra). Therefore I have chosen to focus on Ragga lyrics by male DJ's, principally because what caught my attention about Ragga music is how women as consumers of Ragga lyrics have constructed readings which subvert by 'playing'[3] with and within its hetero/sexist authority. This is principally achieved through the dialogic call and response nature of Ragga performance and consumption, so typical of other forms of Black popular music. Gilroy recognizes this call and response motif as disjunctive of Eurocentric notions of the division between art and social life, which create the moment of performance and consumption. These 'dialogic rituals', in which the authority of the musical text is transformed through 'de/reconstructive procedures', create new meanings (Gilroy 1993a: 34, 40). It is primarily in this interdependent and dialogic relationship between DJ and DJ, and DJ and audience, that Black women have elaborated and extended the Ragga lyrical texts. Expressed in forms of dance and dress, they have produced a Ragga style, or more precisely Ragga dance-hall culture, which actively elaborates a racialized, therefore, in this context, Black, sexual and gender politics. The Ragga 'style' in fashion and dance has been dominated by women, both within the dance-hall and outside, primarily through the production and distribution of Ragga clothing and hairstyles within the predominantly feminized pre/occupations of fashion retailing, dressmaking and hairdressing, and it reveals the second aspect in the elaboration of a specifically Black lower-class female culture.

Ragga Music: 'Slackness' Versus 'Culture'

> Culture in the dance, represented …
> Make we preach pure love and reality
> Slackness in the back yard hiding, hiding, hiding.
> Slackness in the back yard hiding, hiding from Culture.
> Josie Wales, 'Culture A Lick')

Carolyn Cooper (1993) points us to the special status of the terms 'Culture' and 'Slackness' in Jamaican society. She claims that the lyrics of ragga DJs subvert the official culture of Jamaican society, and seek to escape the appropriation of folk culture into what she calls the scribal literary tradition by asserting an urbanized folk ethos, a 'verbal maroonage' (Cooper 1993: 136). Cooper explains that the word 'Culture' represents the authorized values, morality and behaviour of official Jamaican Culture, which seeks to present itself as the representative culture of Jamaica. Slackness represents 'backward', 'rude'[4] folk/ghetto culture, vying for recognition and value within official Jamaican national identity. So, for Cooper, Slackness and Culture represent oppositional values within Jamaican society, centring round the ways that class and patriarchal gender ideology establish 'consensual standards of decency' (p. 141). Cooper defines Slackness as 'an (h)ideology of escape from the authority of omniscient Culture' (p. 141).

To extend Cooper's analysis beyond a local Jamaican particularism, and questions of Jamaican national identity, we must engage with the *diasporicity* (see Hesse, ch. 5, this volume) of reggae music and reggae dance-hall culture. So, to extend Cooper's terminology; if Ragga music of the 1990s is the contemporary 'slack parole' of the dance-hall; what version/s of culture is it seeking to evade?

Peter Wilson, writing as long ago as 1969, argued that the values of respect, reputation and respectability hold great importance within many Caribbean cultures, and that these values are highly gendered in application. Wilson's thesis is that Caribbean women of all classes are particularly invested in the values of respectability, characterized by the 'metropolitan orientated colonial system of social stratification based upon class, colour, wealth, Eurocentric culture, lifestyle and education' (quoted in Besson 1993: 16). Wilson regards reputation as an exclusively male value system, characterized by an emphasis upon male competition for personal rather than social worth, secured by individual skill in verbal virtuosity and sexual virility and anti-establishment activities: 'an indigenous counter-culture based upon the ethos of equality, rooted in personal, as opposed to social worth. It is a response to colonial dependence and *a solution to the scarcity of respectability*' (Besson 1993: 16; emphasis added).

However, Jean Besson challenges Wilson's view that these oppositional values are exclusively gendered in this way and argues that the oppositional values of respectability and reputation are not simple manifestations of conflicting values between men and women. I agree with Besson when she argues for a more complex view, in which class and age and location are factors as important as gender. Besson rejects the view that Caribbean women are more culturally and politically conservative and that the only resistance to Eurocentric cultural dominance comes from the counter-culture of African-Caribbean men. She shows through her study of a rural Jamaican village, Martha Brae, how lower-class African-Caribbean women are also heavily identified with the values of reputation and that this provides a means by which women also articulate a counter-culture of resistance to Eurocentric ideals and values of respectability (Besson 1993: 19) *in ways that are gender specific, but not gender exclusive.* This is a crucial observation for our understanding of Ragga music, because it enables us to recognize the extent to which both the male DJs and Ragga queens are both invested in the values of reputation, and how both men and women in the dance-hall utilize the system of reputation differently to advance their own interests and resist Eurocentric and middle-class standards of respectability.

However, I am also particularly intrigued by the way in which sexuality appears, or more accurately does not appear, in Besson's study of Martha Brae. For while her data clearly show that sexuality is a significant source of women's reputation or honour, Besson never directly focuses upon it. Instead, she alludes to the sexual subjectivity of African-Caribbean women, in a manner that has characterized the literature both academic and fictional. Black women's sexuality is hidden behind a discussion about household and kinship patterns. So, in showing how forms of conjugal relationships and residence patterns are used as sources of reputation, Besson cites the prevalence of bearing children outside of marriage, sometimes in a succession of conjugal unions. Besson correctly offers this as an example of both a pragmatic adaptation to the impact of slavery on Black families and a form of resistance to Eurocentric ideas of marriage, kinship patterns, and gender roles (Besson 1993: 21). Thus the possession of a degree of social and economic independence, sexual freedom and personal autonomy are implied as constituting important aspects of a woman's personal reputation. At the same time, Besson tells us that having children who are not 'owned' by the father, or outside a conjugal relationship, is seen as bringing shame upon a woman. Despite this implied acknowledgement of women's sexual freedom outside marriage, the importance of sex and the erotic in the female economy of reputation is overlooked within Besson's account. She does not examine *how* women utilize sexuality to gain sexual partners who will 'own' their children, and/or live with them, thereby enhancing the woman's social reputation.

It is to Carolyn Cooper's account of Slackness and Culture that we must return to get an idea of how sex and sexuality figure in the contested values of Jamaican society. Although we can read Cooper's account of Slackness and Culture in terms of Wilson's distinction between the oppositional values of Reputation and Respectability, Cooper does not herself directly engage with Wilson's thesis. Cooper notes that the dance-hall DJs eschew respectability and operate at the lower end of social values. Their emphasizing of verbal virtuosity and sexual boasting asserts a claim for social value in terms that correspond with both Wilson and Besson's view of the male system of reputation. Cooper's account of Slackness can be used as a situated example of how the values of reputation are translated into the particular social and cultural space of the dance-hall. In Slackness/Ragga there is stress upon individual performance and skill, sexual prowess and anti-establishment sentiments which we would expect to find circulating within a value system based upon reputation. However, what is distinctive about Ragga, and about Cooper's study of oppositional values in Jamaica, is the unambiguous attention to sex and sexuality, and, perhaps more importantly, to Black female sexuality.[5] Ragga is not expressive of an exclusively male system of reputation, vying with an exclusively female value system of respectability. Ragga shows how Black women also are invested in the values of reputation; how they utilize it to advance their social power and influence over men, and to contest dominant middle-class *and* Eurocentric notions of femininity, marriage and kinship. Sexuality and sex are celebrated as a source of social recognition, reputation and value – hence, social power – for *both men and women* in dance-hall culture. As Cooper rightly points out, Ragga confronts the pious morality which has tended to pervade what she calls 'Jamaican fundamentalist' (Cooper 1993: 141), ideals of sexuality. Jamaican fundamentalism in this context seems to refer to Black or Africa-identified Christian, Rastafarian and secular traditions (e.g. Black Power) which have clearly defined identities for Black women, as strong, courageous or 'nasty':[6] 'Slackness is potentially a politics of subversion. For Slackness is not mere sexual looseness – though it certainly is that. Slackness is a metaphorical revolt against law and order … It is the antithesis of Culture' (p. 141).

In this regard, it seems that Ragga/Slackness seeks to evade and resist the authority of a range of Black cultural values of female respectability, 'in which both the suppression of sexuality and the secondariness of woman are institutionalised' (p. 148). Before analysing this in more detail, we need to consider what is being said in Ragga lyrics.

'Big It Up'[7] – Valuing Black Bodies

The celebration of the Black female body is a particularly strong theme within Ragga music. From the following lyrics we can recognize how in the celebration of particular typical aspects of Black female bodies, Ragga subverts mainstream Eurocentric constructions of the feminine body which have tended to devalue Black women's bodies as 'unfeminine'.

> You turn me on, with your sexy body
> You turn me on – and your bumper[8] heavy …
> You turn me on – you fat and you heavy
> > (Bounty Killer et al., 'You Turn Me On')

The image of the idealized female form as represented within mainstream white mass culture – slim, fragile and acquiescing – is completely overturned. In the context of racism and the domination of Eurocentric standards of beauty in the media and popular culture, just the act of celebrating a common aspect of the Black female form which has so long been devalued or distorted is in itself a powerful and affirmative act. The male DJs' celebration of fatness as sexy and beautiful finds a response in the Ragga dress style. It is a style that invites women to show as much of their body and body shape as they dare. So Black women who previously agonized over their large size now wear the tightest and most revealing of clothing, and flaunt their shapes with feisty confidence.

Many Ragga songs refer to the Black woman's buttocks ('bumper'). Within European gender discourse the Black woman's buttocks has been the sign of her 'exoticism' and her deviation from a European norm of female sexuality. The body of the African woman was appropriated in nineteenth-century medical and public health discourses, through phenological comparisons of the buttocks of Italian prostitutes with that of African women and used to construct a physiognomic link between the Black woman's buttocks as a sign of her excessive sexuality and the 'deviant' sexuality of white prostitutes (Gilman 1992). Therefore, and crucially for Black feminism, dominant notions of an ideal feminine aesthetics were constituted in and through a discourse of race. The Black female form was the deviant, essentially 'Other' to a patriarchal construction of an idealized passive white female sexuality.[9] In the DJs' appreciation of the Black woman's body we see Ragga music's revalorization of the Black female buttocks, reclaiming it from the deviant and exotic, and renaming it as familiar, feminine and erotic.

In saying this we cannot avoid the recognition that this emphasis upon the Black female buttocks as a signifier of rampant sexuality remains problematically confluent with a European discourse of sexuality, race and gender which ties Black subjects to their dismembered and highly exoticized parts (big Black buttocks, the long Black penis, bare Black breasts) as both the location and sign of a licentious Black libido. It seems to me that the shame and discomfort that many Black women feel about the ways in which we are celebrated in Ragga centre round its apparent demand for our complicity with a racist sexual iconography of the Black female body. The racist history of European ideas of sexuality complicates any attempt by Black women to assert their sexual selves in the public domain. The domestication of the white European middle-class wife within the cult of virtuous or true womanhood (cf. Hill Collins 1993; Carby 1998; Etter-Lewis 1993) in the nineteenth century developed hand in hand with imperialism colonialism and the 'defeminization' of Black women (Meis 1986: 95). This has produced a preoccupation with Black women's 'self-liberation ethos' (Beckles 1991), with the gaining and securing of respect *as Black women*, not simply as Black people, or as women. In terms of Caribbean culture, this has tended to require the adoption of Eurocentric standards of decency in order, first, to challenge the gender specificity in the dominant discourse of white racism and also the sexism within the sub-dominant cultures of Black social life. This has tended to produce a Black female tradition that has failed to take seriously or even ignored the contribution of poorly educated and working-class Black women to Black cultural politics (Davies 1998: xiii).

Eroticism and Social Power?

When we look away from the importance of the erotic in the development and sustenance of our power, or when we look away from ourselves as we satisfy our erotic needs in concert with others, we use each other as objects of satisfaction rather than share our joy in the satisfying, rather than make connection with our similarities and differences. To refuse to be conscious of what we are feeling at any time, however comfortable that might seem, is to deny a large part of the experience, and to allow ourselves to be reduced to the pornographic, the abused, and the absurd. (Lorde 1984: 59)

In a great deal of Ragga lyrics, Black women's sexual agency and their ability to use it to control a man are presented as synonymous with material success. 'Gone Up' by Shabba Ranks (1991) illustrates how Ragga texts can convey an image of the 'new (Black) woman' who chooses her man for his sexual and financial potency, which are interlinked (as we can see from the reference in Mega Banton's 'Money First' to a man's wallet needing to be long enough to touch the ground [dirt]) if he is to have sexual success. The Black woman's agency in such lyrics is located in her sexual body, and its ability to control her man's desire and his wallet simultaneously.

> Make sure you collect the money first
> Before you lie down in a bed and start do the 'work'.
> Woman want the money plenty, want the money 'nough
> Woman nah want no man if she know him pocket broke
> Pocket have to long so, till it a touch dirt.
> Put a sign on your door, man, 'Cash before work'.
> (Mega Banton, 'Money First', 1993)

The message of this song is clear: a woman's sexuality has a value in material terms. It is not to be given away for no return; romance certainly is not enough, or even expected. In 'Gone Up', Shabba Ranks is concerned that this is not mistaken for prostitution and goes on to stress the importance of a woman valuing herself and not allowing herself to be exploited by failing to ensure she is rewarded for her 'work', both domestic and sexual:

> Everything a raise so wha' you gonna do
> You nah raise the price of loving too? ...
> Gasoline – Gone up! Gone up! ...
> It's not a matter of fact that you a sell it ...
> You have some woman gwan like them [have] no worth,
> Hitch up in a house like a house robot;
> House to clean – dem clean that up.
> Clothes to wash – dem wash that up.
> Dollars a run – and them nah get enough.
> Don't make no man work you out and park you like old truck.
> (Shabba Ranks, 'Gone Up', 1991)

In this as in many other songs we find the word 'work' used to describe sexual intercourse. Thus, in the song 'Lover Man' by the aptly named

Daddy Screw, the terms 'lover man' and 'worker man' are used alternately to denote a good lover. This deliberate double articulation of the concept of work in my view works in two ways: first, it connotes the history of how Black bodies were marked by our violent insertion into modernity via the slavery which attempted to convert us from human subjects to units of labour. The inversion of work to signify sexual activity can be seen as a valorization and assertion of the playfulness and recreational possibilities of Black bodies in defiance of this alienated corporeality. Second, when sex becomes 'work', it enters the marketplace of consumerism. The best workers, male or female, get the most rewards and power to obtain and possess other commodities, whether these are cars, clothes or other people's sexy bodies. In urban Black communities in the USA, Jamaica or Britain where Black male unemployment is disproportionately high, particularly among the young, there is an important statement being made by shifting the location of the work arena into Black-dominated spaces of the bedroom and the dance-hall. Black popular culture across the diaspora has often been characterized at different moments by resistance to the alienation of the products of Black bodies within arenas of work that are variously viewed as white, western or simply exploitative; the claiming of bodily integrity and autonomy through the celebration of uses of the body in pursuits of leisure and pleasure – song, dance, sport and sex; and the creation and claiming of public spaces of Black autonomy beyond the boundaries of white and/or mainstream authority – notably the Black churches, the dance-hall or bar room. In many regards, modern Black popular culture can be defined as the formation and articulation of public spaces of resistance, reclamation and autonomous creativity against and beyond the hegemony of western modernity and racism.

The Ragga queen's 'sexy' appearance increases her own value as an object of male consumption, but simultaneously her economic power and/or autonomy implied by her expensive clothing and hairstyles, may increase her power over and autonomy from men in the dance-hall.[10] In the Ragga dance-hall, clearly, what is being celebrated and displayed is the highly eroticized female body; the 'Black-woman's-body' spectacularly revealed – near naked – yet tantalizingly 'veiled' in garish shocking pinks, yellows and lime greens. Hairstyles in contrast emphasize false or processed hair, often elaborately bedecked and intricately and rigidly gelled in place, starkly contrasting with the gyrating, twitching fluid 'flexings' of the body below. The Ragga queen in this light can be viewed in her 'loud' appearance as displaying a kind of 'kitsch' and drag style. She is kitsch in that she puts together clothing and contexts to produce a disruptive, jarring, falsifying, irreverent spectacle;[11] wearing iridescent chiffon blouses over beachwear or underwear to go to a night-club. In her fetishistic display of an excessively processed Black femininity she offers a drag style – false hair, false nails, even false identity – but the bodies in drag are female bodies; thus accentuating their power to manipulate, falsify and create their own subjectivities, for surely, 'the fetish is chosen for its nearness to the moment of repression' (Gamman and Makinen 1994: 41) and therein lies the power of Ragga erotic style to play with the sexist gullibility of the male gaze. The Ragga queen is almost a hyper-real image (see Sarap 1998: 93) as resplendent in meanings as she is in her appearance. Her style presents us with a highly processed, commodified appearance, reveling in a kind of consumer fetishism in which women's consumption of style can signify personal economic agency, social power and sexual agency over the consumerism (sexual and material) of men. As Gamman and Makinen have noted:

> The sexual fetishism of the erotic often occurs through processes of consumerism designed to make products appear 'sexy'. We would suggest that the blind spots of gaze theory become most evident when trying to conceptualise the meaning of images in a consumerist society, where spectacle informs all points of the market economy'. (Gamman and Makinen 1994: 183)

Spectacle, eroticism, concealment and revelation, are central pivotal themes of the film *Dancehall Queen*.[12] Marcia is a street vendor, a member of a group we come to learn through the film, which is scorned even by other Kingston poor. Yet, by assuming a false night-time identity as 'sexy bitch' (as one of her dupes calls her) and contender for the title of Dance Hall Queen, Marcia is able both to transcend and escape her everyday, downtrodden and defeminized self. She exploits the concealment of her 'true' identity, not as a form of escape from reality, but to amass economic autonomy and social influence in the pursuit of revenge on two men for the rape of her daughter and the killing of a friend. Her power clearly comes from her willingness to exploit the power of the erotic and to play within the sexism of her male adversaries. She eventually manipulates the two men into a fight which leaves one dead and the other with his crimes exposed; he is humiliated when he discovers who the new Dancehall Queen really is and that he has been duped by a common street vendor. At the end of the film, Marcia has not only become the Dancehall Queen and won the accompanying prize money, she has also won the gender battle against the two men who have blighted her life, and asserted pride in the devalued status of lowly street vendor. Her triumph is not merely a personal triumph; it is a poor Black woman's triumph. The character of Marcia in *Dancehall Queen* exemplifies how a working-class woman can manipulate, revise, resist and recreate new subjectivities and possibilities for herself by playing within the authority of a sexist male culture.

In the split between authenticity and falsification, concealment and exposure, subversion and complicity, Marcia's performative strategies seem to be within a tradition of Black women's self-expression, which Gwendolyn Etter-Lewis (1993) associates with the writing of nineteenth-century African-American novelists. Etter-Lewis describes African-American women's autobiographical writing as 'split at the root', i.e. a strategy of writing constituted in practices of concealment and exposure produced by the split desire to tell one's story while maintaining one's safety from the tyrannies of racism and sexism.

> Speaking/writing their own lives was a risky undertaking embedded in the malevolence of an historically prejudiced society that penalised them at least twice for being both African Americans *and* women. So for these women the act of telling is not only 'split', but also 'nappy'. Like permed or colour-treated hair, the texture of their narrative is often different above and below the surface. Above the surface there is acceptable public appearance (e.g. straight hair/standard language) but close to the root/core is a more natural and appealing form (e.g. nappy hair/the language of resistance that is some-times is disguised or hidden). (Etter-Lewis 1993: 155)

Etter-Lewis is careful to point out that she is not equating straight hair with standard language but is trying to mark out the split between what is revealed (denoted), and what is narrated beneath the surface or (con-noted). This is important. This relation is not simply oppositional – concealment as the opposite of exposure – or simply cumulative – as an addition to it – but rather overlapping and transformative; concealment *as* exposure, exposure *as* concealment. Each is internally deconstructive of the other as well as destabilizing external rules or conventions of repres-entation and accountability. What is revealed not only conceals, but in the very moment of self-revelation can hint at or recall the presence of that which is threatening to emerge, or being repressed. So in the split between the Ragga women's highly falsified, transparently mythical self of purple wigs and sequinned, satined, sensual bodies, there is the undercover 'dirty reality' of the 'nappy head', racism, sexism and poverty. Marcia's identity is not simply split between the false identity of the Dancehall Queen and an 'authentic' identity of the nappy-headed street vendor and single mother; she is both. Both identities are *entangled*; they perform acts of trickery and counterfeiting; they reflect and refract. This split Ragga identity sends out shards of dis/ruptive, dis/locating light on to discourses, myths and practices of gender and race which want to demand Black women's social devaluation and discursive ossification, but which are often refused and evaded through these practices of concealment and exposure.

Ragga lyrics typically emphasize Black women's sexual agency and advocate a libertarian individualism where women have autonomy from patriarchal marital domesticity and the cult of motherhood. This is an unusual feature within Black cultural practices which have typically offered only one honourable feature for Black women's sexuality – as the source of the Black matriarch's power (cf. Hill Collins 1991; Rohlehr 1988). Yet we have to ask how far these representations reveal anything useful about the possibilities for eroticism as a useful source of Black women's autonomous social agency and empowerment. Consider, for example, bell hooks's examination of Nola Darling in Spike Lee's film, *She's Gotta Have It*. Hooks notes that Nola is represented as an active sexual subject, desiring men and not merely being an object of male desire. hooks questions whether Nola Darling is really liberated at all, since, in her view, Nola views herself only through the male gaze of her many lovers, thus concluding that Nola is not liberated at all. We might likewise take the view that in many Ragga lyrics the woman in the song and the women in the audience are being invited into a complicity with this objectifying male gaze. As hooks says of Nola Darling:

> Nola's ... assertive sexuality is most often portrayed as though ... her sexually active body is a reward or gift she bestows on the deserving man ... though desiring subject, Nola acts on the assumption that heterosexual female assertion has legitimacy primarily as a gesture of reward or a means by which men can be manipulated and controlled by women. *What is vulgarly called 'pussy power'*. (hooks 1990, emphasis added)

hooks may indeed have a point in the context of *She's Gotta Have It*, but condemnation alone does not take us very far and closes the possibility of further interrogation of, if or how Black women can use the erotic. It also seems to go against hooks's own call for greater expression of a Black feminist oppositional cultural criticism, which can examine how Black women to come into view in popular culture and connect Black women's real life subjectivity to how we engage with mass culture and create alternative readings, which 'contest, resist, revision, interrogate and invent on multiple levels' (hooks 1992: 129). As hooks herself says, this is vital in order to create new alternative texts; to open up encounters in which Black women can recognize and affirm each other's struggles for visibility and create new spaces for the articulation of radical Black female subjectivities. The very notion of a Black gaze will seem bizarre to many, since it has received very little recognition or attention – much less a Black female gaze. To move beyond disapproval or mere bland compliance with representations of women that seem to collude with, rather than challenge, oppressive images, perhaps we need to rethink the relationship between objectification and agency that seems assumed within hooks's critique of *She's Gotta Have It*.

Avis Lewellan (1988) argues that women as consumers of heterosexual eroticism gain pleasure from viewing women in positions of sexual objectification because they are objectified *for* women (Lewellan 1988: 100). In such representations women are not passive victims of male desire; they desire and (re)turn the desiring gaze on men. The process of desire, and representation itself, Lewellan says, always involve a degree of objectification. In heterosexual eroticism both partners share and exchange the roles of sexual object and subject at different points in the erotic encounter. As the observer of eroticism, the viewing woman places herself either in the position of being the recipient of male desire; or watching another woman who is the recipient of male desire, *as part of her own pleasure* (Lewellan 1988: 100).

To take a more open view on heterosexual eroticism, we must move away from the tendency in much feminist writing to see a necessary correspondence between the structural relations of gender and erotic practices; 'the feminist ideology of heterosexual sex' (Waldby 1995: 267) which views all heterosexual encounters as representative and reinforcing of women's oppression. So, while working-class women, such as Marcia in Dancehall Queen, may at moments appear to collude with their own objectification, they are not fooled. Marcia engages in a well-known 'trickster' strategy within both African-American and Caribbean culture, developed through the demands of surviving the slavery experience; 'playing fool to catch wise'. In other words, appearing to accept one's inferior, less empowered position as a cover for one's own artfulness. As a practice of dissembling, it is another manifestation of concealment and revelation as strategies for self-expression. Women like Marcia know and live the social realities of lone motherhood and poverty, whether in Kingston, London or New York, experiencing the power of male domination that frustrates and makes their lives more difficult. Within a social context where sexuality is an important resource of personal reputation, Marcia can choose between being a passive sexual object or an active sexual subject, using eroticism and sexuality to enhance and sustain her personal power and resist male domination.

Consequently, 'pussy power' is a very significant aspect of the Ragga Queen's style. Just as the male DJ's lyrical emphasis upon the buttocks is picked up and repeated in the women's dances, women extend the appropriation of female genitalia to construct a womanist gender symbolism through dances and clothing that draw attention to the vagina. In dances which simulate coitus upon an absent recumbent and passive male; in hand movements which gesture towards auto-eroticism, or leg movements that expose the female crotch area to full view; in wearing clothing such as 'pum-pum' shorts (literally 'pussy' shorts), so tight as to reveal the imprint of the vagina; or wearing g-string bikinis in the dancehall which may expose the vagina or pubic hair – Ragga women engage in exhibitionism which is crude, vulgar, shocking, sexy and powerful.

What is signified by this vulgar display? We can turn to Shirley Ardener's (1987) essay 'A Note on Gender Iconography: The Vagina' to gain some useful insights on women's uses of vulgarity in gender symbolism. Ardener draws on a wide range of anthropological and artistic examples to demonstrate how women have utilized the symbolism of the vagina to exploit cultural constructions of the vulgar and obscene, in order to harness and make public the repressed powers of the feminine. She draws on ritual behaviour by Bakweri and Belong women of the Cameroons in response to insults inflicted upon women by men. Massed women will engage in verbal and behavioural practices which symbolically 'expose' female genitalia. The aim of these practices is to 'shame' an offending man, group of men or all the men of the village (Ardener 1987: 113–42). These practices, says Ardener, are disciplinary acts of female militancy which seek both to exert power over men and to demonstrate female corporate identity (p. 115).

Similarly, in dances which simulate clitoral masturbation and women in controlling and dominant sexual positions, and clothes that imprint the vagina on the observing gaze, the Ragga Queens construct a sexual subjectivity which is centred on the vagina as the locus of female sexual agency and generative power which does not tie it inevitably to reproduction, that is open and inclusive of a wide continuum of desire: autoeroticism, lesbian desire and an active powerful heterosexual eroticism. Through the elaboration of a gynocentric mode of signification, Ragga women create a gender symbolism that hints at what remains largely unspoken and unacknowledged in the vast majority of Ragga lyrics – that is, the possibility of a Black lesbian or bisexual presence in the dancehall and in Black identity. In many songs the DJs inflame female rivalries and arguments over hairstyles, clothes, possessions and boyfriends.

> Hot gyal, me want you put up unuh hand!
> No borrow-clothes-gyal can tek fe you man!
> Da' gyal a no friend.
> Dem a watch wa' you wear –
> (Cobra, ' Dem Need It', 1998)

The reference to 'borrow-clothes-gyal' clearly seeks to devalue female co-operation and mutuality, evidenced through the lending and borrowing of clothes, and turn them into opportunities for competitiveness and ridicule between women. This interruption into a female space always seeks to place competition over men at the centre of women's relationships. This can be viewed as an attempt both to resist and break down heterosexual female solidarity and to deny the possibility and existence of Black woman-to-woman desire. Consequently, the vaginal symbolism of the women can be reincorporated by the Ragga DJs into an overbearing and overarching phallocentricism – and the women's spectacular vaginal displays become contained by and for the men in the dancehall, within a male heterosexual gaze that refuses the possibility that the display may involve women representing their sexual selves for the hetero-erotic and/or homo-erotic gaze of other women. Yet, perversely, Black women's lesbian or bisexual desire might find room for erotic play and pleasure in the 'public' spaces constructed by the Ragga queens' spectacular gynocentric displays and the relative safety of their invisibility. By this reading, Ragga culture can be viewed as a space within which Black heterosexual men seek to control and contain emerging womanist, gay and lesbian and bisexual identities; while also reassuring themselves of their own representation of phallocentric heterosexuality as the only way to be a 'True Black Man'. This assertion of a governmental Black male identity, in its very moment of articulation, becomes disrupted and questioned by the appearance of that which it seeks to repress – Black queer identity, which appears as a disruption to the assertion of a continuous heterosexed Blackness,[13] since 'queer and Black modify each other's sense of nation' (Harris 1996: 5).

Batty Riders, Batty Men and Black Body Limits

The gynocentricism of the Ragga queens' dances and clothing is confronted by the stark reality of 'compulsory heterosexuality' (Rich 1980) within Ragga culture. Rich uses this term to denote the taken-for-granted assumption of a heterosexual norm, which articulates a governmental (thus naturalized) sexuality by rendering male homosexuality hyper-visible and unnatural, and lesbian or bisexual existence largely invisible. However, while Ragga music naturalizes heterosexuality, it does not assume it. Phallocentric heterosexuality is referenced repeatedly in Ragga lyrics, to such a degree that it does indeed appear that Black heterosexual masculinity is in fact the primary concern of male Ragga DJs.

> All the girls go tell the world that I am wicked in a bed ...
> In a fe me bed me nah want Alfred ...
> Me nah promote mama man,[14]
> All mamma man fe dead
> Pam! Pam! Lick a shot in a mama man head.
> (Shabba Ranks, 'Wicked in Bed')

The erotic narcissism within many lyrics raises a suspicion that perhaps the male Ragga DJs' lyrics, rather than being a celebration of Black women's sexual liberation, are principally the celebration of a particular representation of Black masculinity.[15] As in other forms of Black popular culture which appear so often to articulate a male perspective, one begins to suspect that, like the men in *She's Gotta Have It*: 'In telling us what they think about [Black women] they are telling us what they think about themselves, their values, their desires. She is the object that stimulates the discourse. They are its subject' (hooks 1990:).

Such heterosexist and homophobic lyrics point to an insecurity about the capacity of Black masculinity to secure its it dominance. In requiring the stated disavowal of male homosexuality, many Ragga lyrics posit gay identity as a kind of 'false femininity'. Many songs allude to the dangers of misrecognizing a gay man as a woman, or of gay men seeking to occupy the space reserved for women within a phallocentric desire; a desire that always requires an object for male penetration. However, Ragga does not represent an unbounded sexual libertarianism. There are clearly hierarchies of slackness (Cooper 1993: 149), with homosexuality being regarded as a 'foreign/white/unnatural corruption of 'true' Black values and identities. In 'Fis[t] – A – [W]rist' Shabba Ranks clearly 'accuses' any man who criticizes his emphasis upon heterosexual sex and women's body parts as probably being gay; an offence answerable by immediate expulsion from the space of the dance-hall and Black masculinity.

> Take you fist out of you wrist! You nastiness!
> Look how much woman exist! …
> Tru me talk 'bout punani,[16] some DJ vex
> Mus[t] [b]e in a man pants dem want tek set …
> You don't love woman? Find the exit! …
> (Shabba Ranks, Fis' – A – rist')

Lyrics such as this posit the penis as having an almost independent agency that requires men to maintain a constant surveillance on other men, lest the phallic drive gets misrouted. The power of the phallus means that the 'straight' man is as vulnerable to the power of homosexual phallocentric desire, as women are to the power of heterosexual phallocentric desire – if not more so. What this leaves in place is the discourse of an impenetrable fortified phallic masculinity (Waldby 1995: 270). This produces a psychic investment in a particular sense of the male body, its boundaries and uses, and an imperative of mastery over others through privileging the penis as the sole site of male eroticism. This phallocentrism can lead to an erotic disinvestment in the rest of the male body, an injunction against passivity and '[a]bove all … against "men's secret femininity", receptive anal erotic-ism' (Waldby 1995: 272). Waldby concludes that disavowing anal eroticism is central to the maintenance of phallic masculinity.

As we have observed already, male Ragga DJs are very attentive to the appreciation of the Black female buttocks, which comes to signify the Blackness of both her beauty and her eroticism. We have also noted how gay experience is represented in Ragga discourse as seeking to insinuate itself in the female body space as a false femininity, and so to cheat both heterosexual women and men of their respective powers. The term 'batty man' in denoting gay identity, locates male homosexuality and eroticism exclusively in the anus. The disavowal of male anal eroticism is a recurring theme in many Ragga lyrics, in the frequent warnings to young boys not to 'bend down'. Simultaneously, the attention lavished upon the female buttocks never goes so far as to imply heterosexual anal penetration. The female buttocks, within Ragga erotica, cease in a sense to be anal, but becomes a secondary signifier of the vagina and vaginal penetration. Lyrics emphasize the winding of the female buttocks on the dance floor or the pleasures of vaginal penetration from behind. The buttocks begins to look like a highly unstable signifier within Ragga discourse. Waldby's thesis enables us to understand more theoretically how the Black buttocks (male and female) is used within Ragga sexual signification to reinforce phallo-centricism within the logic of compulsory heterosexuality. Waldby argues that anal eroticism disturbs the idea of the impenetrable, mastering male body by its abandonment of the phallic claim (Waldby 1995: 272). Also the anus is non-gender specific: both men and women have one, it is soft, sensitive and linked to pollution like the vagina:

> All this makes anal eroticism a suasive point for the displacement or erasure of purely phallic boundaries. In a sense then, anal eroticism is the sexual pleasure which conformation to a phallic image most profoundly opposes. If the point of the phallic image is to guard against confusion between the imaginary anatomies of masculine and feminine, and to shore up masculine power, then anal eroticism threatens to explode this ideological body ... But the negative injunction of the phallus against such pleasure is, like all laws, also an invitation to transgression, and it seems likely that this phallic taboo might intensify, rather than disperse, the erotic potential of the anus for heterosexual men. (Waldby 1995: 272)

If we recall the function played by the Black buttocks in early European scientific discourses of gender and sex, we can see more clearly how the eroticized anus becomes a liminal site between discourses of race, gender and sexuality, which are caught within the unresolved historical 'entangle-ment' (Hesse 1999a) of the West and its Others. Hesse uses this term to describe the interconnected experiences in the histories of modernity which frustrate hegemonic political and cultural imaginaries of the West from being able to present tidy and finished political or cultural formations, unimplicated by Other(ed) social imaginaries. Black women and our sexuality are no less entangled in these overlapping histories and discourses, producing discordant interruptions into the imagined communities of feminist and Black social imaginaries.

Conclusion

The exploration of sexuality and the erotic as a means for Black women's self-expression or creativity is fraught with many dangers and fears for Black women's political activism and cultural expression. Black (hetero)-feminism has yet really to address the unresolved and contradictory engagements that Black women have with our desires, our 'complicated female bodies … complicated in relation to each other through [our] own complicated desires and subjectivities' (Harris 1996: 18). Harris alerts us to the silenced contribution of Black lesbian feminism to white lesbian culture and lesbian social theory. I would add that the lesbian identity of much African-American feminist writing, at least in terms of how it has tended to reach Black women in Britain, is largely stripped of this lesbian component. We take the feminism and leave the queer. In this way we often overlook the emphasis African-American lesbian writers have placed upon sexuality as a legitimate arena of attention for Black female empowerment and politics. The demand that Harris makes of queer Black feminism is, for me, a demand that should be made of any Black feminism that would call itself such: 'queer black feminism should have a complicated history of bodies and desires; it has to be able to acknowledge these complications to further resist the shame and oppression some of these bodies are made to be silent about' (Harris 1996: 18).

Ragga music retains value for me because, in its refusal to comply with this silencing, shaming and oppression of Black female desire, it opens up the possibility of acknowledging the ambivalent sentiments we as Black women often have about our bodies. For it is through the mythic figures of the 'Black mammy', 'the Black whore, or sex goddess', and the emasculating and aggressive 'Black bitch' or simply the fertile 'breeder woman', that we have become accustomed to being allowed social and cultural visibility, not only within the dominant culture, but also within the sub-dominant cultures of Black social life. It is through these images that we are accustomed to being the objects of honour or abuse; pity or praise; envy or ridicule; fear or desire; loathing or fascination. Sometimes we even experience all these things at once! Therefore attempts to adjudicate on the value or otherwise of Ragga culture, which do not engage with its inherent irony, ambiguities and contradictions, which are in themselves a manifestation of the complexities it enacts, cannot engage with the complex and discrepant negotiations taking place between race, sex, gender, class and location; negotiations that have always been central concerns of Black feminism.

The construction of the Black female body, and its commodification and sexualization within modernity, place it at a pivotal point in discourses of otherness (Hill Collins 1991: 70). The symbolism of the Ragga woman's highly processed, manufactured, commodified appearance reveals the 'Black-woman's-body' emerging through clothes that stress manufacture and exposure, as opposed to the ideals of feminine 'naturalness' and concealment which dominate 'roots and culture' music, and so expose the hidden veil of discourse which connects the 'natural' body to the 'social' Black body. So the exposure of the constructedness of the social/female/commodified Black body, through 'vulgar' uses of the body, has the (perhaps unintended) consequence of deconstructing and transgressing the discursive separation that seeks to fix and naturalize notions of 'The Good Black Woman' found in many Black diasporic cultures. However, this moment of subversion becomes implicated in the very discourses of sexuality it seeks to evade, because the 'traditional' or African-identified values of femininity are often a reaction against the pornographic images of Black women in Eurocentric discourses. The question of how Black women can articulate ourselves outside these stereotypes, or 'controlling images [which] are designed to make racism, sexism and poverty appear natural, normal, and an everyday part of everyday life' (Hill Collins 1991: 68), remains a profound moral and political dilemma.

Although the Black body has long been an object of intense scientific and cultural scrutiny, little has been done to explore the ontology of the Black body. The challenge for me is to begin to find a way to construct a cultural and social history of the Black body which can analyse it as the site of multiple inscriptions of overlapping discourses, and in which we can try to think about Black people's physical and psychic identifications with our own and other racialized bodies. For, as a Black British woman, I often find myself uncomfortably situated across ambiguous, conflicting and contradictory experiences of my body which engender feelings of pride and shame, pleasure and fear, power and vulnerability, liberation and oppression. In this I know I am not alone. I am glad that Ragga brings the politics of desire and pleasure back on the agenda of Black cultural politics in ways that force many Black women and feminists to confront the repression and disavowal of desire and the Black female body as legitimate sources of Black female agency and oppositional subjectivity. It also demands that we take seriously and allow ourselves to be informed by the concerns of all Black women, so that Black feminism can be informed by and become relevant to the concerns of all sections of Black women, across generational, educational and class differences. This is what I have tried to achieve through engaging with the diverse spectatorship of Black British women in order further to open up the public space in which we can explore share, resist and confront the diverse and multiple imaginaries of Black female subjectivity and Black cultural politics; imaginaries which are often perverse, diverse and contradictory.

Notes

To Barnor Hesse, I thank you for inspiring, supporting and encouraging my ideas and for so many invaluable comments. To Fidel and Ammalika Noble-Bart, for your love, patience and to JC for everything.

1. British Sociological Association annual conference, 'Worlds of the Future: Ethnicity; Nationalism and Globalisation', University of Reading, 1–4 April 1996.

2. The word 'slack' or slackness' has particular cultural and moral connotations in Jamaican parlance, which will be discussed later.

3. Stuart Hall defines 'play' as suggestive of 'instability, the permanent unsettlement, the lack of any final resolution' (Hall 1990: 228) of the fixed binaries.

4. Thus, use of the term 'rude' in this context carries connotations of impudence, insolence and not knowing one's place.

5. See Gordon Rohlehr (1988) for an interesting discussion of images of male and female sexuality in 1930s' calypsoes, similarly regarded as offering a dominantly male cultural and value. Also Peristiany's 1966 account in *Honour and Shame: The Values of Mediterranean Society*.

6. In both Caribbean and African-American cultures, the word 'nasty' can imply moral, sexual and physical defilement. It is a particularly loaded insult when applied to a woman, always implying sexual and moral deviance.

7. To 'big up' is to show appreciation/give respect/praise.

8. 'Bumper' is slang for buttocks.

9. This construction of the married, sexually coy 'feminine' as the ideal sexual identity for the virtuous white woman finds an earlier elaboration in the writings of Mary Wollstonecraft (1977; 1790), who likewise employs the savage woman as a marker against which to compare white womanhood.

10. This may be more a feature of the dance-hall in Jamaica where the economy of the country may pose greater limitations upon women's economic independence from men, than for young Black women in the USA or Britain.

11. See Calinescu 1987 for a discussion of the links between kitsch, modernity and consumerism.

12. *Dancehall Queen*, Cert. 15, Don Letts, 1997, UK.

13. Similarly, we can see in the white gay and lesbian resistance to the homophobia of Ragga music (Skelton 1995) how Blackness enters as an interruption which dislodges any simple notion of an oppositional queer politics or sexuality uncomplicated by questions of race and racism.

14. 'Mama man' is patois for gay man.

15. This is not unique to Black popular culture. Frith and McRobbie (1979, quoted

in Shepherd 1991: 166) use the term 'cock rock' to describe rock music which in its aggressive, dominating boastfulness constantly seeks to remind the audience of the the musicians' power and control – a practice which John Shepherd explains as serving to reinforce male internalization of these images of masculinity.

16. There is a vast lexicon of words in Jamaican patois for vagina, including punani, pum-pum, puni, which regularly appear in Ragga lyrics.

Discography

Bounty Killer, African, Simpleton, Major Mackerel, Colin Roach, Ian Sweetness, Glen Ricks and Jennifer Lara (1992), 'You Turn Me On', Charm.

Cobra (1991), 'Tek Him', Digital-B.

— (1998), 'Hot Gyal', Penthouse.

Daddy Screw (1993), 'Worker Man', New Sound.

Jose Wales (1987), 'Culture A Lick', Jammy's Records.

Mega Banton (1993), 'Money First', on *Bellevue* album, Maxflux.

Shabba Ranks (1990), 'A Mi De Girls Dem Love', on *Raw as Ever* album, Sony Records.

— (1990), 'Fis' – A Wrist', on *Raw as Ever* album, Sony Records.

— (1990), 'Gone Up', on *Raw as Ever* album, Sony Records.

— (1990), 'Wicked In Bed (pt 2)', Greensleeves. Also on *GoldenTouch* album, Digital–B.

Colonial Entanglements: the Discourses of Bermuda's 1995 Referendum on In/Dependence

Roiyah Saltus-Blackwood

> To most people Bermuda is known as an island of rest, a haven to which North Americans flee to escape the aggravations of winter and the vulgarities of American culture. Tourist brochures project this Atlantic Island quite justly as a scenic outpost where it is still possible to find the vestiges of the old colonial society which has long since disappeared from the American mainland. (Ryan 1970: 5)

> Because we are a small island society, we have developed a code of manners which enables us to live – despite all the myriad of frictions that actually exist – in quite good peace and harmony ... There are a very large number of mutual confidences which must be routinely kept by a very large number of people whose paths cross in many different settings ... we do demonstrate ... an inclination to say one thing in public, and do or say something very different in private. (Burchall 1991: 79)

Highlighting the colonial formation of contemporary politics in Bermuda is like trying to film ships or areoplanes as they vanish into the fabled Bermuda Triangle. With one point off the coast of South Carolina and the other off the shores of the Bahamas, Bermuda is the third point and namesake of this mysterious phenomenon.[1] Covering an expanse of the Atlantic Ocean, the Bermuda Triangle phenomenon is rooted in its reputation as an area where ships, planes, navigators and passengers have disappeared without a trace and, to date, for no reasonable explanation. In Bermudian politics a similar disappearance occurs: there is a ritual displacement of references to the colonial themes of its underlying structural antagonisms. This includes the impact of transatlantic slavery, the implications of British colonial administration and the legacy of white, male, minority rule. It is as if the very engagement of the persisting social inequalities rooted in and exacerbated by these legacies is considered unbefitting for acceptable political discourse. Much like the planes, ships and people swept into the Bermuda Triangle, central tenets of local colonialized ruling practices become untraceable. Largely disavowed and rendered unsubstantiated, debate and interrogation become problematic, deemed not only ill-mannered but beyond the realm of what is 'speakable'. Unlike the the Bermuda Triangle, however, is the re/appearance of these same underlying antagonisms. For despite all manner of denial, local legacies and continued colonial imperatives of rule are intricately woven into the fabric of Bermudian society. Pushed beyond the parameters of legitimate political discourse, these formations of localized colonial power have not vanished, but rather have been reworked as dis/appearing and re/appearing signifiers of unresolved structural inequalities that inhabit and inhibit the constitutional anatomy of Bermuda's body politic.

I want to consider this as a metaphorical background to Bermuda's 1995 referendum on whether or not the island should move to establish constitutional independence from Britain. The event marked a rare occasion when the tiny island colony came under the spotlight in international news. In the fleeting images of globally signified political events, however, the legacy of the colonial entanglements surrounding the liberal-democratic question 'Do you favour independence for Bermuda?' were all but airbrushed out. With the fantasy photographs and hype of sun, beauty and tranquillity so often used to describe this tourist destination soon back in place, the momentary but unavoidable exposure of the underlying social antagonisms of political life in Bermuda were largely glossed over. This perhaps is what prompted one British newspaper, the *Daily Telegraph*, to describe the protracted independence episode as 'one of the strangest liberation struggles the Empire has seen' (6 January 1995). My concerns in this chapter lie with the nature of the specific configuration of local and colonial power/discourse in Bermuda that pervaded the independence debate. The momentary exposure and disappearance of the influence of colonial formations in current political discourse is a central theme. Situated in the colonial *absented present*, I will argue that ruling practices in Bermuda remain as much determined by the enduring legacies of the colonial regime as they are by the continual disavowal of these colonial imperatives. The identity of Bermuda lies somewhere between the formations of an *extant* British colony and an *ex*-British colony. It is a place where colonial denial is so pervasive, where notions of colonialism have become so ambiguous, and where the articulation of legacies and continuities of colonial rule seem to evade political discourse. The main question underlying this chapter is: what can the entanglements of colonial societies such as Bermuda tell us about contemporary formations of representation in quasi-colonial political cultures? I begin by providing a brief overview of Bermudian society. Second, I examine how the question of independence was

articulated in different political discourses and how these became implicated
in under-stating colonial and western points of entanglement (Hesse 1999a).
Finally, I consider some of the political and discursive logic involved in
facilitating Bermuda's conjuring tricks and disappearing acts.

Re-mapping the Landscape

Bermuda is a small colony with a history that in many ways differs
from those of other former colonies in this region of Caribbean islands.
Colonized in 1612, Bermuda was the second British colony to be established.[2] Proving an early success, Bermuda started out as a plantation
colony, but by the end of the seventeenth century the land had been
forsaken for the more lucrative sea-faring pursuits. This resulted in a large
white resident population out of which emerged Bermuda's local oligarchy.
This form of local government continued with the rise and decline of the
sea-faring industries that characterized early Bermudian slave society and
the shift to horticulture soon after slave emancipation.[3] A small sea-faring
community with a large number of resident whites (the numerical majority
until the 1830s), Bermuda is also distinct in that, unlike the colonies in the
Caribbean where the local oligarchies (save Barbados and the Bahamas)
were replaced in the making of crown colonies, during the latter part of
the nineteenth century, local oligarchic rule in Bermuda remained intact.
In place since the seventeenth century, the ancien regime of the local
oligarchy was not usurped until 1963. This is what Ryan alludes to when
he reminds us: 'Bermuda is more than a major resort. It is also an Island
on which live a distinct people with a political system and style of life that
is unique' (Ryan 1970: 1). It was under this political regime that tourism
and international trade developed in the first decades of the twentieth
century. This resulted in unprecedented economic growth and
development. Consequently, by the mid-twentieth century, Bermuda, under
the continuing social dictates of a white oligarchy, was ensonced in an
economic boom that was to last unabated until the 1980s.

Describing political life before the transformations of the 1960s, Gordon
Lewis observed that, 'it remained the private game of the Assembly parlia-
mentarians', the political issues, 'the picayune (or petty) matters that
affected their constitutional dignity or their commercial interests, generating
factional passions that left the inert majority unmoved' (Lewis 1968: 313).
In 1950s Bermuda (as in Bermuda's more distant past), a meeting of the
merchants and businessmen who owned the local banks, businesses and
offices along Front Street, the main street of Bermuda's capital, could
easily have been mistaken for a session in the House of Assembly, such was
the overlap. It was these men and their forefathers, brothers, uncles-in-law

and sons who ran the major local businesses and occupied the great majority of the parliamentary seats. Thus until the 1960s economic and political power in Bermuda remained rooted in the cross-currents of inequalities which were an imperative to both local white minority rule and colonial dictate. In describing the logic of this enduring local formation framing colonial Bermuda, Frank Manning observes:

> generally known in Bermuda as either Front Street (their commercial address) or the Forty thieves (their acquisitive style) ... [power] had been maintained through the instruments of economic patronage: jobs, loans, credit, recallable mortgages, charitable donations. Supporters of Front Street found it a paternal, even benevolent oligarchy. Opponents usually lost all they had. (Manning 1978: 17)

Central to the rule of the oligarchy was control of the franchise, racial segregation and clear differentiations between gender, the classes and white ethnic groups. A limited, property-based franchise ensured that political power remained in the hands of a small white minority. With gender as much a constitutive marker of difference as 'race', power remained in the hands of white men. In 1944, when propertied women were granted the right to hold office and vote in municipal, parochial and parliamentary elections, it was done so with the stated understanding that there would be no further changes.[4] With an increasing number of 'coloured' Bermudians becoming eligible to vote and a concerted effort under way to increase their numbers in the House of Assembly, local ruling practices continued to be dictated by those who were white, male and propertied. This had been strenuously guarded and from a population of 43,000 in 1958 only 7,203 people were eligible to vote.

However, although privileged by 'race', in local formations of power and rule, disenfranchised working- and middle-class whites and the descendants of migrant Portuguese workers who had been recruited in the late nineteenth century faced social and political exclusion.[5] The imperatives of white, minority rule worked to exclude all those who were non-white, non-male and non-propertied, and this was reflected in all aspects of Bermudian society. Again unlike many of the colonies in the Caribbean, efforts made to establish trade unions and a political party system in Bermuda were thwarted. Effective resistance against the attempts by the crown to reform, together with the imperatives of local rule framing the emergent tourist and international trade industries, ensured that Bermuda's oligarchy remained economically and politically intact.

In a maiden speech in the House of Assembly during the dawning years of the twentieth century, one white MCP, Colonel Thomas Dill, proudly proclaimed: 'I think the sole reason we have not gone the way of a great many sister colonies is due to the fact that we are not a democratic country. We are an oligarchy … [A]t any rate there is nothing like, and I hope there will never be, anything approaching adult universal suffrage' (Philip 1987: 4). However, although intact, the strident arrogance of such power had by the mid-twentieth century weakened. It was challenged by women from the white elite Woman Suffrage campaign (1921–44), coupled with rising criticism from within sections of the oligarchy, and reinforced by the emerging politicization of the black community who had long fought against the imperatives of white minority rule. By the 1950s oligarchic authority had been considerably undermined. In addition, subsequent influences drawn from contemporaneous anti-colonial struggles in the Third World and the United States civil rights movements catalysed mass demonstrations and boycotts by black Bermudians calling for desegregation and universal suffrage. By 1965, racialized segregation had been outlawed, universal suffrage had been granted and wide-ranging social and economic reforms were being implemented.

It was also during this period that the first political parties were established, the Progressive Labour Party (PLP) and the United Bermuda Party (UBP). With the PLP dedicated to 'promoting the cause of blacks and labour' (*Bermuda Recorder*, 16 February 1963), and the UBP comprising the majority of already elected MCPs, the two parties were very quickly taken to be representative of the racial polarities which had for so long been the basis of local rule.[6] By 1968, the symbols of democratic rule – universal suffrage, political parties and equal rights – had replaced those of white minority rule. However, having the majority of members of parliament already in office, the UBP immediately became the party in power and at the time of the 1995 referendum had been in power for over three decades. Reworked, unresolved legacies of white minority rule continued to shape Bermudian society.

Colonial Articulations and Dis/Appearing Acts

Colonial rule is entangled in Bermuda in the legacy of white minority rule which it for so long legitimized and endorsed. The PLP have contested it since inception, just as the UBP has advocated its continuance since its formation. By the 1970s, however, the UBP government had moved to a more neutral position on independence, albeit one that increasingly defined independence in terms of dollars and cents.[7] This was to continue until 1994 when, quite dramatically, the UBP leader and premier of Bermuda, Sir John Swan, announced that the question of independence was to be put to the people. Raised unexpectedly and catching politicians and Bermudians generally off-guard, by the time the date had been set for the referendum, the issue of independence was at the forefront of political debate and consideration.

It is possible to identify the articulation of three main discourses during the run-up to the 1995 independence referendum: first, that Bermuda enjoyed and must maintain its economic stability, which was largely ensured by political stability and continued coloniality; second, that independence was the next necessary step to be taken in the political development of the island; and third, that independence was inevitable, but that local, constitutional changes must preface a change in Bermuda's status as a colony. These three dominant political discourses clearly reveal the changed considerations facing countries seeking independence in the late twentieth century. In connecting the viability of remaining a British independent territory with the perception of political stability insisted upon by the international business world, the thrust of independence as the liberation of a colonized people that had been such a rallying cry decades before was bizarrely displaced. At a time when colonialism was for so many people and nations a legacy of the distant past, independence as a measure of Bermuda's coming of age was rendered markedly different from the past strident and difficult struggles to end colonial rule. Although the entrenchment of the colonial imperative in the structures and processes of local governance that had also been critical to other countries' desire to end colonialism seemed, on first glance at least, to be equally susceptible to dislocation, careful reflection, however, reveals something else. For Bermuda has been convincingly described quite cynically as a place where there is a 'code of manners' regulating all discourse, where people are by necessity 'public liars and private, very private, tellers of truth' (Burchall 1991). What such an observation reveals is the impact of silenced manifestations of rule and power. As Burchall argues contextually: 'we still have to live, cheek by jowl, with our fellow Bermudians ... [S]imilarly, no matter how strong your disagreement is with someone on this island, he or she will always be visible, and relatively close to you' (Burchall 1991: 178).

This means in the wider realms of political discourse and debate, where subtleties and contradictions are perhaps well established and expected, the loss or the dis/appearance of pertinent aspects governing Bermudian society attain greater significance. It is in the realm of public political discourse in particular that any interrogation or critique of the structural antagonisms underpinning this British colony is necessarily momentary, unstable and fraught with ambiguity. Thus, despite the appeals to economic and cultural considerations seemingly freed from social context and racialized and genderized consequence, these discourses can be (re) read as signifiers of 'otherness'. They can be understood as coded voice-overs with regard to the underlying repertoire of systems of meaning and representation in which cultural differences and inequalities evolve, and contested imaginaries of Bermuda remain rooted. Below I consider in turn each of the three discourses to the independence debate.

Independence as an economic consideration Rooted in an economy which since the opening decades of the twentieth century has depended on foreign investment and tourism, the servicing and dependence of multi-nationals has been seen not as a problem, but rather as a pivotal, though precarious feature of Bermuda's economic base. Unlike ex-colonies faced with recolonization (i.e. 'the further consolidation and exacerbation of capitalist relations and exploitation' (Alexander and Talpade Mohanty 1997: xxi) from powerful nations other than those whose colonial reign they had initially been under), what was seen as paramount in Bermuda was main-taining the economic stability such dependence had long engendered. Unless deemed economically expedient, independence was seen as too great a risk. As James Ahiakpor comments, in his analysis of Bermuda's engage-ment with its status: 'the issue of greatest concern in the debate over political independence for Bermuda is the impact of such a decision on the country's economy' (Ahiakpor 1990: 35). Grounding this economic con-sideration was the narrative of Bermuda's long legacy of local representative government and the suggestion that having had a large measure of self-governing for so long, Bermuda had lost the stain of colonial rule. Eco-nomically prosperous and self-sufficient, allowed to fly its own flag (although the Union Jack is included), having a Bermuda national song much like a national anthem, and with Bermuda Day having replaced Empire Day, Bermuda had taken on the air, if not the status, of a self-governing nation. 'Independence', opponents asked, 'from whom?' (Musson 1979: 65).

This was a discourse in which all other considerations were seen to pale into insignificance. For Elton Trimingham, chairman of the local bank of Bermuda, the 'we' in 'can we afford independence?' was an inclusive 'we' which transcended all others considerations (see *Bermuda Royal Gazette*, 20 July 1995, p. 3). Mention or consideration of 'race' was deemed 'emotive, divisive and unnecessary'. It was insisted by the main instigator of the referendum, the premier, Sir John Swan, that such a move would bring 'the races closer together' but this was 'dismissed as one that could only backfire' (*Bermuda Royal Gazette*, 14 August 1995: 3). It is in the tracking of this particular debate that its coded nature becomes clear. Read as a discursive signifier, the discourse of economic expediency and the drawing on the history of local rule in the island marked less the advent of a new relationship between colonized and colonizer, than the way in which struc-tural antagonisms underlying the legacies of local white minority rule and the continuities of colonialism had now come to be articulated.

Usurped by the socio-political transformations of the 1960s, the residual power of Bermuda's local oligarchy nevertheless remained. The formation of party politics in 1963 resulted in the birth of the United Bermuda Party which, although seeking 'non-white' membership, was nevertheless made up of leading representatives of the political arm of the oligarchy. The outcome had been gradual reform and the denial and silencing of the past. With slogans and election manifestos such as 'Together the United Way' (1968), 'Bermuda on the Move Together: The United Way' (1972) and 'The Partnership that Works' (1976) sending out messages of unity and commonality among all groups, the economic and political processes remained, under the UBP government, dictated by the needs of Bermuda's white elite (Wilson 1978; Manning 1978).

Thus, the legacy of white oligarchy and its racialized logic continued to be largely reflected in the island's areas of economic and political power. Writing on Bermuda in the late 1970s, Jeyaratnam Wilson underlines this point where he observes, it is the 'fear of ultimate black domination on the part of the whites and the resentment by the blacks of continuing white supremacy [that] characterise the socio-political setting in Bermuda' (Wilson 1978: 258). Central to this logic has been negation and denial. This together with the imperatives of integrative partnership and cultural diversity structuring all political discourse since the transformations of the 1960s has meant that the unresolved and discursively forced aside racial antagonisms have become that much more coded.

In the months and weeks leading up to 15 August 1995, the scheduled day of the referendum on independence, the coding of such denials became increasingly fragile and problematic. Although independence was spoken of as an economic consideration that would eat into the pockets of all Bermudians, it was clear that to speak of economic considerations and the legacy of self-rule was to invoke a history of white economic dominance and hegemony. Underlying this particular discourse was a largely coded defence against further destabilization and possible eradication of the socio-economic and political structures which were rooted in the legacies of white minority rule – a power base traditionally legitimated by, although seen to be somewhat removed from, the dictates of the English crown. What was at stake was not only the changing of Bermuda's colonial status, but the ending of a significant symbol, on which the authority and legitimating power to rule had so long rested and which, although transformed, remained ingrained in whiteness.

Independence prefaced by local constitutional change Was this counter-hegemonic discourse or acquiescence? Independence had been advocated by the PLP since its inception. There were those like PLP activist and barrister Phil Perinchief who loudly advocated an affirmative reply. In an newspaper article he asserted that 'the narrow traditional right-wing politics' that produced segregation and a host of other in-equalities are 'dead on their feet. Their burial is imminent. Their days are numbered. The game is up. The black man [sic] is in ascendancy in Bermuda' (*Bermuda Royal Gazette*, 14 August 1995: 3). By the 1990s such militancy and single-minded passion for independence was no longer emanating from the PLP leadership. With independence less of a matter of emancipation and liberation from the yoke of colonialism, as it had been described during the 1960s and 1970s, it was seen more as an in-evitability that must be prefaced with local constitutional change. This is what was articulated most strongly by the opposition party and it was on this basis that the PLP advised its supporters to refrain from voting in the referendum. The thrust of the PLP campaign was that reforms to the local political structure and the constitution had to be implemented before independence could be considered. The reforms included an unfettered electoral system – essentially one person, one vote, each vote of equal value. The PLP had been fighting for these objectives since the revamped electoral system came on line in the early 1960s. With the UBP having neither provided an indication as to the path independence would take, nor addressed the electoral and constitutional reforms insisted on by the PLP, it was argued that to move to independence would be to lock into existing inequalities (*Bermuda Royal Gazette*, 14 July 1995).

Moreover, believing that a referendum was not an ideal way to determine such an important step, the PLP insisted that independence be part of an election platform, so that all the political parties would be forced to present a detailed plan of their vision of an independent Bermuda to the people – a plan that would get the people's endorsement on election day. As the chairman of the PLP referendum campaign committee explained: 'to withhold the vote and not chose to participate in the upcoming referendum is an active means of protest and of registering dissatisfaction with the manner of deciding independence for Bermuda' (*Bermuda Royal Gazette*, 14 August 1995). This point was driven home by the PLP campaign slogan: 'Independence Yes! Referendum No!'

Stigmatized for its ardent opposition to racial and class inequality and unable to break the power of the UBP, who had in the past accused the PLP of fostering 'disharmony and advocating (reverse) racism' (Wilson 1978: 269), it was apparent that by 1995 the PLP had moved away from a pro-black socialist position to one decidedly (though not acknowledged) conservative. It is possible this could be regarded simply as a political tactic with local constitutional change a concern for all Bermudians. But if we trace the historical logic of this discourse, it becomes clear that the constitutional considerations the PLP were so adamantly concerned with were rooted in the political restructuring of the island that had taken place in the early 1960s. It was during this period following the establishment of universal suffrage and desegregation that the electoral districts had been remapped to ensure that if voting was conducted along racial lines there could never be a black majority in power. The 'one man, one vote' campaign, begun in the 1960s, was a direct response to this restructuring. The call for local constitutional change was also a call to change the reworking of a hierarchy of inequalities, revolving chiefly around 'race', which had been put in place in the very dismantling of white minority rule.

During the referendum debate, the PLP's stress on constitutional change perhaps came closest to exposing Bermuda's 'hidden transcript' (Scott 1990) in a more covert interrogation of the continued racialized logic of Bermuda's political structures. But it was also a position that seemed to give succour to strident defences of the colonial past. Many veteran PLP members, such as Phil Perinchief, took exception to this decision and publicly opposed the PLP campaign. Thus, to speak of local electoral reform, much like the their opponents' insistence on the legacy of the island's economic and political stability, was inadvertently to evoke the racialization of those crucial aspects of Bermuda's history that in the political climate of 1995 they had sought to avoid and rework in the coded narrative of constitutionalism. In what Toni Morrison (1992) has called a polite, 'graceful, even generous act' of ignoring 'race', the expansive rhetoric of constitutionalism worked to foster another 'substitute language' in which direct and sustained interrogation of the colonial entanglements were expediently evaded.

Independence as the next step in Bermuda's political evolution

Having initially gained the support of his party, the push for independence came directly from the premier and leader of the UBP, Sir John Swan. Also drawing on the economic success and the long history of self-rule, the argument made was that independence was the next evolutionary step in Bermuda's political development. Rooted in the concern to represent Bermuda as striving to take its place in the modern world, independence was taken to be a sign of the island's maturity and economic stability. This ideal of independence was also constructed as coterminous with the apparent evolution of racial and ethnic power relations in the island, marking a heightened sense of empathy and harmony freed from the legacies of the past. The push was to conceptualize the economic and social successes of the island with a united partnership among all Bermudians, thereby vanquishing, along with colonial rule, all the traces of mono-culturalism and white hegemony. Taking on board the economic stability as well as the cultural legacy of self-rule, the argument was one that sought to promote a new vision of Bermuda. Articulated most vehemently by the premier, it was a vision built neither on the direct negation of the colonial legacy nor on its covert evasion, but one where these factors simply no longer mattered.

Much like the two other discourses disseminated in the months and weeks leading up to 15 August 1995, this discourse proved untenable, and quickly shifted to an insistence that 'this will be our country, each of us will be responsible for it' and that independence could be a 'powerful and incredible catalyst for a subtle shift of attitude' (*Bermuda Royal Gazette*, 19 July 1995: 5). Although the discourse had begun as a step heralding the end of white hegemony and the inequalities of the past, it had reinvented its vision of independence as a panacea for a 'divided society'. It was here that the 'conjuring tricks' of Bermudian political discourse faltered and revealed themselves. If the issue of independence was seen as a litmus test of Bermuda's ability successfully to keep its structural divisions not just displaced and 'somewhere out there' but vanquished, for ever considered of no great consequence, it was contaminated at its point of enunciation by the very opposite message.

In the weeks leading up to the 1995 referendum, the usually latent and hidden notions of white supremacy clashed with the push to end the colonial imperatives which had always underpinned that social order. In addition, the 'code of manners' (Burchall 1991) so central to discourse and representation in Bermuda was breached and the denied and evaded racialized logic continuing to underpin Bermudian society became clearly, albeit momentarily and intermittently, visible. The colonial legacy was something that had to be re-represented in order to be negated; it could not be dismissed without being summoned. In the end, the opponents of independence and the PLP were victorious, the people of Bermuda voted 'No' and the premier resigned as he had promised. Yet, despite the triangular diagreements, each of the competing political discouses appeared incapable of avoiding the social dictates of denying the relevance of contested colonialities.

Political Discourse and Social Dictates

In this section I want to reflect on some implications of the entanglements of the colonial legacy for the meaning of politics in Bermuda, all of which were symbolized by the competing reactions to the independence referendum debate which nevertheless revealed a colonial consensuality. William Connolly (1988) has suggested that the elimination of conflict in political discourse is tantamount to the elimination of politics. In the

Bermudian referendum, despite the existence of three distinct political perspectives, the question of 'race' was consensually expelled from the political agenda. In being naturalized rather than politicized, this meant that the colonial formations of Bermuda had to be emptied of contemporary meaning so there could be no doubt as to what Bermuda signified as a unifying national identity. Yet, paradoxically, it was precisely the different ways in which the logic of denial and disavowal were put to work in these competing political discourses that actually signified Bermuda as an 'essentially contested concept'. And as Connolly points out, 'essentially contested concepts' are central to the formation of *political discourse*. These two aspects of Connolly's analysis must be understood as contextualizing the argument presented in this chapter. First, the concept of political discourse refers to a vocabulary that is commonly employed in the relation between political thought and action. It describes the way in which meanings 'conventionally embodied' in a vocabulary define the framework in which political thought is articulated and the criteria that must be met before an event or reference can be established as political. Only when this framework is endorsed and related criteria met can the status of political be accorded (Connolly 1988). There is, of course, a certain circularity to this reasoning: it means, for example, that within Bermudian political discourse the idea that 'race' and colonialism belonged outside the remit of politics signified the necessary and sufficient criteria of what counted as political discourse. The paradox was, however, that in order to invoke the outside of political discourse, the 'unspeakable' had to be articulated, 'race' and colonialism had to be connotated within political discourse, in this way casting Bermudian national identity within the frame of the second aspect of Connolly's analysis, an *essentially contestable concept*. This can be characterized in two ways. As an 'appraisive' concept, it suggests that a desired state of affairs should be understood as a valued achievement. Thus Bermuda as it was represented in each different political discourse was the contested object not only of different value claims on the future, but of different exclusions in the formation of (post) colonial discourse; while, as an 'internally complex' concept, Bermuda had several dimensions, including agreed and contested rules as to which of its representations were shared and which were open to interpretation. As an essentially contestable concept, then, the meaning of Bermuda was bound to 'involve endless disputes' (Connolly 1988) during the referendum. It was because these disputes were prolonged within the acceptable parameters of political discourse that the intermittent references to 'race' and the colonial legacy successively interrupted attempts to polarize the colonial past and the quasi-colonial present.

We should not of course assume that the configural but denied role that 'race' played here is not unique to colonial Bermuda. It shares similarities with societies such as the Jim Crow states in the southern United States prior to the 1960s and even South Africa, where racial demarcation was 'endemic to their socio-political fabric and heritage' (Higgenbotham 1996: 186). Examining the American south prior to racial desegregation, Evelyn Brook Higgenbotham argues that where racial demarcation is endemic to the socio-political fabric and heritage of a society, 'race' serves as a sign, a 'metalanguage' that 'lends meaning to a host of terms and expression, to a myriad of aspects that would otherwise fall outside the referential domain of race' (Higgenbotham 1996). This is irrespective of whether or not it is denied, as in the case of Bermuda. Similarly the *conjuring away* of 'race' is not unique to Bermuda. This is a theme that Toni Morrison (1992) explores in a powerful series of essays where she reflects on the dis/appearing presence of African-American people in the nationally coded literary imagination. Morrison argues that although hidden and literally silenced in the historically racialized society of the United States, the presence of African-Americans can be tracked in the canonical nineteenth and twentieth-century literary work of writers such as Mark Twain, Edgar Allan Poe, Herman Melville and Ernest Hemingway. For Morrison, the formation of the United States was rooted in the constitution and its necessarily coded language and purposeful restrictions to dealing with 'the racial disingenuousness and moral fragility ' (Morrison 1992: 6) that lay at its heart. This process also shaped US literature, the founding character-istics of which extended into the twentieth century. The consequences of cultural formations of denial, suggests Morrison, oblige us to decode the logic of their 'conjured silence' (p. 51).

Morrison's work helps us to appreciate that the racialized logic under-pinning colonial Bermuda is not unique but has analogous features in the founding and permeating structures of western societies generally. In her (re)reading of (white) American literary writers, Morrison indicates a way of underscoring the hidden Africanist presence. The methodological reward of this approach to analysis is undoubtedly the delight in finding proof of such a presence, rather than remaining at the level of disappointment in the 'uncoded' ways of reading. This points to a need to be ever mindful of the contested historical specificities of place and power in the inscription of political discourse. In the confines of colonial Bermuda, the jettisoning of 'race' beyond the parameters of acceptable political discourse is not simply the necessary discursive erasure of a central, organizing power dynamic of coloniality. Rather, it is also, as Burchall has rightly contended, rooted in the socially consenualizing 'code of practice' which insists that in the small confines of the island, 'despite all the myriad of frictions that actually exist', polite and non-jarring language dictates respectable political practice (Burchall 1991: 79). Hence the apparent crisis when the dream of a Bermuda freed from such constraints revealed what was generally held to be concealed. This was as much a response to the sensibilities and dictates of Bermudian culture as it was to the revelation that these vestiges of colonial rule were so blatantly exposed. If Connolly (1988) provides us with a theoretical understanding for the consensual yet contested logic underpinning political discourse in Bermudian society, then Higgenbotham (1996) and Morrison (1992) provide critical insight into the racialized nature of its systematic disavowals. These cultural specificities are of signal importance in attempting to understand the dis/agreements framing the political in/dependence debates in Bermuda's 1995 referendum.

Conclusion

Both commissioned and official government reports continue to high-light the continued inequalities of Bermuda. Although it has a large black middle class, Bermuda remains a place where white Bermudians and residents still enjoy better jobs and higher rates of income; where significant steps are said to be needed to tackle institutional racism in Bermuda's business sector; and where the presence of Portuguese-Bermudians remains unacknowledged in official statistics differentiating between 'black', 'white' and 'other'.[8] At the same time, Bermuda remains a colony where the interrogation of inequalities is deemed highly problematic and troublesome. In Bermuda, irrespective of major political reforms – the most recent and most dramatic one being the ending of three decades of UBP rule with the election of the PLP in 1998 – the vestiges of the 'old colonial society' are very much alive. These explain the apparent ideological crisis which emerges when we begin to theorize the 'public secret and very private obsession' (Lewis 1968: 325) of 'race' in the island and the entanglements of disavowal it resources. It is only by examining how such avoidance and marginalization become politically encoded as cultural practice and social dictate that we can cease to be perplexed by a country like Bermuda that apparently advocates colonial independence and colonial dependency simul-taneously, as if without contradiction.

Notes

I conducted a series of interviews with a number of Bermudian politicians, writers and political commentators between 1995 and 1997. I would to thank all those I inter-viewed for taking the time to talk with me. Special thanks to Ira Philip, Barnor Hesse and Catherine Hall for their comments and support.

1. Bermuda is located in the Atlantic Ocean, some distance away from the Caribbean

islands. Although they are linked by similar colonial legacies, the overwhelming projection of Bermuda by Bermudians is that the island is distinct and different, and only recently have efforts been made to forge definitive links with the Caribbean.

2. For background on Bermuda, see Lefroy 1877; Craven 1990; and Wilkinson 1973. Books covering Bermudian slave society include Packwood 1975; Smith 1976. Also important is Robinson 1985.

3. For a discussion of Bermuda's political development, see Manning 1978; Wilson 1978; Lewis 1968.

4. The Bermuda Woman Suffrage Society (BWSS) was founded by a small number of white women belonging to Bermuda's ruling class. For twenty-one years, the BWSS campaigned for the right of propertied women to vote. The suffragists' victory did not result in the greater participation of women in the political process, but it was central in the weakening of white minority rule. For an overview of the BWSS, see Benbow 1994.

5. The presence in the colony of people from the islands of the Azores and Madeira dates back to the late 1840s, when indentured workers had been recruited to work as horticultural labourers. Despite objections that their presence would further curtail the economic opportunities of the working class and despite labour policies that effectively tied them to the horticultural industry, the numbers of Portuguese migrant workers grew. By 1939, they made up 8.3 per cent of the total population. Although many still worked in horticulture, some had entered other occupations as land and shop-owners, taxi-drivers and hotel-workers (Richardson 1948). Based on cultural difference (religion, language) and their continuing stigma of their initial recruitment, Portuguese-Bermudians continued to be socially and politically excluded. It was not until 1963 that the first Bermudian of Portuguese descent was elected to the House of Assembly. For information on Portuguese Bermudians see Patricia Mudd (1991).

6. Local writers Ira Philip (1987), Eva Hodgson (1988), Barbara Harris-Hunter (1993) and Walton Brown (1994) have written extensively on the transformations that occurred during this period.

7. The government reports presented during the late 1970s include 'The Green Paper on Independence' (1977) and 'The White Paper on Independence' (1979). Also important is Ahiakpor 1990. Information regarding the debates raging during this period was taken from the local papers, the *Royal Bermuda Gazette* and the *Bermuda Sun*.

8. See Newman 1994.

9

Some Kind of White, Some Kind of Black: Living the Moments of Entanglement in South Africa and its Academy

Zimitri Erasmus

Unaware/unintentional racism drives usually tranquil white liberals wild when they get called on it, and confirms the suspicions of many people of color who feel that white folks are just plain crazy. (Yamato 1990)

roots? ... I swear, if I had a puff for every time black folks drone on about 'roots this' and 'roots that'. I'm more worried about my branches, you know. It's the branches that bear the fruit and tilt for the sky. (Adebayo 1996)

There is a silence in the South African academy.[1] It is a silence about whiteness. There is a barrier to different ways of being black in South Africa. It is essentialism.[2] This chapter focuses, first, on some of the ways in which black and white academics negotiate the racialized spaces of academia. This is a difficult task, since it involves placing academics' informal behaviours under the microscope. This disrupts the policing of what can and cannot be said in contexts constructed as 'scholarly'. Attempts to illustrate who speaks for whom and from what place are very difficult to talk, much less write, about. Here is an attempt to rise to this challenge.

Second, this chapter interrogates black essentialisms.[3] Apartheid South Africa was a racially defined democracy for white citizens. People classified as 'African' were subjects relegated to ethnically defined 'independent states' referred to as the 'bantustans'. People classified as 'coloured'[4] and seen as 'of mixed-race', occupied, along with those classified as 'Indian', a more ambiguous position within the South African polity. The latter groups were neither full citizens (in terms of access to rights before the law), nor complete subjects. The dominant articulation of 'African' identity was in terms of 'tribal' identities while at the same time there was an overarching black/white division of the population. Mamdani aptly conceptualizes the apartheid state as 'the generic form of the colonial state in Africa' in which racial domination was 'mediated through a variety of ethnically organised powers' (Mamdani 1996: 8). This state form shaped resistance movements.[5] Following the non-racial strategy of the Congress Alliance during the 1950s and 1960s, an important shift happened in the 1970s in the wake of the Black Consciousness movement. It emphasized black unity rejecting the racial labelling[6] of apartheid ideology. During this period a general unease and rejection of the notion 'coloured' entered progressive political discourses. Within the United Democratic Front (UDF), a political movement which emerged from a history shaped by both African National Congress (ANC) non-racialism and the Black Consciousness tradition, coloured-african people were referred to as 'so-called coloured'. Despite this discomfort the term 'coloured' was seen as necessary, although always qualified, for mass politics among all South Africans opposed to the apartheid state.

When the ANC was unbanned and eclipsed the UDF, important shifts emerged. These became apparent in the early post-apartheid period when coloured-african activists within the ANC 'rediscovered' their specificity and that of their communities. In the context of an emerging africanist lobby within the ANC nationally and the resulting marginalization of coloured-africans within the party, new contestations arose about the place of coloured activists within the ANC, about who is 'black' and what it means to be 'black' – 'black' here conflated with 'african'. These struggles over racialized identities illuminate one of the central concerns of this chapter: entanglements of blackness, whiteness, colouredness and africanity. In addition, the post-apartheid myth of Rainbow Nationalism, through its production of hegemony for the dominant political party, soothes persistent racially based inequalities and differential racialization among black populations.[7] Here the entanglements involve post-apartheid SA, cross-cultural histories and national identity. It is in the context of this post-apartheid ambiguity that black essentialisms are being articulated.

Webster's Dictionary (1981) defines 'entanglement' as 'the condition of being deeply involved'. It defines an entanglement as 'something that confuses or involves one in difficulties'. These definitions provide only small beginnings for an historicized understanding of entanglement as a social condition. For me this concept also conjures an image from the film *Kundun* (Scorsese, 1998). The Tibetan Buddhist monks in this film create, destroy, and re-create an intricate mandala from multiple colours of sand. The mandala is a spiritually symbolic graphic representation of the universe in the form of multiple images of a circle enclosing a square. Similarly, entanglements are made and remade through crossings of various histories which produce and reproduce multiple cultural formations.

In writing about the silence of whiteness and limits of black essentialisms I weave together various genres – analytical, dramaturgical, literary and personal – in an attempt to provide a rich account of conditions of entanglement, both specific and more common. I enter this process by beginning to share my reflections on a significant event for me. Abrahams, a historian (historically classified coloured) specializing in Khoisan history and the story of Ms Saartjie Baartman,[8] presented a seminar at the African Gender Institute (AGI), University of Cape Town. Her work-in-progress presentation was entitled: *'Ambiguity' is my Middle Name: A Research Diary about Sara Baartman and her Legacy to us Brown Women* (6 August 1996).[9] This chapter is based on two aspects of my experience of this seminar. The first is an experience of white liberal scholars passionately avoiding the terrible fate of being marked as *white*. The second is my discomfort with Abrahams's readiness to take upon herself the mantle of spokesperson for South Africa's 'Brown'[10] people, and my resistance to her essentialist notion of black subjectivity.[11]

The significance of this seminar becomes evident when one examines more explosive and public events in the post-apartheid white South African academy: the Makgoba Affair[12] of 1996 at the University of the Witwatersrand (see Makgoba 1997) and the more recent 'Mamdani Affair'[13] at the University of Cape Town (22 May 1998). These 'affairs' are about black professors/intellectuals making visible and challenging, in their own encounters, the entanglement of racialized power and racialized knowledge in the post-apartheid South African academy. Importantly, experiences of the effects of this power are not limited to these encounters. It is endemic. Similarly, contestations of the violence of this power and knowledge are not confined to the voices of black male intellectuals in professorial positions. Black feminists in South Africa have been among the first to challenge white-centred knowledge.[14] The persistence of this violence despite frequent challenges is indicative of the unyielding imaginary of whiteness as the norm.

This seminar shows the everyday violence of racialized pedagogy experienced by students in historically white universities. It illustrates the inseparability of race and gender and the stubborn denial on the part of some white feminists of the structures that make their experiences different from those of black women. It also illustrates the weaknesses of black essentialist arguments as both instruments of mobilization and vehicles for debate towards the development of critical scholarship.

The Context

The story of Ms Saartjie Baartman must be seen in the context of eugenics, colonialism, slavery and the entanglement of racialized and gendered power relations embedded in these practices at the time (mid-

1600s to mid-1800s). Gould (1995: 293) refers to her as having been a servant to Dutch settlers at the Cape. According to Gould, her master's brother persuaded her to travel to England to exhibit her body to Europeans. On her arrival in London in 1810 she was exhibited in a cage in Piccadilly. Her allegedly large buttocks were to be the key part of the show. After some time she went to Paris where an animal trainer exhibited her. Scientists, among them George Cuvier, analysed her body while she was alive. She was placed in a category of the lowest form of human life. She died in 1815 at the age of twenty-five. Cuvier made a plaster cast of her body before he removed her skeleton, brain and genitals. These organs were preserved and put on display in the Musée de l'Homme in Paris for 150 years. They were removed from public exhibition ten years ago and remain the property of the museum. There is at present a movement to return her remains to SA and to bury her at the Cape in an attempt to restore her human dignity as well as that of her descendants (Gould 1995; Koch 1995). These include a wide range of South Africans across colour, class and cultural lines.

This story as well as that of the Khoena people and their descendants has spawned an industry of academic writing.[15] As illustrated by Abrahams (1996) the historiography and representation of Ms Baartman is a contested terrain. In *'Ambiguity' is My Middle Name* (1996) she examines critical responses to Gilman's 'Black Bodies, White Bodies' (1992). Abrahams argues that white critics are interested in Baartman not *for Baartman* but reduce her, again, to a specimen illustrating colonial wrongs and various intellectual endeavours. In support of this argument she notes, first, that Bal (1991; in Abrahams 1996), a white critic, distances herself from Gilman not 'in defense of Sara, but in defense of the notion that there is somehow a "proper" way in which the colonised can be used as text to aid colonial psychotherapy' (Abrahams 1996: 6). Gould (1982; in Abrahams 1996), she argues, similarly uses the story of Baartman for purposes of an intellectual argument about taxonomy (Abrahams 1996: 11). From her reading of this historiography she finds that most texts are '*never* about Sara Baartman ... [but] always about something else in which she is being used as an example or as evidence' (p. 10). She argues that such practices decontextualize Baartman's story presenting her 'in a timeless unstable present in which all connections to her history and selfhood are lost [making] it that much easier to objectify her and exploit her for whatever textual purpose is at stake' (p. 10).

Abrahams's (1996) message is radical and pointed: white people who write about Ms Baartman are complicit with the racist aims and practices of eugenicists. In other words, these white people are no different from Cuvier. While some white historians would like to think that their retelling of the Baartman story serves to criticize colonial racism, Abrahams suggests that in fact they are simply re-enacting the strategies of white colonial eugenics. In an attempt to place herself in the position of 'legitimate spokesperson' for Ms Baartman, Abrahams (1996) draws on notions of cultural and biological continuity with the Khoena people. As illustrated later in this work, this positioning has its strengths. Its key weakness, however, lies in its lapse into both cultural essentialism and biological determinism.[16] Abrahams's presentation thus requires both an appreciative and a critical response.

Whiteness Waging its Violence

The violence of whiteness surfaced during the presentation. Instead of a measured engagement with her argument, a white scholar snickered at Abrahams's pronunciation of Gould's name. During the discussion some of the white scholars responded defensively, launching into an attack on Abrahams's work and competence. With unbounded, unremitting confidence in their authority and without even a fraction of interest in a dialogue which calls into question this imagined authority, some of these scholars took it upon themselves to tell Abrahams that 'she had better re-read her history and her anthropology'. Yet, the substance of that history and anthropology was not discussed. Instead, the seminar became a parade of some white scholars' fears of the presence of a black voice with a critical perspective. 'You've misunderstood it,' they seemed to be shouting defensively.

In an attempt to participate in the discussion, a white feminist prefaced her contribution with 'I am not black, but ... '. She was interrupted by a white female archaeologist who asked her, incomprehensibly, 'How do you know that you're not a black woman?' To her credit, the former speaker did not reply. Later in the discussion Abrahams asked the following question: Those of you who identify as Khoisan, will you raise your hands?' Now, I was one of the handful of black women present, not one of whom raised her hand. I had difficulty raising my hand since my identity comprises much more than being Khoisan. Yet the white archaeologist saw fit to raise her hand, publicly identifying herself as Khoisan. Furthermore, in an attempt to challenge Abrahams's construction of Baartman's experience as strongly shaped by colonial power relations the archaeologist insisted that because Baartman had agreed to exhibit her body in a cage she was a 'sex worker' and that this had been 'her choice'. So much for history and scholarship. These responses highlight entanglements of race, gender and access to racialized knowledge as a source of power. Not everyone reacted in this way. Sanders Gilman, a white male scholar and target of Abrahams's

(1996) criticism, who was present at the seminar, acknowledged Abrahams's critique but questioned her position of speaking for all black women.

Questions of Location

For me, this event illustrates what is at stake in the logic of two positions in the broader array of historically coloured-african identities in South Africa. One is a position which involves a 'deliberate choice [to] narrow down [one's] subjectivity to one component' (Mama 1995: 118). The second is a choice to live with ambiguities. The first is a position of singularity which reinscribes dominant frames; the second, a position of multiplicity which shifts these frames. Each position carries a power of its own. Each has different implications and particular dangers to guard against. Some of these dangers involve the ways in which some white scholars respond to these particular black articulations by denying their own location of power and race privilege. Others relate to some of the pitfalls in theorizing black identities. These positions are illustrated in Abrahams and my own ways of speaking.

Abrahams defines herself as Brown, Khoisan and Black. The first two identities have been part of recent processes of asserting essentialist forms of coloured-african identities in the Western Cape region of South Africa.[17] Despite the complex history and ancestry of those who identify as Khoisan today, Abrahams is among those who are adamant about privileging their Khoisan heritage and identity over their white heritage. For Khoisan nationalists such as Abrahams their white forefathers are not acknowledged except in so far as they are seen as the masters who raped our slave mothers. In contrast, I embrace and live with these ambiguities. I do not privilege a single aspect of my subjectivity. Nor do I choose to deny my white heritage. This chapter does not examine the reasons behind choosing these two positions. Nor does it explore the details and complexities of each. It simply sketches and attempts to explore the logic of each. This work is an attempt to begin marking out the space from which I, as a coloured-african-woman academic, negotiate the racialized spaces of academia, and to set out some of my own attempts at resistance to having my own identity placed *between* black and white. This involves simultaneous resistance to anti-black racism, white-centred articulations of interpretive authority *and* black essentialism.

Problematizing Whiteness in the South African Academy

I should say that I found it difficult to have too much sympathy with the distress of my white colleagues. Often fatigued by challenging everyday racism, my decision to note but not engage their distress is but one strategy against such fatigue. It is time white people did their own self-interrogation and their own anti-racist work. At the same time it has raised some crucial questions for me which go beyond that particular seminar. How should we understand the significance of these encounters where, more and more frequently, black scholars (and some white ones) try to draw attention to the 'ignoble origins' of modern sociology, history and anthropology and to white academics' profound entanglement with racialized relations of power and interpretation? Why is it that these challenges are met with such violent, shrill, defensive and *unscholarly* responses? Why is it that when we attempt to point out the limitations and politics of the place from which many white scholars speak 'about' and sometimes 'for' black people they immediately assume we're saying they're racist? Should these responses, limitations and assumptions be our concern? Why is it that certain white academics do not want to hear us when we speak as living knowledgeable subjects with critical capacity? Is their acknowledgement of any value? To what extent is there space for a more reflective, calmer and critical discussion in which white and black scholars critically and respectfully can engage with one another? We have more pressing concerns. Our anti-racist practice should not re-centre whiteness. Simultaneously, however, it should not leave whiteness unmarked.

Calling the 'bad word' – 'So you're saying I'm racist' – when a black scholar urges you to take responsibility for your own positioning in relation to those about whom you write and speak is itself a defensive reaction and simultaneously a denial – 'You cannot possibly be saying THAT about ME.' Desiree Lewis (1996) argues that the politics of this defensiveness is embedded in racialized relations of interpretive authority in which white feminist practitioners have a vested interest. Such relations effectively silence black women, often the subjects of white women's research, leaving these relations of authority intact (Lewis 1996: 96, 99). It is easier for white men and women to fly and be suspended in an illusive 'unraced' space of defensiveness than to be grounded on the thin edge of whiteness without its privileges.

Silencing the challenges to white female scholars' positioning in their research as posed by their black female counterparts is neither unusual nor new. Lewis (1996) traces the obstacles to feminist theory and scholarship in South Africa through her examination of this country's first conference proceedings on Women and Gender in 1991. She notes the resistance at these proceedings to creating an interrogative space for examining the position of the 'interpretive [white] subject and her discourse, the politics of knowledge production and the problems surrounding class and racially-bounded definitions of gender and feminism' (Lewis 1996: 94). Lewis points to the positioning of black women primarily as 'subject matter' invited not only 'to witness exhibitions of hegemonic wisdom', but also 'to endorse [both the] diagnoses and proposals [and] the role of 'enlightened' (white, middle-class) feminism in their salvation (p. 94).

Lewis draws significant parallells between the 'logocentric, Othering[18] display of black women on the folders of the Natal conference delegates' (Lewis 1996: 95) and the nineteenth-century western European display of Ms Saartjie Baartman as the stereotypical representation of black women's 'deviance', emphasizing the role of these representations in affirming and consolidating the norm of whiteness, simultaneously so invisible to itself. She observes that '[t]he right to interpret black experience in South Africa has been a white right. Blacks may have emotions and display their experience, but cannot be credited with self-knowledge or interpretive control' (p. 100). This racialized history shapes the relations of power/knowledge[19] production in South Africa that in turn shape the insensitivity within local scholarship to the interlocking of race, class and gender identities (pp. 91, 96). Part of problematizing whiteness in the South African academy entails a recognition and interrogation of the entanglement of white-centred knowledge with the race privilege of whiteness.

It is time to notice that the frontiers of resistance have shifted from burning tyres on Belgravia Road. White dominance today comes in different attire: silk suits as well as flat leather sandals, Doc Martens and dashikis – and we know it. Sites of struggle against it are more widely dispersed. Besides, and here I speak for myself, though something tells me it is not only me: when I voted in April 1994 for the first time at the not-so-tender age of thirty, something significant happened. It felt like part of a rite of passage for coming to voice as a coloured-african and black woman.

With more black people coming into the academy the terrain for knowledge creation is shifting. With this shift white relations of interpretive authority are becoming more visible and are being challenged. The ability of white scholars on the left to erase the ambiguous implications of their own 'dwellings within white[ness]' (Bennett and Friedman 1997: 49); to portray themselves as black people's unquestionable allies against the majority of 'bad whites' is diminishing. 'Good whites' can no longer tell us what our stories are or should be, as if there were a moment when they were not white. Many of them cannot bear it when we stop their show and take the power to name and challenge it. They cannot bear it when we say 'the way in which some of you tell our stories takes US out of the centre, the place we should rightfully occupy in OUR stories'. They do not like it when we tell them 'what you did against apartheid then is not important now; we want to know what you are doing against racism and white dominance today; we want to know how you are living with your whiteness today'.

Coming to Voice in the Hostility of White Dominance

Naming whiteness is one of the ways in which I have come to negotiate this hostile context. In this section I draw mainly on the work of North American authors. Their views are, however, of relevance to South Africa. McIntosh notes that 'white privilege [is] an invisible package of unearned assets' which confers dominance and power and is veiled by layers of denial (McIntosh 1992: 71, 77, 78). For me, white dominance is about using this conferred power to define and describe while itself remaining unnamed. It is the privilege of not having to know, see, listen to and understand the implications for black people of actions based on the use of this power and privilege. In South Africa it is the privilege and illusion of living as a majority even though you are a minority. It is the privilege of denying part of yourself in an attempt to escape your own whiteness.

Whiteness is a subjective position of privilege in the context of white dominance. Frankenburg (1993: 1) names whiteness, first, as 'a location of structural advantage [and] of race privilege, [second, as] a standpoint, a place from which [most] white people look at [or represent themselves, others and society, and, third, as] a set of cultural practices that are usually unmarked and unnamed'. It is 'a space defined only by reference to those named cultures [and races] it has flung out to its perimeter' (p. 231). In similar vein, Pajaczkowska and Young (1992: 202) define whiteness as 'an identity based on power [which] never has to to develop consciousness of itself as responsible, it has no sense of its limits except as these are perceived in opposition to others'.

In naming whiteness one 'avert[s] the critical gaze from the racial object to the racial subject; from the described and imagined to the describers and imaginers; from the serving to the served' (Morrison 1992: 90). Shifting the gaze is an important political act. It is a first step in the process by which black and white scholars can begin to transform the meaning of whiteness.[20] It allows us to talk about our 'social interpretations *as* social interpretations, as socially constructed and mutable re-presentations rather than as common sense facts' (Bonnett 1993: 167). In so doing it disrupts power and brings into focus the politics of white dominance.

This first step is crucial in transforming racialized relations of social power. It allows us to divest whiteness of the power it imagines itself to have, and which we sometimes attribute to it. In this way it helps us bring blackness in its various forms to centre-stage and give it new meaning. Furthermore, naming whiteness rather than being complicit with its unspoken assumptions shapes one's conception of anti-racism and the processes necessary to work towards an anti-racist society. The endemic nature of white dominance in the academy implies that 'anti-racism [is not] ... a polite professional campaign ... [it is] a necessarily militant struggle' (Bonnett 1993: 171) on the part of both blacks and whites. In the process of such struggle it is crucial that we are not only aware of our subjective location at the time, but also of its fluidity. At this point I return to my conversation with Abrahams. In the paragraphs that follow I explore the strengths and limitations of her work as well as the contradictions faced by me in wanting to show solidarity with her in the hostile white dominant environment of this specific seminar.

The Power of Black Essentialism(s)

One might find fault with Abrahams's rather crude way of lumping Gould, Gilman and his white leftist critics with the likes of Cuvier. At the same time I still value Abrahams's work for the challenge it poses to relations of interpretive authority. There are three points of power in Abrahams's work. First, she shifts the gaze from Ms Saartjie Baartman to the white male scientists, academics and commentators who objectify, sexualize and describe her and use their 'findings' as 'evidence' for their reading (from physical features) of social and sexual practices among the 'Hottentots and Bushmen'. Identifying personally with the Khoisan she dares to wonder what a white male academic would be looking at or for when looking at *her*. Through this process she pinpoints the reinscription of black women's place in the margins: 'What [Gould] was saying was not only that Khoisan women play with themselves, but that this was what mattered about us. This was our point of entry into academic discourses ... [which] ... held no place for Brown brains, only for Brown bodies' (Abrahams 1996: 11, 12).

It is Abrahams's particular location at the margins which allows her to see academics writing from the centre with different eyes. Hers is a vision not often articulated yet sorely needed in academic writing. A vision which frightens some white academics (male and female) because it shows up their own location in the power/knowledge/practice relationship. Second, the author unsubtly yet powerfully locates herself. When reading her paper one hears her saying out loud: 'I am a black/brown woman who sees, feels and experiences this story differently from a white person.' More specifically, she says, 'I am a Khoisan woman writing about a Khoisan woman.' She draws on her vernacular, her cultural references and proceeds to read and write from this place. Her interpretation of the message from white male historiography on Ms Baartman translates into 'swearwords and insults ... whitey is taking you for a c ... t' (Abrahams 1995: 15). This juxtaposition of voices highlights the rude power of location. She talks about the pain and struggle of eventually finding this position of enunciation outside of the imagined but real power of white male historiography: 'With Sara Baartman's story, the genital preoccupation of white male historiography operated so as to turn my own vernacular against me. A problem I could not even begin to phrase in my language was a problem I could not solve' (p. 14).

Abrahams's work is part of the struggle to shift the power relations embedded in knowledge creation; to shift the relations of oberserver and observed; and to resist seeing and experiencing ourselves as sexualized 'Other': 'To be a Brown woman observing was, in the narratives surrounding Sara Baartman, a contradiction in terms' (Abrahams 1996: 12).

Finally, the author's essentialist position is attractive for the purposes of political mobilization in SA today. Hall (1993a: 393), Fuss (1989) and Calhoun (1994: 17) argue that we should not underestimate the importance of essentialism(s) as discourses of resistance. Abrahams's claim to/of 'Khoisan-ness' has the power to sew together the contradictory fragments which constitute coloured-african identities by providing an imaginary coherence around a singular identity so that we are no longer '*stukkende mense*' (a broken people).

Limitations of Black Essentialism(s)

There is a serious downside to this essentialism in the current South African conjuncture. Abrahams places herself in the position of 'niece' to Baartman (Abrahams 1996: 13). In this way she arrogates to herself the role of representative, saying: 'My position [as woman descended from the Khoisan] does allow me certain privileged information' (p. 4). In taking this position she relies on biological determinism to assert her position of privilege in relation to the life of Baartman. She argues that the objectification of Baartman and of black women generally boils down to an issue 'about Black women and white men' (p. 7) and notes that: 'this whole race/gender thing ... begins with blood ... I was born Brown ... blood is family' (pp. 7, 8).

At some points she seems to be on the verge of articulating a more nuanced view of identity as when she notes that researching the life of Baartman 'was a process of ... finding out who I was' (p. 4). Yet ultimately she seems to lapse into a biological determinism oddly reminiscent of the eugenicists she criticises:

[W]e all knew I was going to be born Brown. There was a whole Brown history, culture and family just waiting for me to be born into ... Like any African, I was taught to take blood very seriously. No matter what, blood is still family, which means you have to stand up for them. So no matter how hard this gender thing divides us – and I can scold a man out as well as the next person – they still my blood [sic] (Abrahams 1996: 7, 8).

It may be her complicity with race-science that makes her fall into the trap of the 'damaged black' discourse. Amina Mama (1995: 43–63) reviews the growth and development of academic psychological research and theory about black people in North America. She notes that the conceptualization of black people as 'damaged' 'concurred with dominant post-slavery discourses' (p. 46) and constructed the black person as 'a psychologically tormented individual whose entire identity was dictated by white racism' (p. 47). This discourse constructed blackness as a pathology. In this regard Abrahams refers to '[p]aranoid schizophrenia [as] an old coping mechanism' among black people (Abrahams 1996: 14). Despite the strengths of her work she notes this same pathology as the cause of her not being in a 'good state for analytic thinking'. In this way she challlenges the power white male historiography imagines itself to have, only to affirm it in the same breath.

Although Abrahams critiques white male historiography for presenting Ms Saartjie Baartman in a 'timeless unstable present' (Abrahams 1996: 10), she presents Brown history and culture as 'just waiting' (p. 8), untouched by history, timeless and stable, for her to be born into. Essentialist claims which grope desperately at a mythical ethnic purity based in selectively reconstructed mythical pasts and notions of biological continuity feed the ideologies of Brown Nationalist movements in the Western Cape. Mervyn Ross of the Kleurling Weerstands Beweging (Coloured Resistance Movement) represents the voice of ethnic nationalism:[21]

We are proud that we are ethnic. And once we are ethnic and being recognised by various other people, we can also go further and say, 'Look we are ethnic. We have our own language, our own culture, our own land and we want to govern ourselves'. We are not prepared to be governed by the white man anymore – he has made a mess of it for 300 years. We are not prepared to be governed by black people. (Ross in Caliguire 1996: 10)

This ethnic nationalism falls back on racial and cultural essentialism and so becomes a bedfellow with apartheid discourse and right-wing movements such as the Afrikaner Weerstandsbeweging.[22] This language harks back to the frightening era of separate development – the preferred term for apartheid in the 1960s. Furthermore, seemingly oblivious of the power relations between intellectuals, the communities from which we come and the people we study, Abrahams also claims to 'reject the position of intellectual' (Abrahams 1996: 14) in order to come to the point of challenging white male historiography. In addition, she takes it upon herself to speak for all african men and women – black and brown. This raises important questions: Who is eligible to write about whom? Who is eligible to speak for whom?

Her singular and totalizing definitions of Brown and Black feed into discourses of ethno/cultural-nationalism, specifically Brown Nationalism. For her, 'Black' refers to 'people descended from Africans, who owe allegiance only to Africa' (Abrahams 1996: fn. 6: 6); while 'Brown' refers to 'people descended from the Khoisan and imported slave, who owe allegiance only to the Khoisan' (fn. 9: 7). One wonders, too, where others who have borne the brunt of anti-black racism – for example, in Australia – fit in. Some lived black experiences, the more untidy ones, are excluded from these definitions. Black people descended partly from Africans who do not owe allegiance *only* to Africa are not 'black' in her defnition. Similarly, people (like me) partly descended from the Khoisan who do not owe allegiance to these ancestors *only* are excluded from her universalist notions of Black and Brown.

Such totalizing notions of identity often silence dissent and tar over differences *within* black communities. In this sense Abrahams's voice is as silencing as voices of white dominance, just in a different way. It is through her attempts to claim monopoly over the expression of black identities that *she* defines and describes, simply from a different location.

The Difficulties of Entanglement

Abrahams and I have a different sense of our relationship to the past. Against all odds she seems to find coherence when looking to the past. I find fragments. My identity is ex-slave – Malaysian, Javanese, St Helenian; it is a particular unknown fragment of being Khoisan; it is an unknown factor of being Dutch. From a very early age, I, as many others from various coloured experiences, have learnt that blackness is equated with being african. This discourse has placed and continues to place me in a position of dislocation because my ancestry is not exclusively african. What do I make of these ghostly unknowns; of this dislocation? I live with them from day to day not knowing what they are. So I create myself, not ahistorically, and call myself both black and coloured-african.

Many fellow South Africans from various racialized experiences would urge me to choose between being black or coloured. Their argument would be that I am confused; I can only choose one; choosing both is contra-dictory; choosing to be coloured is reactionary; after all 'coloured' is a term imposed by the apartheid regime and the time has now come to reject this term. Implicit in such argument is the simplistic notion that one can be either black or white, never differently black and definitely not both; that choosing to be black is inherently progressive while choosing to be coloured is inherently reactionary. Such argument constructs 'black' as the nodal identity with 'coloured' defined in terms of its relation to black and white. The reality is that I cannot choose. Choosing to be only black would deny the specificity of my experience. Besides, no identity is inherently progressive or reactionary. Am I confused? Should I have a greater sense of certainty about my identity? No, I am not confused. Nor do I have to seek such certainty. As Amina Mama points out: 'We are formed out of contradictions which do not have to be resolved for us to live with them' (AGI seminar, 8 October 1996).

Choosing to be coloured, african *and* black is not about being ambiguous – doubtful about whether I am black, coloured *or* african. It is about being neither exclusively black, exclusively coloured, nor exclusively african.

It is from this place that I responded to Abrahams in the seminar.

When Abrahams asked the audience: 'Those of you who identify yourselves as Khoisan, will you raise your hands?' I was about to raise mine when I thought: But that's not all I am, it's only one part of me. Calling myself Khoisan would do violence to the moments of entanglement in my ancestral and personal histories. In contradistinction to the title of her paper, her question presented Khoisan as a unitary, closed and completed identity – something I do not have nor wish to claim.

I felt I could not choose only one part of my identity. Identifying only as Khoisan denies my ('imported') slave heritage as well as my Dutch heritage. At this historical moment my Dutch heritage is something I would rather shy away from. Who can be proud of a heritage associated with violence, genocide and rape? I prefer not to be politically correct (or incorrect) and so acknowledge my Dutch heritage no matter how painful the possibilities of the violence may be. Beyond the pain there is my presence here today – a clear indication of generations of survivors. It is in this sense that I remember/acknowledge my Dutch heritage. I think about my ancestors surviving this heritage and through this transforming it and creating their own understandings of who they may be.

All this happens simply at the level of my imagination. I no longer have a grandmother or great-grandmother who can tell me her version of our family story.

The thought of my ancestors – Khoi, San, Dutch and slave – creating their own understandings of who they may be, and my own practice of creating and re-creating my own subjectivity in the process of becoming black, coloured and african resonates with Amina Mama's argument that we do not simply internalize what the dominant culture says about us. Instead, in our struggles against racism and sexism we create new subjectivities as black men and women (Mama 1995: i). Besides, our being black is not exhausted by these struggles. There are other cultural, creative and innovative aspects of our black identities. Furthermore, in the context of different forms of racism and different cultural contexts there are many ways of being black in the world.

The moment I realized I could not raise my hand in support of Abrahams's question was a moment during which I refused to be complicit in Abrahams's notion that she was speaking *for me*. This moment revealed to me both the simultaneous power and dangers of difference. Abrahams assumed the power to speak *for* me in a discourse which challenged the dominant racialized and gendered discourse of academe. She lost me in silencing crucial parts of me. I took the power to resist an essentialist discourse of Khoisan-ness. In this seminar both Abrahams and I stepped into the danger zone of white appropriations of such difference.

'Hi-*bredie*-ty'

To acknowledge multiplicity embedded in the entanglements of whiteness, blackness, colouredness and africanness is *not* to live in a dislocated space where all identities are equal. Significantly, this does not imply being an apolitical, precarious, fence-sitting subject. The historical reality of differential black experiences under apartheid and particular contexts of white dominance and black essentialisms constrain and shape our choices. We cannot be whatever we want. This brings me to the 'knowns' in my identity.

I know that my subjectivity is racialized and racially gendered. For me, my subjectivity is not an ethnic identity which can be objectively defined in terms of a single language, culture and/or religion. It is the locus of multiple subjectivities/various other identities, some of which are racialized – it is the junction in which other identities meet.

The Jazzart choreographer and dancer Dawn Langdown, who has danced the painful history of coloured-african people on stage, refers to her identity in the following way: *'Ek is wat ek is. Ek is 'n mixed bredie'* (I am what I am. I am a mixed bredie). By using the word *bredie* – the Afrikaans name for a very specifically South African meat stew – Langdown names her multiplicity without losing locatedness. Like Langdown's, my coloured identity is all about 'hi-*bredie*-ty' – a hybrid identity located in a specific place with a specific history; an identity formed and re-formed in the context of specific social relations of power. If ever there is an unstable, restless, highly differentiated, hybrid place to be, it is the one which I occupy. Yes, I am a 'disquieting, untidy presence' (Miller 1990: 35). Too untidy for some whites. Too untidy for some blacks. With the former I am often seen as the 'safe black' woman. The one who is 'not really black'. And when I articulate some kind of black voice, they're shocked. The latter are left disappointed because mine is, often, not the voice they want to hear, not a 'truly' black voice. Unlike untidy, disquieting me, Abrahams has chosen a clear, stable, tidy answer to fill in the blank space in 'I am … '

'The Specifics are Mine, The Condition is Common'[23]

How reconcilable is my insistence on being aware of the complexity of my roots with my insistence on articulating a critical black perspective? I have discovered an interesting echo of this state of being in a novel rooted in a very different context: *Some Kind of Black* by Diran Adebayo, who is of Nigerian descent, black and British. Rather oddly for a Virago publication, the characters speak in a sexist masculine discourse which makes it a not so easy read for any woman. You cannot but want vehemently to resist being referred to as 'meat' and 'thing' (Adebayo 1996: 15, 19). Yet there are moments for a black woman when his depictions of those whites who exoticize black men and women are painfully familiar. He writes of those whites in search of a particular notion of black sexuality as 'desperately seeking some dark continent concentrate' (p. 29). His is a novel about the uncomfortable complexity of blackness(es) and is itself an uncomfortable read because of its masculine voice.

Dele is the central character. He is a second generation black British man of Nigerian descent. We meet him at the end of his studies at Oxford. He no longer harks back to the 'Old Country', but finds no comfort zone in London, where he is equally uncomfortable with the exoticizing practices of some whites, the pompous nationalism of the Nubians and the shallowness of the Love Has No Colour Brigade. Dele is very clearly UK Blak[24] with a double consciousness.[25] He is not concerned with 'roots' nor is he impressed by 'speaky-spoky' [folks who are] as Oxford as yards of ale' (Adebayo: 9, 19). He lives in a place of dislocation which has but a 'fragile edifice' (p. 190). This fragility surfaces strongly when he is with one of his white girlfriends, Andria. He spends his time 'shuttling from one [racialized] world to another' (p. 187) hating white worlds for their seeming happiness with 'his basking in the mainstream' (p. 190) and black worlds for their assumptions that 'because he was with a white girl, and had acted how he did, he was one of *them*' (p. 190; my emphasis). This 'shuttling' begins to end when a violent encounter with the *Babylon* (the police) sends his sister, Dapo, into a coma. Dapo suffers from sickle-cell anaemia. This event grounds Dele, forcing him to reflect on his hatred 'for the police and the system and all those white things' (p. 185), and Andria's place in all of this. After all, she was less of the establishment than he, 'the Oxbridge man'. Differently violent is the jostling among several 'Blacker than You' (p. 105) organizations which compete to appropriate Dapo's story for their own political ends, almost erasing her from the story in the process. Dapo's inert black body, dressed in scientific instruments and housed in the intensive therapy unit of the Middlesex Hospital, occupies a space very reminiscent of that of Abrahams's 'auntie Sara' (Abrahams 1996: 13).

Adebayo's novel is set in London, not Cape Town. His hero does not have white ancestry. Yet, his resistance to both Africentrist/cultural/ethnonationalist and exoticizing white discourses speak to my own experiences in South Africa. This condition of complex blackness(es) is a transnational one. Yet the dislocation of diaspora has its local specificities.

For Dele, some of the black worlds of London are divided into Nigerian-Nigerians, UK Africans, Caribbeans who 'lack a coherent identity', Small Islanders and some Jamaicans who speak of 'dark, ugly Africans and bubuheads' (Adebayo 1996: 13, 21, 47). For me, some of the black worlds in Cape Town are divided into AfriKan-Africans who possess the resources and integrity of 'pure and strong' African cultures; this includes Chief Joe Little[26] who drapes himself in a *Karos*[27] for special occasions; 'illegal alien' Africans who are from Africa in a way that South Africans 'are not'; coloured people who 'lack a coherent identity' and thus 'do not know who they are'; Muslim coloured people who '*do* know who they are'; and coloured people who speak of 'dark, ugly Africans' and of '*kroes*-haired coloureds'.[28] My choice not to be exclusively Khoisan is about resisting a totalizing narrative about african ways of being african, coloured kinds of blackness(es) and coloured kinds of colouredness(es) in SA.

Considering both my black and white heritage as well as my suffering under and resistance to white domination, I would be 'some kind of black'. Certainly not a 'pure' black because historically my identity was formed in close relation with whiteness. It is the latter which denies me the resources of a 'pure' africanity, and my acknowledgement of it that denies me the resources of 'pure' Khoisan-ness. My roots are too messy; my branches cast too wide. Yes, for the moment I am 'some kind of black'. For me, being coloured-african is being 'some kind of black' – a space which has no comfort zone in between. And as I name this identity 'coloured', even hyphenated with 'african', I fear that I am fixing it, limiting it, robbing it of its differentiation, its diversity, of its power to challenge notions of 'pure' blackness, 'pure' whiteness, 'pure' brownness or 'pure' colouredness for that matter.

Living the Moments of Entanglement

The Caribbean poet Derek Walcott encapsulates living with entangled fragments. He challenges 'broken people' to ease the burden of a fragmented past through valuing the now reassembled pieces of our African, Asian and

European heritages – 'the cracked heirlooms whose restoration shows its white scars' (Walcott 1992). We have had losses – too many – some of which can never be recovered. And we need to live with ourselves today.

Edouard Glissant (1989), writing from the same location as Walcott (1992), and on the Caribbean slave experience and the formation of Caribbean identities, illuminates the meaning of entanglement when he writes that 'we are the roots of a cross-cultural relationship ... [s]ubmarine roots ... not fixed in some primordial spot, but extending in all directions in our world through its network of branches' (Glissant 1989: 66, 67).

For me, the concept of entanglement has two components: a relationship of engagement both historically and in the present, and the creation and re-creation of newness and/or difference from that engagement. In the context of colonialism, dislocation and cultural dispossession a key survival mechanism for the dominated was to appropriate the dominant culture and, in so doing, to create their own 'new' cultures. In this sense coloured-african identities and cultures are less about what was lost culturally along the Middle Passage and as a result of genocide, and more about the articulation of these diverse identities and fragments of cultural formations with the colonial culture. Creolization of the Dutch language and the subsequent formation of the Afrikaans[29] language is one manifestation of this process of cultural and identity formation among slave communities in the Western Cape.

In the case of coloured-african identities in SA, the engagements are multiple: with whiteness and western cultural practices; with various forms of africanity present at the Cape before colonists arrived; with ways in which to maintain remnants of cultural formations which slaves through the Middle Passage brought with them. They involve re-memoring/re-membering the 'coral-become bodies of those slaves drowned in the Middle Passage' (Baucom 1997: 9) and the links these bodies make with waters washing several shores across the globe – Dutch, East Indian, Malaysian, African among others.

These engagements have multiple, seemingly contradictory political effects. In relation to coloured-african identities in the Western Cape, SA, relationships of antagonism are among such effects – antagonism with whiteness, with notions of blackness as 'pure', with notions of cultural purity. Simultaneously, collusions and often fragile solidarities result from such engagements. Examples from the Western Cape of collusions as means of survival abound in the context of relationships between coloured farm workers and the white farmers who employ them. Furthermore, the refraction of gendered and classed identities through racialized and creolized african identities brings to the fore multi-vocality.

There is often a yearning for an illusive wholeness, rootedness, belonging, fixity; wanting to glue together the fragments in the hope of finding wholeness. This occurs in a context in which one is fixed by others; positioned as rootless in relation to those who imagine themselves to be rooted. With this process comes 'Othering' as articulated in the meanings of *ilau* among the Xhosa and *malau*, a term within Xhosa language sometimes used to refer to coloured-africans – meaning the one who is not rooted in his/her tradition; the one who does not know whether s/he is black or white. And, coloured-africans are not only 'Othered' by other South African africans, they themselves participate in processes of 'Othering'.

The interaction between the above processes and those of differential racialization on the part of the apartheid state results in hierarchies of oppression. In this context these generally construct africans as more oppressed than coloured-africans and thus more deserving in the post-1994 context of transformation and redistribution. The political effects of such hierarchies require serious interrogation – an issue beyond the bounds of this chapter.

The concept and the social condition of entanglement have significant consequences for hegemonic binarisms and notions of 'pure' and singular identities. Among these is the trangressive effect of engagements in entanglement through its disruption of the hegemonic black/white binary frame and singular notions of blackness and whiteness, of woman, of man. Coloured-african identities 'are not caught athwart frames, [they] are shifting frames' (Busia 1994: 213). This concept has significant consequences for understanding the cultural history of the African present and for engaging newly emerging notions of African Renaissance. This is the analytical power of the concept of entanglement.

Glissant notes:

> We must return to the point from which we started. Diversion is not a useful ploy unless it is nourished by reversion: not a return to the longing for origins, to some immutable state of Being, but a return to the point of entanglement, from which we were forcefully turned away; that is where we must ultimately put to work the forces of creolisation, or perish. (Glissant 1989: 26)

Glissant's insights are useful in understanding the different choices made by Abrahams and I respectively. Reversion refers to an 'obsession with a single, [coherent] origin' (Glissant 1989: 16) and the need to 'return to roots' on the part of displaced peoples. In the context of coloured experiences in SA, 'return' refers to a 'return' to cultural roots embedded in the past rather than to a particular geographical place. Such 'return' is usually for the purposes of building a coherent story. It is in these ways that Abrahams favours reversion. This preference for a singular identity somehow fixed in time loses the 'tangled nature of lived experience and promot[es] the idea of 'uncontaminated survival' (p. 14).

Diversion comes with an awareness that a return to origins in search of coherence is impossible (Glissant 1989: 19, 23). It is an acceptance of living with fragments of origins, silences about slavery, and entanglements with whiteness – outcomes of the violence of colonialism and apartheid. Diversion entails reclaiming all elements of our pasts, however fragmented, including those 'scorned, repressed [and] denied' (p. 24) – African, Malaysian and European – and re-creating new stories which do not have to be coherent and/or complete. It is a detour through the conditions of 'racialized displacement' (Hesse 1996b: 138) for the purposes of living with ourselves today and resisting domination and description.

There is power to living the moments of entanglement. It acknowledges both destructive and inventive moments of colonial encounters, in so doing recognizing that the survivors of colonialism and slavery may have been weak but seldom passive (Clifford 1988: 16), thus affirming black agency. It facilitates an understanding of local identity formations as emerging from historical compromises between a mixture of 'resistance to incorporation into a larger whole and of elements of accommodation to this larger order' (Marcus 1992: 313). This approach challenges essentialist notions of subjectivity and highlights the complexity of subjectivity as an encounter with difficulty. Furthermore, through its acknowledgement of racialized colonial relations of social power, it challenges a pluralist, apolitical conceptualization of black subjectivity. Simultaneously, it challenges the simple binary of black/white relations and identities, noting the presence of the Other in the Self destabilizing any notions of 'pure' selves. Living the moments of entanglement is itself a form of resistance.

There is pain to living the moments of entanglement. Walcott (1992) notes that gathering together broken pieces which do not fit 'contain[s] more pain than their original sculpture'. The challenge is to contain this pain while simultaneously living with different articulations of blackness within contexts of white dominance. None of this erases the sense of loss. None of this eases the pain of 'nostalgia without [coherent] memory' (Adebayo 1996: 169). None of this erases the white scars of colonialism, slavery and apartheid. And, we need to keep living with ourselves today.

Notes

Many thanks to Zine Magubane, Gabeba Baderoon, Desiree Lewis, Cheryl Hendricks, Edgar Pieterse, Karen Farquharson, Angelo Fick, Pumla Qgola, Andries du Toit and Robin Cohen for the various ways in which they have affirmed the place from which I speak in this piece. Special thanks to Andries du Toit for reading and commenting on several drafts, and to Barnor Hesse for detailed and constructive editorial comments.

1. I pay specific attention to the South African academy since it is important to distinguish the latter from academies elsewhere on the African continent. In this regard it is important to note the roles of the University of Dar es Salaam, Tanzania, and the University of Dakar, Senegal (among others) in challenging racialized knowledge production. Developments at these institutions are today reflected in the work of the Council for the Development of Social and Economic Research in Africa (CODSERIA) among other research organizations based on the African continent. Furthermore, in post-apartheid South Africa, white dominance is endemic in specific spheres such as the academy, the big business world, tourism and advertising. Although the arguments I develop with regard to whiteness in the South African academy may be of wider significance and relevance (Europe and the USA), it is important to note the specificity of its dominance in the African context.

2. For the purposes of this work, 'black' refers to a transnational political category defining the experiences of people who have suffered and continue to suffer white domination. In the South African context this would include those historically classified Indian, Coloured and African/Black.

3. Essentialism is generally understood as a belief in the unchanging and transhistorical true essence of identities. Diana Fuss (1989) brings our attention to the argument that essentialisms can be used as resources for resistance. Essentialist standpoints are inherently neither progressive nor reactionary. Black essentialisms can be understood as positions which advocate one way of being black, a monolithic blackness. Such positions have a totalizing function often erasing gendered and various other ways of being black.

4. The majority (56 per cent) of the voting population in the Western Cape Province of South Africa is historically classified coloured (Eldridge and Seekings 1996: 520). In this work I use the terms 'coloured' and 'coloured-african' interchangeably. The latter asserts the african location of coloured identities. Use of the lower case is an attempt to resist centring any one of these identities.

5. The historical information on resistance movements is adapted from joint work with Edgar Pieterse. See Erasmus and Pieterse (1999).

6. This construction of 'coloured' as an identity imposed by apartheid occurs despite historical evidence that slave communities at the Cape referred to themselves as 'coloured' in the late 1800s (Bickford-Smith 1994: 289).

7. Differential racialization refers to the various ways in which different black people have been and continue to be racialized. This conceptualization is based on an understanding of racisms and racializtion as processes which are not uniform and immutable. Racisms and racialized identities are formed in the context of and so shaped by very specific relations of social power.

8. Ms Saartjie Baartman was a Khoena woman subjected to the horrors of eugenicist practices of the nineteenth century. The term 'Khoena' is also sometimes spelt 'Quena'. It refers to the indigenous peoples of South Africa also known as the Khoi and the San, and by the derogatory terms 'Hottentot' and 'Bushmen'. She was referred to by colonialists as the 'Hottentot Venus'. This derogatory naming continues in particular circles today.

9. Although Abrahams has published other writings, this particular piece is as yet unpublished at the time of writing. It can, however, be obtained from the Documentation Centre at the African Gender Institute, University of Cape Town (e.mail: agi@agi. uct.ac.za).

10. People classified coloured in apartheid SA were also referred to as 'bruinmense' (brown people) by the National Party at the time. This naming was and continues to be

used today by some people historically classified coloured – mainly those who support National Party politics and ethnic-based national movements.

11. Thus far Abrahams has been among the first to articulate this particular essentialist position in academia. Her position can, however, be located within broader popular debates in the media shaped by the recent emergence of several cultural heritage organizations such as the Cape Cultural Heritage Development Council and political organizations such as the Kleurling Weerstands Beweging (KWB). For Mervyn Ross of the KWB the politics of heritage and history relegates both black africans and white europeans to the position of colonizer, leaving Khoi and San the innocent victims. Although these movements are marginal, their popular appeal cannot be ignored. Furthermore, such movements are increasingly gaining academic attention as illustrated by the conference held in Cape Town on Khoisan Identities and Cultural Heritage (July 1997) and the publication of these proceedings edited by Andrew Bank. The conference papers are concerned more with historical than contemporary issues in Khoisan identities with several focusing on the articulation of these identities in Namibia and Botswana.

12. *Mokoko: The Makgoba Affair* (1997) is Professor William Makgoba's reflections on the politics of transformation at a historically white university – the University of the Witwatersrand, Johannesburg. This reflection is based on his experience at the hands of thirteen university deans (mostly white and male) who expended much effort to prove a lack of intellectual integrity on the part of Makgoba at the time of his appointment as deputy vice chancellor of this university. They attempted to do this by pointing to alleged dishonesties in his curriculum vitae. This process happened in the wake of Makgoba's support for striking students and workers who hold an administrator hostage. His account illustrates the colour of excellence and the continued uncritical assumption of a white right to knowledge production in the South African academy. It points to the relationship between power and knowledge in post-apartheid South African academe.

13. The 'Mamdani Affair' took place at the University of Cape Town (UCT), a historically white university. Central to this 'affair' was Professor Mahmood Mamdani's public academic challenge of the racialized structure of a course entitled 'Introduction to Africa'. This was a core course in the newly established foundation semester in the Faculty of Social Sciences and Humanities. It was prepared as a substitute for the course Mamdani was initially requested to design and from which he was later formally suspended by the deputy dean of this faculty. In similar vein to the Makgoba Affair, this process highlights the relationship between racialized power and control of knowledge production in the post-apartheid South African academy. It also illustrates the complex collusions with this relationship on the part of the university administration.

14. The work of Desiree Lewis on the politics of South African feminisms (1996) and issues of *Agenda*, a South African-based feminist journal, during the years 1992 and 1993 provide some examples of such contestations. Further examples of such events are discussed in the works of Bennett and Friedman (1997) and Van der Spuy (1997).

15. Gould 1985; Gilman 1985, 1992; Skotnes 1996; Critical Arts 1995; Robins 1997; Douglas 1997; Sharp 1997; Collection of Conference Papers on Khoisan Identities and Cultural Heritage, 1997 (in the library of University of Cape Town, Department of Sociology); among many others.

16. Biological determinism is a perspective which attributes one's identity as black to biologically inherited characteristics. Often 'blood' is used as a metaphor in essentialist arguments. However, as will be shown later in this piece, Abrahams's use of 'blood' comes very close to a notion of identity fixed in biology.

17. Among these are the Kleurling Weerstands Beweging (Coloured Resistance

Movement), the Brown Nationalist Movement, the National Liberation Front and the Coloured Forum among others. These movements generally construct coloured people as an ethnic group and argue for self-determination of coloured people in a post-apartheid context which they see as hostile towards this group of people.

18. Processes of constructing an 'Other' are embedded in relations of domination, for example, gendered and racialized relations of social power. The consequences (whether intended or unintended) of Othering entail representing the 'Other' in a distorted fashion with the effect of maintaining the privilege of the dominant. Priority is given to the dominant viewpoint and experience as the standard or universal measure against which all other viewpoints and experiences are evaluated.

19. 'Power/knowledge' refers to the intricate links between knowledge production and relations of power. Central to an acknowledgement of these links is the conceptualization of knowledge as located, that is, not separate from the maker of knowledge or from the historical period of its making. For the purposes of this chapter, racialized relations of power in the production of knowledge are of central concern. (See Foucault 1980.)

20. Among new works in this field is a collection entitled *Whiteness: A Critical Reader* edited by Mike Hill (1997).

21. Michael Ignatieff (1994: 3–6) distinguishes between civic and ethnic nationalism. For him the former is based on a conceptualization of the nation as based on common citizenship; a community of equal citizens holding rights before the law and with a shared attachment to certain institutions, practices and values. Ethnic nationalism, on the other hand, has its history in the German Romantic notion that the unity of a nation is not based on shared rights but on 'the people's pre-existing ethnic characteristics: their language, religion, customs and traditions' (p. 4). The key to ethnic nationalism is that an individual's attachments to a nation are 'inherited, not chosen' (p. 5).

22. The Afrikaner Weerstands Beweging (Afrikaner Resistance Movement) is an extra-parliamentary, para-military, white, right-wing political movement in South Africa. It emerged in the 1980s under the leadership of Eugene Terreblanche. Central to its rhetoric is the notion of an Afkrikaner *volk* with rights to self-government in an all-white state.

23. Busia 1994: 204.

24. UK Blak refers to cultural formations specifically expressive of blackness(es) as lived in Britain. These point to the significance of black cultural formations in the history and politics of race and citizenship in Britain as shaped by processes of migration (Gilroy 1993a: 81–7).

25. The concept of 'double consciousness' was developed by W. E. B Du Bois and used by Gilroy (1993a). In the case of Dele it refers to being both black and British and to the challenges which arise from living this doubleness as illustrated in the novel discussed.

26. Mr Joe Little is a self-proclaimed chief of a Khoi grouping, the Hancumqua. He founded the Cape Cultural Heritage Development Council for the purposes of building pride in origin among coloured people through an emphasis on Khoi lineages.

27. A *Karos* is the animal skin with which the Khoena/Khoisan covered themselves; it is usually draped around the shoulders.

28. Coloured people with kinky hair.

29. Afrikaans has generally been seen as the language of the dominant in South Africa. Historical research on the development of Afrikaans as a language has, however, shown that it is historically the language of the slaves. The first Afrikaans texts were written in Arabic.

Conclusion: the Multi-cultural Question

Stuart Hall

This chapter addresses many of the themes rehearsed in the Introduction and elsewhere in this volume. Its starting point is Homi Bhabha's quoted observation that 'multiculturalism' is a heterogeneously expanded port-manteau term and that 'multi-cultural' has become a floating signifier. The first part of the chapter undertakes a deconstructive critique of these key terms. It considers their conditions of emergence and disseminated exist-ence in contemporary British society and political discourse. The second half picks up from Barnor Hesse's idea of the 'transruptive effects' of the multi-cultural question, and traces these in a number of domains. The chapter ends by trying in a tentative way to rescue a new multicultural political 'logic' from the debris of existing political vocabularies which the eruption of the multi-cultural question has left in its wake.

The term 'multiculturalism' is now universally deployed. However, this proliferation has neither stabilized nor clarified its meaning. Like other related terms – for example, 'race', ethnicity, identity, diaspora – multi-culturalism is now so discursively entangled that it can only be used 'under erasure' (Hall 1996a). Nevertheless, since we have no less implicated concepts to think this problem with, we have no alternative but to go on using and interrogating it.

The Multi-cultural/Multiculturalism Distinction

It might be useful to draw a distinction here between 'multi-cultural' and 'multiculturalism'.[1] Here multi-cultural is used adjectivally. It describes the social characteristics and problems of governance posed by any society in which different cultural communities live together and attempt to build a common life while retaining something of their 'original' identity. By contrast, 'multiculturalism' is substantive. It references the strategies and policies adopted to govern or manage the problems of diversity and multi-plicity which multi-cultural societies throw up. It is usually used in the singular, signifying the distinctive philosophy or doctrine which underpins multi-cultural strategies. 'Multi-cultural', however, is by definition plural. There are many kinds of multi-cultural society. The USA, Canada, Britain, France, Malaysia, Sri Lanka, New Zealand, Indonesia, South Africa, Nigeria all qualify. They are 'multi-cultural' in significantly different ways. However, they all share one characteristic. They are by definition culturally heterogeneous. They differ in this respect from liberal-constitutional, 'modern', western nation-states which are predicated on the (usually unspoken) assumption of cultural homogeneity organized around 'universal' liberal-individualist secular values (Goldberg 1994).

The two terms are now so interdependent that it is virutally impossible to disentangle them. However, 'multiculturalism' presents specific difficulties. It stands for 'a wide range of social articulations, ideals and practices'. The problem is that the '-*ism*' tends to convert 'multiculturalism' into a political doctrine and 'reduces [it] to a formal singularity, fixing it into a cemented condition ... Thus converted ... the heterogeneity characteristic of multi-cultural conditions is reduced to a pat and pedestrian doctrine' (Caws 1994). In fact, 'multiculturalism' is not a single doctrine, does not characterize one political strategy, and does not represent an already achieved state of affairs. It is not a covert way of endorsing some ideal, utopian state. It describes a variety of political strategies and processes which are everywhere incomplete. Just as there are different multi-cultural societies so there are very different 'multiculturalisms'. Conservative multiculturalism follows Hume (Goldberg 1994) in insisting on the assimilation of difference into the traditions and customs of the majority. Liberal multiculturalism seeks to integrate the different cultural groups as fast as possible into the 'mainstream' provided by a universal individual citizenship, tolerating only in private certain particularistic cultural practices. Pluralist multiculturalism formally enfranchises the differences between groups along cultural lines and accords different group-rights to different communities within a more communal or communitarian political order. Commercial multiculturalism assumes that if the diversity of individuals from different communities is recognized in the marketplace, then the problems of cultural difference will be (dis)solved through private consumption, without any need for a redistribution of power and resources. Corporate multiculturalism (public or private) seeks to 'manage' minority cultural differences in the interests of the centre. Critical or 'revolutionary' multiculturalism foregrounds power, privilege, the hierarchy of oppressions and the movements of resistance (McLaren 1997). It seeks to be 'insurgent, polyvocal, heteroglossial and anti-foundational' (Goldberg 1994). And so on.

Far from being a settled doctrine, 'multiculturalism' is a deeply contested idea (May 1999). It is contested by the conservative Right, in defence of the purity and cultural integrity of the nation. It is contested by liberals, who claim that the 'cult of ethnicity' and the pursuit of difference threaten the universalism and neutrality of the liberal state, undermining personal autonomy, individual liberty and formal equality. Multiculturalism, some liberals also say, legitimates the idea of 'group rights'. But this subverts the dream that one nation and one citizenship can be constructed out of the diverse cultures of different peoples – *e pluribus unum*.[2] Multiculturalism is also contested by modernizers of different political persuasions. For them, the triumph of the universalism of western civilization over the particularism of ethnic and racial belonging established in the Enlightenment marked a fateful and irreversible transition from Traditionalism to Modernity. This shift must never be reversed. Some postmodern versions of 'cosmopolitanism', which treat 'the subject' as wholly contingent and unencumbered, are sharply opposed to Multiculturalism, where subjects are more located. It is also challenged from several positions on the Left. Anti-racists argue that it – wrongly – privileges culture and identity over economic and material questions. Radicals believe it divides the united front of race-and-class against injustice and exploitation along ethnically and racially particularistic lines. Others point to various versions of commercialized, consumerist or 'boutique' multiculturalism (Fish 1998) which celebrate difference without making a difference.[3] There is also what Sarat Maharaj (in an unpublished paper) felicitously calls 'multicultural managerialism', which is often indistinguishable from 'a spook-lookalike of Apartheid logic'.

Can a concept which means so many different things and so effectively draws the fire of such diverse and contradictory enemies really have anything to say to us? Alternatively, is its contested status precisely its value? After all, 'A sign which has been withdrawn from the pressures of the social struggle..inevitably loses force, degenerating into allegory and becoming the object ... of [mere] philological comprehension' (Volosinov/Bakhtin 1973). For good or ill, we are inevitably implicated in its practices, which characterize and define 'late-modern societies'. In Michele Wallace's terms:

> everybody knows ... that multiculturalism is not the promised land ... [However] even at its most cynical and pragmatic, there is something about multiculturalism which continues to be worth pursuing ... we do need to find ways of publicly manifesting the significance of cultural diversity, [and] of integrating the contributions of people of colour into the fabric of society. (Wallace 1994)

Conditions of Emergence

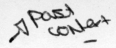

Multi-cultural societies are not new. Long before the age of European expansion (from the fifteenth century onwards) – and with increasing intensity since – the migration and movement of peoples has been the rule rather than the exception, producing societies which are ethnically or culturally 'mixed'. 'Movement and migration ... are the defining socio-historical conditions of humanity' (Goldberg 1994). People have moved for many reasons: natural disasters, climate and ecological change, war, conquest, famine, poverty, labour exploitation, colonization, slavery, indenture, political repression, civil war, economic underdevelopment. Empires, the product of conquest and domination, are often multi-cultural. The Greek, Roman, Islamic, Ottoman and European empires were all, in different ways, both multi-ethnic and multi-cultural. Colonialism – always a double inscription – attempted to convene the colonized within the 'empty, homogeneous time' of global modernity, without effacing deep differences or disjunctures of time, place and tradition (Bhabha 1994; Hall 1996a). The plantation systems of the western world, the indentured systems of South-East Asia, colonial India, as well as the many nation-states consciously carved out of a more fluid ethnic canvas – in Africa, by the colonizing powers, in the Middle East, the Balkans and Central Europe, by the Great Powers – all loosely fit the multi-cultural description.

These historical examples are not irrelevant to how multiculturalism has surfaced in the post-war world. They provide some of the latter's conditions of emergence. But there is no linear connection between the colonial and the post-colonial. Since the Second World War, the multi-cultural question has not only changed its forms but become intensified. It has also become more salient, taking centre-stage in the field of political contestation. This is the result of a series of decisive shifts, a strategic reconfiguration of social forces and relations across the globe.

First, the winding up of the old European imperial system and the completion of the decolonizing and national independence struggles. In the wake of the dismantling of the old empires, many *new* multi-ethnic and multi-cultural nation-states were created. However, they continue to reflect their prior conditions of existence under colonialism.[4] These new states are relatively weak, economically and militarily. Many lack a developed civil society. They remain dominated by the imperatives of the early independence nationalist movements. They govern populations with a variety of different ethnic, cultural or religious traditions. The indigenous cultures, dislocated if not destroyed by colonialism, are not inclusive enough to provide the basis for a new national or civic culture. These difficulties are compounded by extensive poverty and underdevelopment, in the context of deepening global inequality and an unregulated neo-liberal economic world order. Increasingly, crises in these societies assume a multi-cultural or ethnicized form.

There is a close relationship between the re-emergence of 'the multi-cultural question' and the phenomenon of the 'post-colonial'. The latter concept could take us on a detour through a conceptual labyrinth from which few travellers return. It must suffice at this point simply to assert that the 'post-colonial' does *not* signal a simple before/after chronological succession. The movement from colonization to post-colonial times does *not* imply that the problems of colonialism have been resolved, or replaced by some conflict-free era. Rather, the 'post-colonial' marks the passage from one historical power-configuration or conjuncture to another (Hall 1996a).[5] Problems of dependency, underdevelopment and marginalization, typical of the 'high' colonial period, persist into the post-colonial. However, these relations are *resumed* in a new configuration. Once they were articulated as unequal relations of power and exploitation between colonized and colonizing societies. Now they are restaged and displaced as struggles between indigenous social forces, as internal contradictions and sources of destabilization *within* the decolonized society, or between them and the wider global system. Think of the ways in which the instability of democratic rule in, say, Pakistan, Iraq, Iran, Indonesia, Nigeria, or Algeria, or the continuing problems of political legitimacy and stability in Afghanistan, Namibia, Mozambique or Angola have clear roots in their recent imperial history. This post-colonial 'double inscription' is taking place in a global context where direct rule, governance or protectorship by an imperial power has been replaced by an asymmetric globalized system of power which is post-national, transnational and neo-imperial in character. Its main features are structural inequality, within a deregulated free-trade and free capital-flow system dominated by the First World, and programmes of structural readjustment, in which western interests and models of governance are paramount.

The second factor is the ending of the Cold War. Its main features are the post-1989 break-up of the Soviet Union as a trans-ethnic, trans-national formation, the decline of state communism as an alternative model of industrial development and the waning of the Soviet sphere of influence, especially in Eastern Europe and the Central Asia. This has had regional effects similar in certain ways to the dismantling of the old imperial systems. Nineteen eighty-nine has been followed by the attempt, under US leadership, to construct 'a new world order'. One aspect of this drive has been the relentless pressure by the West, designed to drag these very different, relatively underdeveloped East European societies kicking and screaming, overnight, into what is called '*the* market'. This mysterious entity is propelled into old, complex cultures and authoritarian polities as an abstract and denuded principle, without any attention to the cultural, political, social and institutional embeddedness which markets *always* require. One result is that the unsolved problems of social development have combined with the resurgent traces of older, still unrequited, ethnic and religious nationalisms, allowing the tensions in these societies to resurface in a multi-cultural form.

It should be emphasized that this is no simple revival of archaic ethnicities, though such elements persist. Older traces are combined with new, emergent, forms of 'ethnicity', which are often a product of uneven globalization and failed modernization. This explosive mix selectively revalorizes older discourses, condensing in a lethal combination what Hobsbawm and Ranger (1993) called 'the invention of tradition' with what Michael Ignatieff (1994) has called (after Freud) 'the narcissism of minor differences'. (Serbian nationalism and ethnic cleansing in Bosnia and Kosovo are obvious examples.) Their reinvention of the past-in-the-present is reminiscent of the Janus-faced character of nationalist discourse (Nairn 1997). These revivalist movements remain deeply attached to the idea of 'the nation'.[6] They see the nation as an engine of modernization and a guarantor of a place in the new world system. at precisely the moment when globalization is bringing the nation-state-driven phase of capitalist modernity to a hesitant close.

The third factor is our old friend 'globalization'. Again, globalization is not new. European exploration, conquest and colonization were early forms of the same secular, historical process (Marx once called it 'the formation of the world market'). But since the 1970s, the process has assumed new forms while being, also, intensified (Held et al. 1999). Contemporary globalization is associated with the rise of new, deregulated financial markets, with global capital and currency flows large enough to destabilize medium-sized economies, transnational forms of production and consumption, the exponential growth of the new cultural industries powered by the new information technologies, and the rise of 'the knowledge economy'. Characteristic of this phase is time–space compression (Harvey 1989), which struggles, however incompletely, to cohere particular times, places, histories and markets within a homogeneous, 'global' space–time chronotope. It is also marked by the uneven disembedding of social relations and processes of de-traditionalization (Giddens 1999) which are not restricted to developing societies. Western societies can no more defend themselves against these effects than societies of the periphery.

This system is global, in the sense that its sphere of operations is planetary. Few places are beyond the reach of its destabilizing interdependencies. It has significantly weakened national sovereignty and eroded the 'reach' of the older western nation-states (the engines of earlier phases of globalization), without entirely displacing them. The system, however, is *not* global, if by that we understand that the process is uniform in character, impacts everywhere in the same way, operates without contradictory effects or produces equal outcomes across the globe. It remains a system of deep, indeed deepening, global inequalities and instabilities, of which no power – not even the USA, which is the most economically and militarily powerful nation on earth – is any longer completely in control.

Like the post-colonial, contemporary globalization is both novel and contradictory. Its economic, financial and cultural circuits are western-driven and US-dominated. Ideologically, it is governed by a global neo-liberalism which is fast becoming the common sense of the age (Fukayama 1992). Its dominant cultural tendency is homogenization. However, this is not the only trend. It has also had extensive *differentiating* effects within and between different societies. From this perspective, globalization is *not* a natural and inevitable process whose imperatives, like Fate, cannot be resisted or inflected, only obeyed.[7] Rather, it is a hegemonizing process, in the proper Gramscian sense. It is 'structured in dominance', but it cannot control or saturate everything within its orbit. Indeed, it produces as one of its unintended effects subaltern formations and emergent tendencies which it cannot control but must try to 'hegemonize' or harness to its wider purposes. It is a system for *con-forming difference*, rather than a convenient synonym for the obliteration of difference. This argument is critical if we are to take account of how and where resistances and counter-strategies are likely successfully to develop. This perspective entails a more discursive model of power in the new global environment than is common among the 'hyper-globalizers' (Held et al. 1999).

The Subaltern Proliferation of Difference

Alongside globalization's homogenizing tendencies, there is 'the subaltern proliferation of difference'. It is a paradox of contemporary globalization that, culturally, things appear to look more alike (a sort of Americanization of global culture, for example); however, at the same time, there is a proliferation of 'differences'. The 'vertical' of American cultural, economic, technological power seems to be constantly cross-cut and off-set by a set of lateral connections, producing the sense of a world composed of many 'local' differences, with which the 'global-vertical' is obliged to reckon (Hall 1991). In this model, the classic Enlightenment binary between Traditionalism and Modernity is displaced by a disseminated set of 'vernacular modernities'. Consider, for example, the way News International's effort to saturate India and China with the staple diet of western television

was forced into a tactical retreat. It could advance only through an 'indigen-
ization' of the local television industries which greatly complicates the
range of images offered locally and sets in motion the development of an
indigenous industry rooted in different cultural traditions. Some see this
as just a slower version of the westernization of Indian and Chinese culture
when exposed to the global market. Others see it as the way in which the
peoples in these areas try to enter 'modernity', acquire the fruits of its
technologies, and yet do so to some extent on their terms. In the global
context, the struggle here between 'local' and ' global' interests is not yet
finally resolved.

This is what, in another context, Derrida calls *différance:* 'the playing
movement that "produces ... these differences, these effects of difference'
(Derrida 1982).[8] This is *not* the binary form of difference, between what
is absolutely the same, and what is absolutely 'Other'. It is a 'weave'
of similarities and differences that refuse to separate into fixed binary
oppositions. *Différance* characterizes a system, where 'every concept [or
meaning] is inscribed in a chain or in a system within which it refers to
the other, to other concepts [meanings], by means of the systematic play
of differences' (Derrida 1972). Meaning here has no origin or final destination, cannot be finally fixed, is always *in process*, 'positional' along a
spectrum. Its political value cannot be essentialized, but only relationally
determined.

Strategies of *différance* are not able to inaugurate totally different forms
of life (they do not work with the notion of a totalizing dialectical 'overcoming'). They cannot conserve older, traditional ways of life intact. They
operate best in what Homi Bhabha calls 'the borderline time' of minorities
(Bhabha 1994). However, *différance* does prevent any system from stabil-
izing itself as a fully sutured totality. It arises in the gaps and aporias
which constitute potential sites of resistance, intervention and translation.
Within these interstices lies the possibility of a disseminated set of vernacular modernities. Culturally, these cannot frontally stem the tide of
westernizing techno-modernity. However, they continue to inflect, deflect
and 'translate' its imperatives from below.[9] They constitute the basis for a
new kind of 'localism' that is not self-sufficiently particular, but which
arises *within*, without being simply a simulacrum of, the global (Hall 1991).
This 'localism' is no mere residue of the past. It is something new –
globalization's accompanying shadow; what is left aside in globalization's
panoramic sweep, but returns to trouble and disturb globalization's cultural
settlements. It is globalization's 'constituitive outside' (Laclau and Mouffe
1985; Butler 1993). Here we find the 'return' of the particular and specific
– of the specifically different – at the centre of globalization's universalist,
panoptic aspiration to closure. 'The local' has no stable, trans-historical

character. It resists universalism's homogenizing sweep with different, conjunctural times. It has no fixed political inscription. It can be either progressive or regressive and fundamentalist – open or closed – in different contexts (Hall 1993b). Its political thrust is not determined by its essential content (usually caricatured as 'Tradition's resistance to modernity'), but by its articulation with other forces. It emerges at many sites, one of the most significant being that planned and unplanned, compelled and so-called 'free' migration, which has brought the margins to the centre, the multi-cultural disseminated 'particular' to the heart of the metropolitan western city. Only in such a context can we understand why what threatens to become the moment of the West's global closure – the apotheosis of its global universalizing mission – is *at the same time* the moment of the West's slow, uncertain, protracted de-centring.

The Margins in the Centre: the British Case

How has this untimely appearance of the margins in the centre – the heart of 'the multi-cultural question' – become what Barnor Hesse (see Introduction) calls 'a transruptive force' within the political and social institution of western states and societies?

The British case can be briefly put in place in relation to the wider argument. The national story assumes that Britain was a unified and homogeneous culture until the post-war migrations from the Caribbean and the Asian sub-continent. This is a highly simplistic version of a complex history (Hall 1999a, 1999b, 1999c, 1999d). Britain is not a sceptred isle which arose, fully formed and separate, as an integral nation-state, from the North Sea. Though 'assumed to be fixed and eternal', it was in fact constituted out of a series of conquests, invasions and settlements (Davis 1999). It was part of the European land-mass until the sixth century BC; dominated for centuries by the French; and integrally related to Europe until the Reformation. Britain has existed as a nation-state only since the eighteenth century, by virtue of the civil pact (rooted, in fact, in an Anglo-Saxon, Protestant ascendancy) that associated significantly different cultures – Scotland and Wales – with England. The Act of Union with Ireland (1801) which ended in Partition never succeeded in integrating the Irish people or the Celtic-Catholic element into the British imaginary. Indeed, Ireland has been Britain's earliest 'colony' and the Irish the first group to be systematically 'racialized'. The so-called homogeneity of 'Britishness' as a national culture has been considerably exaggerated. It was always contested by the Scots, Welsh and Irish; challenged by rival local and regional allegiances; and cross-cut by class, gender and generation. There have always been many different ways of being 'British'. Most national achievements – from free speech and a universal franchise to the welfare state and NHS – were won as bitter struggles between one kind of British person and another. Only retrospectively were these radical differences smoothly reintegrated into the seamless web of a transcendent 'Britishness'. Britain was also the centre of the largest *imperium* of modern times, governing a variety of different cultures. This imperial experience profoundly shaped British national identity and British ideas of greatness and its place in the world (C. Hall 1992). This more-or-less continuous intercourse with 'difference', which was at the heart of colonization, has framed the 'other' as a constitutive element of British identity.

There has been a 'black' presence in Britain since the sixteenth century, an Asian presence since the eighteenth. But the type and scale of migration into Britain from the non-white global periphery, which has seriously challenged the settled notion of British identity and posed 'the multi-cultural question', is a post-Second World War, post-colonial, phenomenon. Historically, it began with the arrival of the SS *Empire Windrush* in 1948, bringing returning Caribbean volunteer-servicement and the first civilian Caribbean migrants who left the depressed economies of the region in search of a better life. The flow was quickly reinforced from the Caribbean, then from the Asian sub-continent and Asians expelled from East Africa, together with Africans and others from the Third World, until the late 1970s when immigration legislation effectively closed the door.

The old relations of colonization, slavery and colonial rule, linking Britain with the empire for over 400 years, marked out the pathways which these migrants followed. But these historic relations of dependency and subordination were *reconfigured* – in the now-classic post-colonial way – when reconvened on domestic British soil. In the wake of decolonization, and masked by a collective amnesia about, and systematic disavowal of, 'empire' (which descended like a Cloud of Unknowing in the 1960s), this encounter was interpreted as 'a new beginning'. Most British people looked at these 'children of empire' as if they could not imagine where 'they' had come from, why, or what possible connection they could possibly have with Britain.

By and large migrants found poor housing and unskilled, poorly paid jobs in the cities and industrial regions, themselves recovering from the war, and affected by the steep decline in Britain's economic fortunes. Today, they and their offspring constitute about 7 per cent of the British popu-lation.[10] However, they already constitute 25 per cent of the London population, reflecting the selective density of settlement. They have been subjected to all the processes of social exclusion, racialized disadvantage, informal and institutionalized racism that are typical across western Europe today in the face of similar processes affecting France, Spain, Portugal,

Germany and Italy. Their post-war history has been marked by struggles against racialized disadvantage, confrontations with racist groups and the police, and institutional racism in those institutions and public authorities which differentially manage and distribute the support systems on which migrant communities are heavily dependent. In broad terms, the majority are clustered at the lower end of the social deprivation spectrum, characterized by high relative levels of poverty, unemployment and educational underachievement. In 1991, less than two-thirds of the men and under half of the women of working age were actually in work.

However, their social and economic positioning has become markedly more differentiated over time (Modood et al. 1997) Some Indians, East African Asians and the Chinese, despite being highly qualified, are experiencing the 'glass ceiling' of blocked promotion at the upper levels of the professional ladder. The Pakistani communities are considerably active, entrepreneurially, in the small business sector. Nevertheless, a few Asian millionaires cannot disguise the fact that some Indian and many Pakistani families still live in serious household poverty. Bangladeshis are on average four times more 'deprived' than any other identifiable group. Gender differences play a critical role. Young Afro-Caribbean men are seriously vulnerable to unemployment and educational underachievement, and are over-represented in school exclusions, stop-and-search arrests and the prison population. Afro-Caribbean women, however, now have higher job mobility and earnings rates than their white counterparts. The picture is no longer one of uniform deprivation, though socio-economic disadvantage continues to be extensive.

What kinds of 'community' have they formed? How unified and homogeneous are their cultures? What is their relationship to so-called 'mainstream' society? What strategies are appropriate to their fuller integration within mainstream British society?

The term 'community' (as in 'ethnic minority communities') accurately reflects the strong sense of group identity found among these groups. However, it can be dangerously misleading. The model is an idealization of the face-to-face relationships of the one-class village, connoting homogeneous groups with strong, binding, internal ties and very clear boundaries separating them from the outside world. So-called 'ethnic minorities' have indeed formed strongly marked, cultural communities, and maintain in everyday life, especially in familial and domestic contexts, distinctive social customs and practices. There are continuing links with their places of origin. This is especially the case in the densely settled areas, such as Afro-Caribbean communities in Brixton, Peckham and Tottenham, in Manchester's Moss Side, Liverpool and Handsworth; or Asian communities in places like Southall, Tower Hamlets, Birmingham's Balsall Heath, Bradford and Leeds. But there are also differences which refuse to be consolidated. Caribbeans from the different islands come from quite distinctive racial and ethnic mixes, though they all tend (wrongly) to be seen as 'Jamaican'. Asians are also lumped together as a single group. However, 'Despite sharing some cultural traits in common … [Asians] belong to different ethnic, religious and linguistic groups and bring with them different fears and historical memories' (Parekh 1999). All these communities are ethnically and racially mixed, with substantial white populations. None is a racially- or ethnically-segregated ghetto. They are significantly less segregated than, say, non-white minorities are in many US cities. As with the white popula- tion, class and gender are highly significant in determining differential positioning across British society (Brah 1996; Yuval-Davis 1997; Phoenix 1998). A more accurate picture would have to begin with the lived complexity emerging in these diaspora communities, where so-called 'tradi- tional' ways of life derived from the cultures of origin remain important to community self-definitions, but consistently operate alongside extensive daily interaction at every level, with British mainstream social life.

Maintaining racialized, ethno-cultural and religious identities is clearly important to self-understanding in these communities. 'Blackness' is as critical to third-generation Afro-Caribbeans identity[11] as the Hindu or Muslim faiths are to some second-generation Asians. But these are certainly not communities immured in an unchanging Tradition. As in most di- asporas, traditions are variable from person to person, and even within persons, and are constantly being revised and transformed in response to the migration experience. There is very considerable variation, both of commitment and of practice, between and within different communities – between different nationalities and linguistic groups, within religious faiths, between men and women, and across the generations. Young people from all the communities express some continuing allegiance to their 'traditions', alongside a visible decline in actual practice. Identities declare not some primordial identity but rather a positional choice of the group with which they wish to be associated. Identity choices are more political than anthropological, more 'associational', less ascribed (Modood et al. 1997).

Generalizations are therefore extremely difficult to make in the face of this multi-cultural complexity. Bhikhu Parekh, an acute observer, adopts a *strong* definition of 'ethnic communities': 'the Asian and Afro-Caribbean communities are ethnic in nature, that is, physically distinguishable, bonded by social ties arising out of shared customs, language and practice of inter- marriage, and having their distinct history, collective memories, geographical origins, views of life and modes of social organization.' Nevertheless, he recognizes that:

> Contrary to popular impression, great changes are afoot within ethnic com-
> munities and every family has become a terrain of subdued or explosive
> struggles. In every family, husband and wife, parents and children, brothers
> and sisters are having to re-negotiate and re-define their patterns of relation-
> ship in a manner that takes account both of their traditional values and
> those characteristic of their adopted country. Different families reach their
> own inherently tentative conclusions. (Parekh 1991)

It is therefore a fundamental error to mistake their diasporic ways of
life as simply in slow transition to full assimilation (an idea quietly and
decisively laid to rest, in Britain at least, in the 1970s). They represent a
novel cultural configuration – 'cosmopolitan communities' – marked by
extensive trans-culturation (Pratt 1992). In turn, they have had a massive,
pluralizing impact on public and private social life in Britain, transforming
many British cities into multi-cultural metropolises. They were the 'cool'
in that transient New Labour phenomenon, 'Cool Britannia'. One sign
that they have outrun the common-sense categories is that they are simultaneously invoked as representing that 'sense of community' that liberal
society is supposed to have lost, and as the most advanced signifers of the
urban postmodern metropolitan experience!

Readers may want to quarrel with the detail of the process as described
(which is, of necessity, generalized and abstract). However, unless the
fundamental picture is substantively challenged, it is worth reflecting on
the enormous dis- or (as Barnor Hesse puts it in his Introduction) 'transruptive' consequences for a political strategy or approach to the multi-
cultural question which these developments pose. The rest of this chapter
is concerned with tracing through some of these trans-ruptive effects.

Disrupting the Language of 'Race' and Ethnicity

The first of these is the transruptive impact on the traditional categories
of 'race' and ethnicity. The emergence of the multi-cultural question has
produced a differentiated 'racialization' of central areas of British life and
culture.[12] Increasingly, the British have been obliged to think of themselves
and their relations with others within the UK in racialized terms. Ethnicity,
too, has entered the British domestic vocabulary. Whereas in the American
self-understanding the USA is a society composed of ethnicities, Britain
(though in origins quite diverse) has always applied the term to everyone
else – Britishness being the empty signifier, the norm, against which 'difference' (ethnicity) is measured. The rising visibility of ethnic communities
together with the movement towards devolved government have posed
questions about the 'homogeneity' of British culture and 'Englishness' as

an ethnicity, precipitating the multi-cultural question at the centre of a crisis of national identity.

Of course, Britishness as a category has always been racialized through and through – when has it connoted anything but 'whiteness'? But this fact has been carefully segregated from the national discourse, popular and scholarly. 'Race' has struggled to be seriously acknowledged in mainstream political theory, journalistic or scholarly thinking.[13] This silencing is breaking down as these terms force their way into public consciousness. Their growing visibility is, inevitably, a fraught and difficult process. What is more, this is now 'race' in quotation marks, 'race' under erasure, 'race' in a new configuration with ethnicity. This epistemic shift is one of the multi-cultural's most transruptive effects.

Of the two largest non-white post-migration communities in Britain, 'race' is usually applied to Afro-Caribbeans, 'ethnicity' to Asians. In fact, these terms map only very roughly on to these actual communities. 'Race' makes sense of Afro-Caribbean experience because of the significance of skin colour, a biologically derived idea. In fact, the colour spectrum among Afro-Caribbeans is extremely wide – the result of the extensive miscegenation of Caribbean plantation society and centuries of 'trans-culturation' (Ortiz 1940; Brathwaite 1971; Glissant 1981; Pratt 1992). Asians are not a 'race' at all, nor indeed a single 'ethnicity'. Nationality is often as important as ethnicity. However, Indians, Pakistanis, Bangladeshis, Sri Lankans, Ugandans, Kenyans, the Chinese are all cross-cut by regional, urban/ rural, cultural, ethnic and religious differences.

Conceptually, 'race' is not a scientific category. The differences attributable to 'race' within a population are as great as that between racially defined populations. 'Race' is a political and social construct. It is the organizing discursive category around which has been constructed a system of socio-economic power, exploitation and exclusion – i.e. racism. However, as a discursive practice, racism has its own 'logic' (Hall 1990). It claims to ground the social and cultural differences which legitimate racialized exclusion in genetic and biological differences: i.e. in Nature. This 'natualizing effect' appears to make racial difference a fixed, scientific 'fact', unresponsive to change or reformist social engineering. This discursive reference to Nature is something which anti-black racism shares with anti-Semitism and sexism (where, too, 'biology is destiny), though less with class. The problem is that the genetic level is not immediately visible. Hence, in this type of discourse, genetic differences (supposed to be hidden in the gene structure) are 'materialized' and can be 'read off' in easily recognizable, visible signifiers such as skin colour, physical characteristics of hair, features (e.g. the Jewish hooked nose), body-type etc., enabling them to function as closure mechanisms in everyday situations.[14]

'Ethnicity', by contrast, generates a discourse where difference is grounded in *cultural and religious* features. It is often, on these grounds, counter-posed to 'race'. But this binary opposition can be too simplistically drawn. Biological racism privileges markers like skin colour, but those signifiers have always also been used, by discursive extension, to connote social and cultural differences. 'Blackness' has functioned as a sign that people of African descent are closer to Nature, and *therefore* more likely to be lazy, indolent, lacking the higher intellectual faculties, driven by emotion and feeling rather than Reason, over-sexualized, with low self-control and prone to violence, etc. Correspondingly, those who are stigmatized on ethnic grounds, because they are 'culturally different' and therefore inferior, are often *also* characterized as physically different in significant ways (though not perhaps as visibly as blacks), underpinned by sexual sterotypes (blacks being over-masculinized, Orientals feminized). The biological referent is therefore never wholly absent from discourses of ethnicity, though it is more indirect. The more 'ethnicity' matters, the more its characteristics are represented as relatively fixed, inherent within a group, transmitted from generation to generation, not just by culture and education, but by biological inheritance, stabilized above all by kinship and endogamous marriage rules that ensure that the ethnic group remains genetically, and therefore culturally, 'pure'. Ethnicity is underpinned by characteristics which are 'physically distinguishable ... arising out of ... [the] practice of inter-marriage' (Parekh 1991). In short, the articulation of difference with Nature (biology and the genetic) is present, but displaced *through kinship and inter-marriage*.

Both the discourses of 'race' and 'ethnicity', then, work by establishing a discursive articulation or 'chain of equivalences' (Laclau and Mouffe 1985) between the social/cultural and the biological registers that allows differences in one signifying system to be 'read off' against equivalents in the other chain (Hall 1990). Biological racism and cultural differentialism, therefore, constitute not two different systems, but racism's two registers. In most situations, the discourses of biological and cultural difference are simultaneously in play. In anti-Semitism, Jews were multiply racialized on biological, cultural and religious grounds. As Wieviorka argues, racism exists 'where there is an association of these two main strategies, whose unique combination depends on the specificities of experience, the historical moment and individual preference' (Wieviorka 1995). It seems therefore more appropriate to speak, not of 'racism' *vs* 'cultural difference', but of racism's 'two logics'.[15]

There seem to be three reasons for the current conceptual confusion. The first is empirical. Afro-Caribbean migrants – viewed largely in racialized terms – arrived in Britain earlier. Asians, characterized by religious and cultural difference, arrived and became visible as a so-called 'problem' later. In the 1970s, anti-racist struggles by both groups tended to cluster under the affirmative identity of 'black', defined by their shared racialized difference from white society. However, one unintended effect was to privilege the Afro-Caribbean experience over that experienced by Asians. As the salience of what Taylor (1994) has called 'the politics of recognition' has grown, stressing the right to cultural difference, so the two trajectories have become more separate. 'Black' has become descriptively normalized for people of African descent and Asians have tended to revert to ethnically-specific terms of identification. Hence the anomalous current description 'black and Asian', which combines 'race' and 'ethnicity'. Second, there are many more situations in the world where ethnicity rather than 'race' has provided the focus of violent exclusionary conflict (e.g. Indonesia, Sri-Lanka, Rwanda, Bosnia and Kosovo). Third, there has been a significant rise in discrimination and exclusion either based on religion or with a strong religious component (Richardson 1999), in particular against Muslim communities, related to the worldwide politicization of Islam. Some writers feel that a multiculturalism focused on biological racism rather than cultural differentialism ignores this religious dimension (e.g. Modood et al. 1997).

In the 1980s some commentators observed a decline in biologically based racism and a rise in 'the new cultural racism' (Barker 1981). Modood indeed speaks of an 'effacing of colour racism' and a 'reinforcing [of] cultural racism at a micro-level' in Britain. It is not clear that current developments bear this zero-sum account out empirically (racist attacks on Asian families and violent assaults in the street on black youths continue apace) or that it is particularly helpful to trade one against the other in this either/or way. What seems more appropriate is an expanded conception of racism that acknowledges the way in which, in its discursive structure, biological racism and cultural differentialism are articulated and combine. These two 'logics' are always present, though in different combinations and differently foregrounded in different contexts and in relation to different subject populations. Of course, the actual histories of racialized and ethnicized closure are very different in different places (e.g. the USA and the UK), emerge at different moments and in different forms, and have very different political and social effects. They should not be homogenized. However, the conflation of biological and culturally inferiorizing discourses seems to be a defining characteristic of 'the multi-cultural moment'.[16]

Given the way 'black' – originally a negative epithet – has become a term of positive cultural identitification (Bonnett 1999), we may speak here of the 'ethnicization' of 'race'.[17] At the same time, cultural difference has taken on a more violent, politicized and oppositional meaning – which we might think of as the 'racialization' of ethnicity (e.g. 'ethnic cleansing'). The consequence is to place on the agenda of a British multiculturalism two related but different political demands which have hitherto been considered mutually exclusive: the demand (against a differentiated racism) for social equality and racial justice; and the demand (against a universalizing ethnocentrism) for the recognition of cultural difference. We return to the political significance of this double demand below.

Unsettling 'Culture'

The second transruptive effect is that which 'the multicultural question' has on our understanding of culture. The binary opposition derived from the Enlightenment – Particularism *vs* Universalism, or Tradition *vs* Modernity – produces a certain way of understanding culture. There are the distinctive, homogeneous, self-contained, strongly bounded cultures of so-called traditional societies. In this anthropological definition, cultural tradition saturates whole communities, subordinating individuals to a communally-sanctioned form of life. This is counter-posed to the 'culture of modernity' – open, rational, universalist and individualistic. In the latter, particular cultural attachments must be set aside in public life – always trumped by the neutrality of the civic state – so that the the individual is formally free to write his/her own script. These characteristics are held to be fixed by the essentialized content of each. The idea that liberal society could act in a 'fundamentalist' way or that the 'traditionalism' of, say, Islam could combine with modern ways of life appears to be a contradiction in terms. Tradition is represented as set in stone.[18]

However, since the inception of the global 'project' of the West at the end of the fifteenth century, this Tradition/Modernity binary has been progressively undermined. Colonized traditional cultures remained distinctive; but they inevitably became 'conscripts of modernity'.[19] They may be more strongly bounded than so-called modern societies, but they are no longer (if ever they were) organic, fixed, self-sustaining, self-sufficient entities. As a result of globalization in its longer, historical sense, they have become more 'hybrid' formations. Tradition functions less as doctrine than as *repertoires of meaning*. Increasingly, individuals draw upon these frameworks and the attachments they inscribe to help them to make sense of the world, without being rigorously bound by and into them in every detail of existence.[20] They have become part of a larger dialogical relation to the other. Pre-colonial cultures were, to very different degrees, progressively *convened*, globally under the rubric of western capitalist modernity and the imperial system without their distinctiveness being wholly erased. This left them (as C. L. R. James once remarked of the Caribbean) 'in but not

of Europe'. As Aijaz Ahmad (no natural ally of the hybridizing intel-
ligentsia) has observed: 'the cross fertilization of cultures has been endemic
to all movements of people ... and all such movements in history have
involved travel, contact, transmutation, hybridization of ideas, values and
behavioural norms' (Ahmad 1995).

One term which has been used to characterize the increasingly mixed
and diasporic cultures of such societies communities is 'hybridity'. Its
meaning, however, has been widely misunderstood.[21] Hybridity is not a
reference to the mixed racial composition of populations. It is really another
term for the cultural logic of *translation*. This logic is increasingly evident
in the multi-cultural diasporas and other mixed and minority communities
of the post-colonial world. New and old diasporas governed by this
ambivalent, inside/outside position are to be found everywhere. It defines
the combined and uneven cultural logic of the way so-called western
'modernity' has impacted on the rest of the world ever since the onset of
Europe's globalizing project (Hall 1996a).

Hybridity does *not* refer to hybrid individuals, who can be contrasted
as fully-formed subjects with 'traditionals' and 'moderns'. It is a process
of cultural translation, which is agonistic because it is never completed,
but rests with its undecidability. It

is not simply appropriation or adaptation; it is a process through which
cultures are required to revise their own systems of reference, norms and
values by departing from their habitual or 'inbred' rules of transformation.
Ambivalence and antagonism accompany any act of cultural translation
because negotiating with the 'difference of the other' reveals the radical
insufficiency of our own systems of meaning and signification. (Bhabha
1997)

In its many variants, 'tradition' and 'translation' are variously combined
(Robbins 1991). It is not simply celebratory, because it has deep and
disabling 'costs' deriving from its multiple forms of dislocation and habita-
tion (Clifford 1997). As Homi Bhabha has suggested, it signifies an

ambiguous, anxious moment of ... transition, that nervously accompanies
any mode of social transformation [which is] without the promise of celebratory closure or transcendance of the complex, even conflictual conditions
that attend the process ... [It] insists on displaying ... the dissonances that
have to be crossed despite the proximate relations; the disjunctions of power
or position that have to be contested; the values, ethical and aesthetic, that
have to be 'translated' but will not seamlessly transcend the process of
transfer. (Bhabha 1997).

However, it is also often 'how newness enters the world' (Rushdie 1991).

The idea of culture embedded in 'ethnic minority communities' does not reference a fixed relation between Tradition and Modernity. It neither remains within one boundary, nor transcends boundaries. In practice it refuses those binaries.[22] *Necessarily*, its notion of 'community' covers a wide variety of actual practices. Some individuals remain deeply committed to traditional practices and values (though rarely without a diasporic inflection). For others, so-called traditional identifications have been transformed by being intensified (e.g. by hostility from the 'host' community, racism, or by changing world conditions, such as the rising salience of Islam). For others, still, hybridization is far advanced, but rarely in any assimilationist sense. This is a radically dislocated, and more complex, picture of culture and community than is inscribed in the conventional sociological or anthropological literature. 'Hybridity' marks the place of this incommensurability.

In diasporic conditions people are often obliged to adopt shifting, multiple or hyphenated positions of identification. About two-thirds of those from minority communities asked in the *Fourth National Survey of Ethnic Minorities* whether they thought of themselves as 'British' agreed, though they also felt that, for example, being British and Pakistani did not compete strongly in their minds (Modood et al. 1997). Black-and-British or British-Asian are increasingly identities the young are willing to answer to. Some women, who believe that their communities have a right to have their differences respected, do not wish their lives as women, their rights to education or their marital choices to be governed by norms which are communally regulated and policed. Even where the more traditionally oriented sections are concerned, the principle of *heterogeneity* continues to be strongly operative. In our terms, then, the besuited Asian chartered accountant vividly invoked by Modood (1998), who lives in suburbia, sends his children to private school and reads *Readers Digest* and the *Bhagavad-Gita*, or the black teenager who is a dance-hall DJ, plays jungle music but supports Manchester United or the Muslim student who wears baggy, hip-hop, street-style jeans but is never absent from Friday prayers, are *all*, in their different ways, 'hybridized'. Were they to return to their villages of origin, the most traditional would be regarded as 'westernized', if not as hopelessly diaspora-ized. They are all negotiating culturally somewhere along the spectrum of *différance*, in which disjunctures of time, generation, spatialization and dissemination refuse to be neatly aligned.

Unsettling the Foundations of the Liberal-Constitutional State

A third transruptive effect of 'the multi-cultural question', is its challenge to the dominant discourses of western political theory and the foundations of the liberal state. In the face of the dissemination of unstable differences, the settled argument between liberals and communitarians, which now dominates the western political tradition, has been seriously disturbed.

The post-Enlightenment, liberal, rational, humanist universalism of western culture looks, not less historically significant but, less *universal* by the minute. Many great ideas – liberty, equality, autonomy, democracy – have been honed within the liberal tradition. However, it is now clear that liberalism is not the 'culture that is beyond cultures' but the culture that won: that particularism which successfully universalized and hegemonized itself across the globe. Its triumph in virtually setting the limits to the domain of 'the political' was not, in retrospect, the result of a disinterested mass conversion to the Rule of Universal Reason, but something closer to a more earthy, Foucauldean, power-knowledge sort of 'game'. There have been theoretical critiques of the 'dark' sides of the Enlightenment project before, but it is 'the multi-cultural question' which has most effectively blown its contemporary cover.

Universal citizenship and the cultural neutrality of the state are two cornerstones of western liberal-universalism. Of course, citizenship rights have never been universally applicable, either to African-Americans at the hands of the Founding Fathers or to colonial subjects at the dispensation of imperial rule. This gap between ideal and practice, between formal and substantive equality, negative and positive freedom, has haunted liberalism's conception of citizenship from its inception. As to the cultural neutrality of the liberal state, its achievements are not to be lightly discarded. Religious toleration, free speech, the rule of law, formal equality and procedural legality, a universal franchise – though seriously contested – are positive achievements. However, the neutrality of the state works only when a broad cultural homogeneity among the governed can be assumed. This assumption has indeed underpinned western liberal democracies until recently. Under the new multi-cultural conditions, however, this premise seems less and less valid.

The claim is that the liberal state has sloughed off its ethnic-particularistic skin and emerged in its culturally cleansed, universalistic, civic form. Britain, however, like all civic nationalisms, is not only a sovereign political and territorial entity but also 'an imagined community'. It is the latter which is the focus of identification and belongingness. The discourses of the nation do not, as we are led to suppose, reflect an already achieved unified state. Their purpose is, rather, to forge or construct a unified form of identification out of the many differences of class, gender, region, religion and locality which actually cross-cut the nation (Hall 1992; Bhabha 1990) To achieve this, these discourses must deeply embed and enmesh the so-called culture-free 'civic' state in a dense entanglement of cultural meanings, traditions and values which come to stand for or represent the nation. It is only *within* culture and representation that identification with this 'imagined 'community' can be constructed at all .

All so-called modern, liberal nation-states thus combine the so-called rational, reflective, civic form of allegiance to the state with a so-called intuitive, instinctual, ethnic or allegiance to the nation. That heterogeneous formation, 'Britishness' grounds the United Kingdom, the political entity, as an 'imagined community' . As that great patriot Enoch Powell observed: 'the life of nations, no less than of men [sic], is lived largely in the mind.' Britain's rational and constitutional foundations are given lived meaning and texture through a system of representation. They are grounded in the customs, habits and rituals of everyday life, the social codes and conventions, the dominant versions of masculinity and feminity, the socially-constructed memory of national triumphs and disasters, the imagery, imagined landscapes and distinctive national characteristics which produce the idea of Britain. These aspects are no less important because many of them are 'invented' (Hobsbawm and Ranger 1993). Though the nation constantly reinvents itself as an on-going process, it is represented as something which has existed from the origins of time (See Davis 1999). Of course, it does not follow that because the 'universal' state is grounded in very distinct cultural particularities, the state is nothing but a playground for rival definitions of the good. What, however, can no longer be sustained in the face of 'the multi-cultural question', is the binary contrast between the particularism of 'their' demands for the recognition of difference versus the universalism of 'our' civic rationality.[23]

In fact, the so-called homogeneity of British culture has been massively overstated. There have always been very different ways of 'being British'. Britain was always cross-cut by deep cleavages around gender, class and region. Serious differences in material and cultural power between the different 'kingdoms' of the UK were masked by the hegemony of the English over the rest and 'Englishness' over 'Britishness'. The Irish never properly belonged. The poor have always been excluded. The mass of the people were not enfranchised until the beginning of the twentieth century. To this we must add the growing cultural diversity of British social life itself. The effects of globalization, the decline of Britain's economic fortunes and world position, the end of empire, the rising pressures to devolve government and power, the growth of internal nationalisms, local and regional sentiment, and the challenge of Europe have all unsettled the so-called homogeneity of Britishness, producing a major internal crisis of national identity. There is also the astonishing pace of social pluralism and economic and techological change that have undermined the older class and gender settlements, made British society a less predictable place, and are the sources of a massive internal diversification of social life.[24] Today, it would be difficult to find a significant national consensus around any of the critical social issues about which there are deep differences of opinion and lived experience. People belong to many different, overlapping, 'communities' which sometimes exert contrary pulls. Britain is 'a multi-culturally diverse' society, long before one begins to consider the impact of post-migration multi-ethnic communities. Indeed, it sometimes appears as if the latter are the symbolic bearers of a complex pattern of change, diversification and 'loss' for which they are only the most convenient scapegoats.

The multi-cultural question has also helped to deconstruct some of the other incoherences of the liberal-constitutional state. The 'neutrality' of the liberal state (i.e. the fact that it is represented as pursuing in the *public* realm no particular notion of 'the good') is said to secure the personal autonomy and liberty of the individual to pursue his/her own conception of 'the good', provided it is done *in private*. The ethically neutral legal order of the liberal state thus depends on the strict separation between the public and private spheres. This is harder and harder to deliver in a stable form. The law and politics increasingly intervene in the so-called private realm. Public judgements draw their justification from the private realm. Post-feminism, we understand better how the sexual contract underpins the social contract. Domains like the family, sexuality, health, food, dress, which used to belong quintessentially to the private, have become part of an expanded public and political realm of contestation. The easy dis-tinctions between the public and the domestic spheres is no longer tenable, especially since the massive entry of women, and the 'privatized' activities which used to be associated with that sphere. Everywhere, 'the personal' has become 'the political'.

What Michael Walzer famously called 'Liberalism 1' constitutes one of the great discursive systems of the modern world, in recent years making virtually a clean sweep of political theory. Only a thin definition of culture and a highly attenuated notion of collective rights are compatible with the individualist emphasis at the centre of this market-liberal conception.[25] It does not recognize the degree to which the individual is what Taylor (1994) calls 'dialogic' – not in the binary sense of dialogue between two already constituted subjects, but in the sense of its relation to the other being fundamentally constitutive of the subject, which can position itself as an 'identity' only in relation to what it lacks – its other, its 'constitutive outside' (Lacan 1977; Laclau and Mouffe 1985; Butler 1993). The meaning-ful individual life is always embedded in cultural contexts within which alone its 'free choices' make sense.

From a normative point of view, the integrity of the individual legal person cannot be guaranteed without protecting the inter-subjectively shared experiences and life-contexts in which the person has been socialized and formed his or her identity. The identity of the individual is interwoven with collective identities and can be stabilized only in a cultural network that cannot be appropriated as private property, any more than the mother tongue itself can. Hence the individual remains the bearer of 'rights to cultural membership'. (Habermas 1994)

In practice, under the pressure of multi-cultural difference, some western constitutional states like Britain have been obliged to move to what Walzer calls 'Liberalism 2', or what in a less constricted vocabulary in Europe would be called a 'social democratic' reformist programme.[26] The state has formally recognized and reflects publicly the differentiated social needs and growing cultural diversity of its citizens, acknowledging some group rights as well as individually defined rights. It has had to develop redistributive public support strategies (e.g. affirmative action programmes, equal opportunities legislation, publicly funded compensatory grants and a welfare state for deprived groups, etc.), even to ensure the 'level playing field' so beloved by formal liberalism. It has adopted into law some alternative definitions of 'the good life' and legalized certain 'exceptions' on essentially cultural grounds. For example, in recognizing the right of Sikhs to wear turbans without suspending the obligations of employers under health-and-safety regulations, or by accepting consensual arranged marriages as legal but declaring the imposition of an arranged marriage on a non-consenting woman to be coercive and thus illegal, British law has gone in practice some way to striking a balance between *cultural pluralism* defined in relation to communities and *liberal conceptions* of the liberty of the individual subject.[27] In Britain, however, this move has so far been piecemeal and, since the New Labour erosion of the commitment to the welfare state, uncertain: a haphazard response to the growing visibility and presence of the ethnicized communities at the heart of British life. It has constituted a species of 'multi-cultural drift' (Hall 1999a).

Beyond the Existing Political Vocabularies

What would be required for this 'drift' to become a sustained movement, a concerted effort of political will? To put it another way, what are the premises behind a radically distinctive form of British multiculturalism? It would need to be grounded not in some abstract notion of nation and community, but in the analysis of what 'community' actually means and how the different communities which now compose the nation actually interact on the ground. In addressing the sources of disadvantage, it would have to reflect what we have called 'racism's two registers' – the inter-dependence of biological racism and cultural differentialism. The commit-ment to expose and confront racism in any of its forms would have to become a positive objective of, and a statutory obligation on, government, on which its claims to representative legitimacy would be seen to depend. It would have to address the double political demand that arises from this interplay between the gross inequalities and injustices arising from the absence of substantive equality and justice, and exclusion and inferiorization arising from the lack of recognition and insensitivity to difference. Finally, rather than a strategy for improving the lot of the so-called 'ethnic' or racialized minorities alone, it would have to be a strategy which broke with that majoritarian logic and attempted to reconfigure or reimagine the nation as a whole in a radical post-national form (Hall 1999b).

The double demand for equality and difference appears to outrun our existing political vocabularies. Liberalism has consistently failed to come to terms with cultural difference or to deliver equality and justice for minority citizens. By contrast, communitarians argue that, since the self cannot be independent of its ends, the conceptions of 'the good life' embedded in communities should take precedence over the individual. Cultural pluralists ground this idea in a very strong definition of community: 'distinct cultures which embody concepts charged with historical memories and associations … which shape their understandings and approach to the world and constitute cultures of distinct and cohesive communities' (Parekh 1991).

As we have tried to show, ethnic minority communities are not integrated collective actors, such as would allow them to become the legal subjects of all-encompassing community rights. The temptation to essentialize 'com-munity' has to be resisted – it is a fantasy of plenitude in circumstances of imagined loss. Migrant communities bear the imprint of diaspora, 'hybridization' and *différance* in their very constitution. Their vertical integration into their traditions of origin exist side-by-side with their lateral linkages to other 'communities' of interest, practice and aspiration, real and symbolic. Individual members, especially the younger generations, experience the contradictory pulls which these different forces exert. Many are making their own, negotiated 'settlements' within and outside their communities. Women who respect the traditions of their communities feel free to challenge their patriarchal character and the sexism with which their authority is sometimes exercised. Some are happy to conform. Others, while unwilling to trade identities, insist on their individual right to consent, where there is no consent, on the 'right to exit' and the support of the law and other social agencies to make the exercise of that right practically effective.[28] The same is true of political and religious dissent.

In making the move towards greater cultural diversity at the heart of modernity, therefore, we must have a care lest we simply reverse into new forms of ethnic closure. We should remember that 'ethnicity', with its naturalized relationship to 'community', is another term operating 'under erasure'. We all locate ourselves in cultural vocabularies and without them we are incapable of enunciation as cultural subjects. We all come from and speak from 'somewhere'; we are located – and in that sense even the most 'modern' bear the traces of an 'ethnicity' . As Laclau paraphrases Derrida, we can only think 'within a tradition'. However, he reminds us that this is possible only 'if one conceives one's relation to that past as a critical reception' (Laclau 1996). Cosmopolitan critics are right to remind us that in late-modernity, we tend to draw on the fragmented traces and broken repertoires of several cultural and ethical languages. It is not a denial of culture to insist that 'the social world [does not] divide up neatly into distinct particular cultures, one to every community, [nor] that what every-one needs is just *one* of those entities -- a single, coherent culture – to give shape and meaning to … life' (Waldron 1992). We often operate with too simplistic a conception of 'belonging'. Sometimes we are most 'spoken' by our attachments when we struggle to be free of them, quarrel with, criticize or dissent radically from them. Like parental relationships, cultural tradi-tions shape us *both* when they nurture and sustain us *and* when we have to break irrevocably with them in order to survive. And beyond – though we don't always recognize it – there are always the 'attachments' we have to those who share our world with us but who are different from us. The pure assertion of difference is viable only in a rigidly segregated society. Its ultimate logic is that of *apartheid*.

Must personal liberty and individual choice, then, in the end, trump every particularity in modern societies, as liberalism always claimed? Not necessarily. The right to live one's life 'from within', which is at the heart of a modern conception of individuality, was indeed honed and developed within the western liberal tradition. But it is no longer a value restricted to the West, in part because the forms of life in which it developed are no longer exclusively 'western'. It has become a cosmopolitan value and, in the form of the discourse of human rights, is as pertinent to Third World workers struggling at the periphery of the global system, women in the developing world up against patriarchal conceptions of a woman's role, or political dissenters subject to the threat of torture, as it is to western consumers in the weightless economy. In that sense, paradoxically, cultural belongingness (ethnicity) is something, in its very specificity, of which everyone partakes. It is a universal particular, a 'concrete universal'.

Another way of putting the point would be to note that, by definition, a multi-cultural society always involves more than one group. There has to be some framework in which serious conflicts of outlook, belief and interest can be negotiated, and this cannot be simply the framework of one group writ large, which was the problem with Eurocentric assimilationism. The specific and particular 'difference' of a group or community cannot be asserted absolutely, without regard to the wider context provided by all those 'others' in relation to whom 'particularity' acquires a relative value. Philosophically, the logic of *différance* means that the meaning/identity of every concept is constituted in relation to all the other concepts in the system, in terms of which alone it signifies. A particular cultural identity cannot be defined only by its positive presence and content. All identity terms depend on marking their limits – defining what they are in relation to what they are not. As Laclau argues: 'I cannot assert a differential identity without distinguishing it from a context, and in the process of making the distinction, I am asserting the context at the same time' (Laclau 1996). Identities, then, are constructed within power relations (Foucault 1986). Every identity is founded on an exclusion and, in that sense, is an 'effect of power'. There must be something which is external to an identity (Laclau and Mouffe 1985; Butler 1993). That 'outside' is constituted by all the other terms of the system, whose 'absence' or lack is constituitive of its 'presence' (Hall 1996b). 'I am a subject precisely because I cannot be an absolute consciousness, because something constitutively alien confronts me.' Each particular identity, then, is *radically insufficient* in terms of its 'others'. 'This means that the universal is part of my identity as far as I am penetrated by a constitutive lack' (Laclau 1996).[29]

The problem is that this argument seems to provide an alibi for the surreptitious return by the back door of the old liberal universalism. However, as Laclau notes: 'European imperialist expansion had to be presented in terms of a universalizing civilizing function, modernization and so forth. The resistances of other cultures were ... presented not as struggles between particular identities and cultures, but as part of an all-embracing and epochal struggle between universality and particularisms' (Laclau 1996). In short, western particularism was rewritten as a global universalism.

In this paradigm, then, universalism is opposed at every point to particularity and difference. However, if the 'other' in fact is part of the difference we are asserting (the absence that allows a presence to signify), then any generalized claim which includes the 'other' does not come from outer space but arises from *within the particular*. 'The universal emerges out of the particular, not as some principle underlying and explaining the particular but as an incomplete horizon suturing a dislocated particular identity' (Laclau 1996). Why incomplete? Because it cannot – as it is in the liberal conception – be filled by a specific and unchanging content. It will be redefined whenever a particular identity, in taking account of its others and its own radical insufficiency, expands the horizon within which the demands of all can and must be negotiated. Laclau is right to insist that its content cannot be known in advance – in this sense the universal is an empty sign, an 'always receding signifier'. It is that horizon to which every particular difference must orient itself if it is not to fall back into absolute difference (which, of course, is the antithesis of a multi-cultural society). What we said about the generalizing across cultures of the individual's wish to live his/her life 'from within' is an example of this process. A demand, arising from within a particular culture, is expanded and its link with the originating culture transformed as it is obliged to negotiate its meaning with other traditions within a wider 'horizon' which now includes them both.

How then can the particular and the universal, the claims of both difference and equality, be recognized? This is the dilemma, the conundrum – the multi-cultural question – at the heart of the multi-cultural's trans-ruptive and reconfigurative impact. It requires us to think beyond the traditional boundaries of the existing political discourses and their ever-ready 'solutions'. It suggests that we have to put our minds seriously not to reiterating the sterile arguments between liberals and communitarians, but to some new and novel ways of *combining* difference and identity, drawing together on the same terrain those formal incommensurables of political vocabularies – liberty and equality *with* difference, 'the good' *and* 'the right'.

Formally, this antagonism may not be amenable to resolution in the abstract; but it can be negotiated in practice. A process of final political adjudication between rival definitions of 'the good' would be inimical to the whole multi-cultural project, since its effect would be to constitute every political space as a 'war of manoeuvre' between entrenched and absolutized particular differences. The only circumstances in which this is not a simple zero-sum game is within the framework of an agonistic form of democratic negotiation (Mouffe 1993). However, the emphasis needs to be on the 'agonistic' – democracy as an on-going struggle without final resolution. We cannot simply reaffirm 'democracy'. But the multi-cultural question also suggests that the moment of 'difference' is essential to defining democracy *as a genuinely heterogeneous space*. In our anxiety to identify the points of possible articulation, we must be careful not em-phasize the ineradicable necessity of this moment of *différance*.[30] However, what is clear is that the process cannot be allowed to remain with this political assertion of a radical particularity. It must attempt to construct a diversity of new public spheres in which all the particulars will be transformed by being obliged to negotiate within a broader horizon. It is essential for this space to remain heterogeneous and pluralistic, and for the elements negotiating within it to retain their *différance*. They must resist the drive to be integrated by a process of formal equivalence, such as is inscribed in a liberal conception of citizenship, that is to recoup an Enlightenment assimilationist strategy via a long detour. As Laclau recognizes: 'This universalization and its open character certainly condemns all identity to an unavoidable hybridization, but hybridization does not necessarily mean decline through the loss of identity. It can also mean empowering existing identities through the opening of new possibilities. Only a conservative identity, closed on itself could experience hybridization as loss' (Laclau 1996).

Towards a New Political Logic

In the latter part of the chapter, we have been struggling to identify and disinter the bare outlines of a new multi-cultural political logic. Such a strategy would seek to do, conjuncturally, what is said in the liberal-constitutional model to be incommensurable in principle: to effect a radical reconfiguration of the particular and the universal, of liberty and equality with difference. The aim has been to begin to reframe the inheritances from the liberal, pluralist, cosmopolitan and democratic discourses in the light of the multi-cultural character of late-modern societies. No easy final resolution seems possible. Instead, we have tried to sketch an approach in which, in pushing for vigorous and uncompromising strategies to be adopted which confront and try to eradicate racism, exclusion and inferiorization (the old anti-racist or race equality agenda, which is as relevant today as it ever was), certain limits have nevertheless to be respected (in the new multi-cultural circumstances of difference in which those strategies now operate).

Thus, we cannot simply reaffirm individual liberty and formal equality, (what New Labour disarmingly calls 'equality of worth'!) because we can see both their inadequacy to the complexities of attachment, belongingness and identity that multi-cultural society introduces and the deep injustices of inequality, social exclusion and injustice that continue to be perpetrated in their name. Individual choice, however tarted up with a thin veneer of communitarianism, cannot supply the bonds of recognition, reciprocity and connection which give meaning to our lives as social beings. *This is the cultural or communitarian limit on liberal (including 'market-liberal') forms of multiculturalism.* On the other hand, we cannot enfranchise the claims of community cultures and norms over individuals without at the same time expanding – not only ideally but in practice – the right of individuals as bearers of rights to dissent from, exit from and oppose if necessary their communities of origin. There are palpable dangers in slipping into a more

formally separate, plural form of political representation. There is a danger
in simply valorizing the distinctive values of 'community' as if they are
not always in a moving relationship to all the other competing values
around them. The return to ethnicity in its 'ethnically absolutist' form
(Gilroy 1993a, 1993b) is only too capable of producing its own kinds of
violence. It over-essentializes cultural difference, fixes racial binaries,
freezes them in time and history, gives power to established authority over
others, privileges 'the fathers and the Law', and leads to the policing of
difference. This seems to be the critical frontier where cultural pluralism
or ethnic communitarianism *encounters its liberal limit.*

However, the fact is that neither individuals as free-floating entities nor
communities as solidaristic wholes occupy the social space on their own.
Each is constituted in and through its relation to that which is other and
different from itself. If this is not to result in either 'the war of all against
all' or a segregated communalism, then we must look for how both the
greater recognition of difference and greater equality and justice for all
can become part of a common 'horizon'. It seems to be the case, as Laclau
suggests, *both* that 'the universal is incommensurable with the particular'
and that the former 'cannot exist without the latter'. Far from undermining
democracy, this so-called 'failure' is 'the precondition for democracy'
(Laclau 1996). Accordingly, this multicultural political logic requires at
least two further conditions of existence: a deepening, expansion and
radicalization of democratic practices in our social life; and the unrelenting
contestation of every form of racialized and ethnicized exclusionary closure
(whether practised by others on minority communities, or within communities). For racialized disadvantage and exclusion block the access of
everyone, including 'minorities' of *all* kinds, to the process of defining a
more inclusive 'Britishness' with which, *only then*, might everyone be
legitimately invited to identify. This constitutes *the democratic or cosmopolitan limit on both liberal and communitarian alternatives.*

The difficulties in the way of practically and politically expanding this
multi-cultural political logic are legion, and it has not been possible within
the scope of this chapter to address them. However, one could not leave
the argument without at least indicating the difficulties. On the one hand,
in Britain, this is a propitious moment to raise the multi-cultural question
because Britishness as a national identity is in a transitional state, beset by
problems and up for extensive renovation and renegotiation. However,
such opportunities are also always moments of profound danger. For, just
as the multi-cultural question opens up from below issues which were
considered closed (settled) in the western political institution, so it is seen
by many as the straw that broke the camel's back. It points towards the
redefinition of what it means to be British, where the unthinkable might

come to pass – it might be possible to be Black-and-British or Asian-and-British (or even British-and-gay!). However, the idea that *everyone* should have access to the processes by which such new forms of 'Britishness' are redefined, coupled with the loss of empire and decline as a world power, is literally driving some of its citizens crazy. The 'pollution' of Little England – as the latter see it – is calculated to produce not just a resurgence of the old biological stereotypes, but a proliferating lexicon of new exclusionary binaries, grounded in a racialized 'cultural difference'; a British version of the the new racisms which are abroad everywhere and gaining ground.

Both processes are alive and well in Britain at the turn of the millennium. Both thrive hand-in-hand, in a fateful symbiosis. The celebration of the anniversary of the arrival of the SS *Empire Windrush* – described by some as 'the irresistible rise of multi-racial Britain' (Phillips and Phillips 1998) – occurred within a year of the long-delayed Macpherson Inquiry into the murder of the black teenager Stephen Lawrence, by five white youths, with its finding of 'institutional racism' (Macpherson 1999). Both these events are deeply paradigmatic of the contradictory state of British multiculturalism and their appearance together, in the same conjuncture, is essential to an understanding of Britain's confused and problematic response to 'the multi-cultural question'.

Notes

Parts of this chapter were given as lectures at Johns Hopkins University, Baltimore; the University of Michigan, Ann Arbor, as the Herbert Gutman Memorial Lecture at the City University of New York Graduate Center; and the Amiel and Melburn Trust Annual Lecture 'Race Against Time' at the Institute of Education, University of London. I am grateful to all those who commented on aspects of the paper on those occasions.

1. To some extent, this distinction overlaps with that offered in the Introduction but also departs from it in certain important respects.

2. In fact, as Kymlicka (1989) has argued, the problems posed by multiculturalism are not adequately represented as necessitating a strong conception of collective rights since, in his perspective, individuals must remain the bearers of rights. On the other hand, Parekh (1991) argues that many rights already acknowledged by liberal societies (for example, trade union legislation, the race relations and equal opportunities Acts, Sikh exemption from health and safety requirements) are in fact group-based or collectivity defined.

3. Hazel Carby (1998) has remarked on the 'stark reversal of visibility of the black male body', where images of Black men have made a remarkable transition straight from the drug-soaked ghetto to the front covers of the fashion magazines while their actual bodies have remained largely where they were (an inordinate number of them in gaol).

4. 'In 1983 there were 144 recognized nations in the world. By the late 1990s this number had grown to just under 200. More will certainly come into being over the next

few years as local ethnic groups and nations without a state press for greater autonomy (Giddens 2000: 153).

5. No conjuncture is ever wholly new. It is always a transformed combination of existing and emergent elements – in Gramsci's terms, the re-articulation of a dis-articulation. Cf. Gramsci (1971) and Hall (1998).

6. 'Globalization in a post-imperial age only permits a post-nationalist consciousness for cosmopolitans who are lucky enough to live in the wealthy west' (Ignatieff 1994).

7. Globalization-as-fate seems to be a key feature of the Blair/New Labour/Third Way position. Giddens, who also advanced similar arguments, now makes a stronger argument for the regulation of global corporate power (cf. Giddens 2000).

8. I am, of course, translating from philosophy to culture, and expanding Derrida's concept without warrant – though not, I hope, against the spirit of his meaning (cf. Derrida 1972).

9. For Derrida, *différance* is both 'to differ' and 'to defer'. It is grounded in strategies of delay, reprieve, referal, elision, detour, postponement, reserving (cf. Derrida 1972).

10. One needs to compare this figure with the size of the African-American, Latino, Caribbean, Korean and Vietnamese populations in the USA to get a sense of comparative scale

11. There is some evidence to suggest that 'blackness' was not strongly marked among the earliest Caribbean migrants and developed in Britain in the 1960's as a response to racism.

12. The impact of the official inquiry into the death of Stephen Lawrence and the Macpherson Report (1999) is the most striking recent example of this.

13. Paul Gilroy speaks correctly of 'the inability to take race seriously and an iron-jawed disinclination to recognize the equal human worth and dignity of people who are not white' (Gilroy 1999).

14. In discursive terms, racism has a metonymnic structure – the genetic differences which are hidden being displaced along the chain of signification through their inscription on to the surface of the body, which is visible. This is what Frantz Fanon meant by *epidermalization* or the 'corporeal schema' (cf. Hall 1990, 1996b).

15. This is the position adopted by Balibar (1991b) in his discussion of 'differentialist racism', a term borrowed from Taguieff, and by Wieviorka (1995). Modood (1997), however, in my opinion, goes too far in attempting to distinguish 'cultural racism from any connection with fixity or the biological' and draws too a sharp opposition between 'biological racism' and 'cultural differentialism'. I think this misreading comes from not taking the *discursive* character of racism sufficiently into account. Modood is therefore misled into taking the biological referent in 'biological racism' too literally.

16. Here I differ from the way the race/ethnicity distinction is drawn by, for example, Pnina Werbner in an important contribution (Werbner 1997).

17. This was a result of an extensive struggle of re-signification. Judith Butler (1993) makes the argument that what is important about terms such as 'black' or 'queer', which have moved from a negative to a positive connotation, is that they retain the traces of the struggle to change within them. This may constitute an alternative strategy to 'political correctness' which attempts to cleanse the language of all traces of negativity.

18. Whereas it needs to be understood as 'the changing same' (Gilroy 1993a) or as 'a discursive concept ... [which] seeks to connect, authoritatively, within the structure of its narrative, a relation amongst past, community and identity' (Scott 1999). Fixture is

something which *happens* to tradition under certain conditions – how it ceases to be creative and becomes immured in 'authority'.

19. See David Scott (1999).

20. This is the important distinction between the conception of culture as a 'way of life' and the conception of culture as 'signifying practice' (Hall 1998).

21. Thus, I do not take seriously Robert Young's argument (that the use of the term 'hybridity' simply restores the old racialized discourse of difference which one was attempting to supersede). This is semantic quibbling. Surely terms can be dis-articulated and re-articulated from their originary meanings: what is this pre-post-structuralist conception of language in which meaning is fixed eternally to its racialized referent? Clearly, my concern has been throughout with *cultural* hybridity, which I relate to the novel combination of heterogeneous cultural elements in a new synthesis – e.g. 'creol-ization' and 'trans-culturation' – and which cannot be fixed by, or be dependent on, the so-called racial character of the people whose culture I am discussing.

22. Tradition does not mean something fixed. It is, rather, a recognition of the em-bodied character of all discourse. 'It is a special sort of discursive concept in the sense that it performs a distinctive kind of labour; it seeks to connect authoritatively, within the structure of its narrative, a relation among past, community and identity ... It depends upon a play of conflict and contention. It is a space of dispute as much as of consensus, of discourse as much as of accord' (Scott 1999).

23. Rawls made an important concession to his communitarian critics in recognizing that his theory of justice was particularly appropriate for a liberal-pluralist society, where the desire for political co-operation is already widespread (i.e. dependent on certain particularistic cultural assumptions). 1998.

24. This includes uneven patterns of economic and technological change, the revolu-tion in the position of women and the feminization of the workforce, the decline in manual male working-class culture and the older occupational communities; new patterns of consumption and the religion of the free market, new family forms and styles of parenting, generational differences in an ageing population, the decline of organized religion, profound shifts in sexual behaviour and moral culture, the decline of deference, the rise of managerialism, the heroization of the entrepreneur, the new individualism and the new hedonism.

25. Walzer talks, confusingly (and, in view of recent developments, optimistically), about the USA 'choosing Liberalism 1 from within Liberalism 2'. In fact, recent Amer-ican public policy with its assault against affirmative action programmes in the name of individual liberty looks more like a concerted effort to drag the USA back to Liberalism 1 from its brief flirtation with Liberalism 2! Kymlicka, from a Canadian perspective, argues that certain individually-defined group rights are compatible with the liberal conception, and stretches the liberal conception to its limits in order to make them so. Taylor (1994) suggests that they are not; first, because of the individualistic foundational assumptions of liberalism, and, second, because the protection of collective identities conflicts with the right to individual liberties. Liberalism therefore requires to be re-formed in order to accommodate the multi-cultural demand for 'recognition'. Habermas (1994), however, argues that, of course, individuality is constituted intersubjectively, but that, correctly understood, a theory of rights not only accommodates but requires a politics of recognition that protects the integrity of the individual as a bearer of rights; this is compatible with liberalism provided there is 'the consistent actualization of the system of rights'.

26. John Rex, who supports the general proposition of the cultural neutrality of the state, correctly argues that this approach differs from that of liberal individualism. It has been underpinned, at least until the advent of New Labour, by a social-democratic welfare programme including substantial redistributive measures, which it would be misleading to subsume under an all-inclusive liberal rubric just because it respects the rights of the individual.

27. For a persuasive argument on the complexities of evaluating differences between cultural practices in a non-absolutist way, see Parekh (1999).

28. See the extended debates on this question by Women Against Fundamentalism.

29. In what follows I am particularly indebted to the way the argument about universalism/particularism is conducted in Ernesto Laclau's recent work, especially *Emancipations* (1996).

30. This may be a matter of emphasis rather than fundamental disagreement. Laclau, for example, writes as if the proliferation of identities is something which has simply happened to late-modern societies; his focus is on how such a disseminated field could nevertheless be hegemonized through a certain type of 'universalization'. When advanced by some proponents, this often becomes a recuperation of difference and a reassertion of the old Enlightenment universalist argument. However, from the multi-cultural perspective, the heterogenization of the social field – the pluralization of positionalities – is itself a necessary and positive, though not sufficient, moment and must be retained (in its hybridized forms), alongside the efforts (always incomplete) to define, from within their particularities, a more universal horizon.

Bibliography

Abrahams, Y. (1996) *'Ambiguity' is my Middle Name: A Research Diary about Sara Baartman and her Legacy to us Brown Women*. Paper presented at African Gender Institute Colloquium, University of Cape Town, 6 August 1996 and at Gender Equity Unit, University of the Western Cape, 26 September 1996).

Adebayo, D. (1996) *Some Kind of Black* (London: Virago).

Adeleke, T. (1998) *UnAfrican Americans – Nineteenth-Century Black Nationalists and the Civilizing Mission* (University of Kentucky Press).

Adi, H. (1998) *West Africans in Britain 1990–1960* (London: Lawrence and Wishart).

Adi, H. and M. Sherwood (1995) *The 1945 Manchester Pan-African Congress Revisited* (London: New Beacon Books).

Adorno T. and Horkheimer (1969) *Dialectic of Englightenment* (London: Verso).

Ahiakpor, J. (1990) *The Economic Consequences of Political Independence. The Case of Bermuda* (Canada: Fraser Institute Press).

Ahmad, A. (1995) 'The Politics of Literary Post-Coloniality', *Race and Class*, vol. 36, no. 3.

Aktay, Y. (1997) 'Body, Text, Identity: The Islamist Discourse of Authenticity in Modern Turkey', unpublished PhD thesis, Middle East Technical University, Turkey.

Alexander, C. (1996) *The Art of Being Black* (Oxford: Oxford University Press).

— (1998) 'Re-imagining the Muslim Community', *Innovations*, vol. 11, no. 4, pp. 439–50.

Alexander, J. and Chandra Talpade Mohanty (1997) *Feminist Genealogies, Colonial Legacies, Democratic Futures* (New York: Routledge).

Allen, J. (1995) 'Global Worlds', in J. Allen and D. Massey (eds), *Geographical Worlds* (Oxford: Oxford University Press in association with the Open University).

Althusser, L. (1969) *For Marx*, trans. B. Brewster (London: Allen Lane).

Anderson, B. (1983) *Imagined Communities* (London: Verso).

Anthias, F. (1998) 'Evaluating "Diaspora": Beyond Ethnicity?' *Sociology*, vol. 32, no. 3, August, pp. 557–80.

Anthias, F. and Yuval-Davis, N. (1992) *Racialized Boundaries* (London: Routledge).

Appadurai, A. (1990) 'Disjuncture and Difference in the Global Cultural Economy', in M. Featherstone (ed.), *Global Culture* (London: Sage).

— (1996a) *Modernity at Large: Cultural Dimensions of Globalization* (Minneapolis: University of Minnesota Press).

— (1996b) 'Sovereignty without Territoriality: Notes for a Postnational Geography', in P. Yaeger (ed.), *The Geography of Identity* (Ann Arbor: University of Michigan Press).

Ardener, S. (1987) 'A Note On Gender Iconography: The Vagina', in P. Caplan (ed.), *The Cultural Construction of Sexuality* (London: Routledge).

⸱⸱ H. (1973) *The Origins of Totalitarianism* (New York: Harcourt Brace).

⸱⸱ (1983) *Nations before Nationalism* (Chapel Hill: University of North Carolina

Back, L. (1996) *New Ethnicities and Urban Culture* (London: UCL Press).

Bal, M. (1991) 'The Politics of Citation', , vol. 21, no. 1, pp. 25–45.

Baldwin, J. (1995) 'The Fire Next Time' [1963], in *The Price of the Ticket: Collected Non-Fiction* (New York: St Martin's/Marek).

Balibar, E. (1991a) 'Es Gibt Keinen Staat in Europa: Racism and Politics in Europe Today', *New Left Review*, no. 186 (April/May).

— (1991b) 'Is there a "Neo-Racisim"', in E. Balibar and I. Wallerstein, *Race, Nation, Class* (London: Verso).

Ball, W. and J. Solomos (1990) *Local Politics and 'Race'* (London: Macmillan).

Barber, B. R. (1996) *Jihad vs. McWorld* (New York: Ballantine).

Barker, M. (1981) *The New Racism* (London: Junction Books).

Barrett, L. (1977) *The Rastafarians – Sounds of Cultural Dissonance* (Boston: Beacon Press).

Baucom, I. (1997) 'Charting the Black Atlantic', *Post-Modern Culture* website.

Baudrillard, J. (1981) *Towards a Political Economy of the Sign* (St Louis: Telos Press).

— (1998) *The Consumer Society: Myths and Structures* (London: Sage).

Bauman, Z. (1989) *Modernity and the Holocaust* (London: Polity Press).

Beckles, H. (1991) 'Caribbean Anti-slavery: The Self-Liberation Ethos of Enslaved Blacks', in H. Beckles and V. Shepherd (eds), *Caribbean Slave Society and Economy: A Student Reader* (London: James Currey).

Bell, D. and G. Valentine (1997) *Consuming Geographies: We are Where We Eat* (London: Routledge).

Benbow, C. (1994) *Gladys Morrell and the Woman Suffrage Movement in Bermuda* (Bermuda: Writer's Machine).

Bennett, J. and M. Friedman (1997) 'White Women and Racial Autobiography', *Agenda* 32, pp. 49–55.

Benson, S. (1996) 'Asians Have Culture, West Indians Have Problems', in T. Ranger, Y. Samad and O. Stuart (eds), *Culture, Identity, Politics* (Aldershot: Avebury).

Berger, M., B. Wallis and S. Watson (eds) (1995) *Constructing Masculinity* (London: Routledge).

Berman, P. (ed.) (1992) *Debating P.C. – The Controversy over Political Correctness on College Campuses* (New York: Laurel).

Bernal, M. (1987) *Black Athena: The Afroasiatic Roots of Classical Civilization* (London: Free Association Books).

Besson, Jean (1993) 'Reputation and Respectability Reconsidered: A New Perspective on Afro-Caribbean Peasant Women', in J. H. Momsen (ed.), *Women and Change in the Caribbean* (London: James Currey; Jamaica: Ian Randle; Bloomington: Indiana University Press).

Bhabha, H. (1990) *Nation and Narration* (London: Routledge).

— (1994) *The Location of Culture* (London: Routledge).

— (1997) 'The Voice of the Dom', *Times Literary Supplement*, no. 4923.

— (1998) 'Culture's in Between', in D. Bennett (ed.), *Multicultural States – Rethinking Difference and Identity* (London: Routledge).

Bhattacharyya, G. (1998) 'Riding Multiculturalism', in D. Bennett (ed.), *Multicultural States – Rethinking Difference and Identity* (London: Routledge).

Bickford-Smith, V. (1994) 'Meanings of Freedom: Social Position and Identity among Ex-Slaves and their descendants in Cape Town, 1875–1910', in N. Worden and C. Crais (eds), *Breaking the Chains* (Johannesburg: Witwatersrand University Press).

Blount, M. and G. P. Cunningham (eds) (1996) *Representing Black Men* (London: Routledge).

Boahen, A. A. (1987) *African Perspectives on Colonialism* (London: Johns Hopkins University Press).

Bocock, R. (1993) *Consumption* (London and New York: Routledge).

Bolster, W. J. (1997) *Black Jacks – African American Seamen in the Age of Sail* (London: Harvard University Press).

Bonnett, A. (1993) 'Contours of Crisis: Anti-racism and Reflexivity', in P. Jackson and J. Penrose (eds), *Constructions of Race, Place and Nation* (London: University College London Press).

Bonnett, A. (1999) 'Anti-Racist Dilemmas', *Race and Class*, vol. 36, no. 3.

Bourdieu, P. (1977) *Outline of a Theory of Practice* (Cambridge: Cambridge University Press).

— (1981) 'Men and Machines', in K. Knorr-Cetina and A. Cicourel (eds), *Advances in Social Theory and Methodology* (Boston, Routledge and Kegan Paul).

— (1984) *Distinction: A Social Critique of Taste*, trans. R. Nice (London: Routledge).

— (1990a) *In Other Words* (Cambridge: Polity Press).

— (1990b) *The Logic of Practice* (Cambridge: Polity Press).

— (1997) *Méditations pascaliennes* (Paris: Seuil).

Boyce Davies, C. (1994) *Black Women, Writing and Identity – Migrations of the Subject* (London: Routledge).

Boyd, H. and R. L. Allen (eds) (1995) *Brotherman: The Odessey of Black Men in America: An Anthology* (New York: Ballantine Books).

Brah, A. (1996) *Cartographies of Diaspora* (London and New York: Routledge).

Brathwaite, E. K. (1971) *The Development of Creole Society in Jamaica, 1770–1820* (Oxford: Oxford University Press).

Brohm, J.-M. (1978) *Sport: A Prison of Measured Time* (Worcester: Pluto).

Brown, J. N. (1998) 'Black Liverpool, Black America and the Gendering of Diasporic Space', *Cultural Anthropology*, vol. 13, no. 3, pp. 291–325.

Brown, Walton (1994) 'Desegregation, Universal Suffrage and the Politics of Direct Action in Bermuda, 1950-1963', unpublished paper presented at the Conference of Caribbean Historians.

Bryan, B., S. Dadzie and S. Scafe (1985) *Heart of the Race – Black Women's Lives in Britain* (London: Virago).

Burchall, L. (1991) *The Other Side: Looking Behind the Shield* (Detroit: Harlo Press).

Burchell, G., C. Gordon and P. Miller (eds) (1991) *The Foucault Effect: Studies in Governmentality* (London: Harvester Wheatsheaf).

Bush, B. (1999) *Imperialism, Race and Resistance – Africa and Britain 1919–1945* (London: Routledge).

Busia, A. P. A. (1994) 'Performance, Transcription and the Languages of the Self: Interrogating Identity as a "post-colonial" poet', in S. M. James and A. P. A. Busia (eds), *Theorising Black Feminisms* (London and New York: Routledge), ch. 13.

Butler, J. (1993) *Bodies That Matter* (London: Routledge).

Calhoun, C. (1994) 'Social Theory and the Politics of Identity', in C. Calhoun (ed.), *Social Theory and the Politics of Identity* (Oxford and Cambridge, MA: Basil Blackwell).

Caliguire, D. (1996) 'Voices from the Communities', in W. James et al. (eds), *Now That We are Free: Coloured Communities in Democratic South Africa* (Cape Town: Idasa).

Calinsecu, M. (1987) *Five Faces of Modernity* (Durham, NC : Duke University Press).

Carby, H. V. (1986) '"On the Threshold of Women's Era": Lynching, Empire, and Sexuality in Black Feminist Theory', in H. L. Gates Jr (ed.), *'Race', Writing and Difference* (Chicago: University of Chicago Press).

— (1998) *Race Men: The W. E. B. DuBois Lectures* (Cambridge, MA: Harvard University Press).

E.. (1982) *Black Sportsmen* (London: Routledge and Kegan Paul).

* *Sense of Sports* (2nd edn) (London: Routledge).

oyna (eds) (1982) *Black Youth in Crisis* (London: Allen and Unwin).

Castells, M. (1997) *The Rise of the Network Society* (Oxford: Basil Blackwell).

Caws, P. (1994) 'Identity, Trans-cultural and Multi-cultural', in D. Goldberg (ed.), *Multi-culturalism* (London: Blackwell).

CCCS (Centre for Contemporary Cultural Studies) Collective (1982) *The Empire Strikes Back* (London: Hutchinson).

Césaire, A. (1972) *Discourse on Colonialism* (New York: Monthly Review Press).

— (1995) *Notebook of a Return to My Native Land*, trans. M. Rosello and A. Pritchard (Newcastle upon Tyne: Bloodaxe).

Chambers, I. and L. Curti (eds) (1996) *The Post-Colonial Question* (London: Routledge).

Chapman, R. and J. Rutherford (eds) (1988) *Male Order: Unwrapping Masculinity* (London: Lawrence and Wishart).

Clegg, J. (1994) *Fu Manchu and the Yellow Peril: The Making of a Racist Myth* (Stoke on Trent: Trentham Books).

Clifford, J. (1988) 'Introduction: The Pure Products Go Crazy', in J. Clifford (ed.), *The Predicament of Culture* (Cambridge, MA and London: Harvard University Press).

— (1997) *Routes* (Cambridge, MA: Harvard University Press).

Cohen, P. (1988) 'The Perversion of Inheritance: Studies in the Making of Multi-Racist Britain', in P. Cohen and H. S. Bains (eds), *Multi-Racist Britain* (London: Macmillan).

— (1997) 'Labouring under Whiteness', in R. Frankenberg (ed.), *Displacing Whiteness* (Durham, NC and London: Duke University Press).

Cohen, R. (1997) *Global Diasporas: An Introduction* (London: UCL Press).

Cohen, S. (1980) *Folk Devils and Moral Panics* (Oxford: Basil Blackwell).

Connell, R. (1987) *Gender and Power* (Cambridge: Polity Press).

— (1995) *Masculinities* (Cambridge: Polity Press).

Connolly, P. (1997) 'Racism and Postmodernism: Towards a Theory of Practice', in D. Owen (ed.), *Sociology after Postmodernism* (London: Sage).

Connolly, W. E. (1988) *The Terms of Political Discourse* (London: Basil Blackwell).

— (1991) *Identity/Difference* (Ithaca, NY: Cornell University Press).

Cooper, C. (1993) *Noises in the Blood: Orality, Gender and the 'Vulgar' Body of Jamaican Culture* (London: Macmillan).

Craven, W. (1990) *An Introduction to Bermuda* (Bermuda: Maritime Press).

Critical Arts (1995) (A Journal of Cultural Studies) *Recuperating the San*, vol. 9, no. 2 (Croom Helm).

Davies, A. (1998) *Blues Legacies and Black Feminism* (Toronto: Random House).

Davis, N. (1999) *The Isles* (Basingstoke: Macmillan).

Dawson, R. (1967) *The Chinese Chameleon: An Analysis of European Conceptions of Chinese Civilization* (London: Oxford University Press).

Dear, M. (1997) 'Postmodern Bloodlines', in G. Benko and U. Strohmayer (eds), *Space and Social Theory* (Oxford: Blackwell).

Deleuze, G. and Guattari, F. (1977) *Anti-Oedipus: Capitalism and Schizophrenia* (New York: Viking Press).

Dennis, F. (1988) *Behind the Frontlines* (London: Victor Gollancz).

Derrida, J. (1972) *Positions* (Chicago: University of Chicago Press).

— (1981) *Dissemination* (London: Althone Press).

— (1982) *Margins of Philosophy* (Brighton: Harvester).

— (1994) *Specters of Marx – The State of Debt, the Work of Mourning and the New International* (London: Routledge).

Douglas, S. (1997) 'Reflections on State Intervention and the Schmidtsdrift Bushmen', *Journal of Contemporary African Studies*, vol. 15, no 1, pp. 45–66.

Driver, C. (1983) *The British at table 1940–1980* (London: Chatto and Windus).

Dunant, S. (ed.) (1994) *The War of the Words - the Political Correctness Debate* (London: Virago).

Duneier, M. (1992) *Slim's Table* (Chicago: University of Chicago Press).

Dunn, A. (1998) 'Who Needs a Sociology of the Aesthetic? Freedom and Value in Pierre Bourdieu's Rules of Art', *Boundary 2*, vol. 25, no. 1, pp. 87–110.

Economist Intelligence Unit (1993) *Eating Out in the UK* (London: Economist).

Eldridge, M. and Seekings, J. (1996) 'Mandela's Lost Province: The African National Congress and the Western Cape Electorate in the 1994 South African Elections', *Journal of Southern African Studies*, vol. 22, no. 4, pp. 517–41).

Erasmus, Z. and E. Pieterse (1999) 'Conceptualising Coloured Identities in the Western Cape, South Africa', in M. Palmberg (ed.), *National Identity and Democracy in Africa* (Cape Town: Mayibuye Centre, Human Sciences Research Council and Nordic Africa Institute).

Etter-Lewis, G. (1993) *My Soul Is My Own. Oral Narratives of African-American Women in the Professions* (London: Routledge).

Eze, E. C. (ed.) (1997) *Post-Colonial African Philosophy* (London: Basil Blackwell).

Fanon, F. (1963) *Wretched of the Earth* (London: Penguin).

— (1986) *Black Skin, White Masks* [1967] (London: Pluto).

Fay, B. (1996) *Contemporary Philosophy of Social Science – A Multicultural Approach* (Oxford: Blackwell).

Fish, S. (1998) 'Boutique Multiculturalism', in A. Melzer et al. (eds), *Multiculturalism and American Democracy* (Lawrence: University of Kansas Press).

Fogelin, R. J. (1995) *Wittgenstein* (2nd edn) (London: Routledge).

Foster, L. and P. Herzog (eds) (1994) *Defending Diversity – Contemporary Philosophical Perspectives on Pluralism and Multiculturalism* (Amherst: University of Massachusetts Press).

Foucault, M. (1972) *The Archeology of Knowledge* (London: Tavistock Publications).

— (1977) *Language, Counter-memory, Practice* (Ithaca, NY: Cornell University Press).

— (1980) *Power/Knowledge* (Brighton: Harvester Press).

Frankenburg, R. (1993) *White Women, Race Matters: The Social Construction of Whiteness* (London: Routledge).

Frost, D. (1999) *Work and Community among West African Migrant Workers since the Nineteenth Century* (Liverpool: Liverpool University Press).

Fryer, P. (1984) *Staying Power – The History of Black People in Britain* (London: Pluto Presss).

Fukuyama, F. (1992) *The End of History* (New York: Free Press).

Fuss, D. (1989) *'Essentially Speaking: Feminism, Nature and Difference* (New York and London: Routledge).

Gamman, L. and M. Makinen (1994) *Female Fetishism: A New Look* (London: Lawrence and Wishart).

Geiss, I. (1974) *The Pan-African Connection* (London: Methuen).

Geyer, M. and C. Bright (1995) 'World History in a Global Age', *American Historical Review*, vol. 100, no. 4 (Ocotber), pp. 1034–60.

Giddens, A. (1998) *The Third Way* (London: Polity Press).

— (1999) *Runaway World* (London: Profile Books).

— (2000) *The Third Way and its Critics* (London: Polity Press).

Gilman, S. (1985) *Difference and Pathology* (Ithaca, NY and London: Cornell University Press).

⸻ (1992) 'Black Bodies, White Bodies: Toward an Iconography of Female Sexuality in Late ⸺⸺enth-Century Art, Medicine and Literature', in J. Donald and A. Rattansi (eds), ⸻⸺*ure and Difference* (London: Sage).

⸻⸺*re Ain't No Black in the Union Jack: The Cultural Politics of Race and* ⸻⸺*ersity of Chicago Press).

— (1993a) *The Black Atlantic: Modernity and Double Consciousness* (London: Verso).

— (1993b) *Small Acts* (London: Serpent's Tail).

— (1997) 'Modern Tones', in J. Skipwith (ed.), *Rhapsodies in Black: Art of the Harlem Renaissance* (Berkeley, CA and London: University of California Press).

— (1999) 'Joined-up Politics and Post-colonial Melancholia', the 1999 Diversity Lecture (London: Institute of Contemporary Arts).

Glissant, E. (1981) *Le Discours Antillais* (Paris: Seuil).

— (1989) *Caribbean Discourse* (University of Virginia Press).

Goldberg, D. (ed.) (1993) *Racist Culture* (London: Basil Blackwell).

— (1994) 'Introduction', in D. Golberg (ed.), *Multiculturalism* (London: Blackwell).

Gould, S. (1995) *The Flamingo's Smile: Reflections in Natural History* (Harmondsworth: Penguin).

Gramsci, A. (1971) *Selections From the Prison Notebooks*, ed. and trans. Q. Hoare and G. Nowell Smith (New York: International Publishers).

Grossberg, L. (ed.) (1996) 'On Postmodernism and Articulation: an Interview with Stuart Hall', in D. Morley and K.-H. Chen (eds), *Stuart Hall: Critical Dialogues in Cultural Studies* (London and New York: Routledge).

Gutman, A. (ed.) (19)*Multiculturalism and the Politics of Recognition* (Princeton, NJ: Princeton University Press).

Habermas, J. (1994) 'Struggles for Recognition in the Democratic Constitutional State', in A. Gutman (ed.), *Multiculturalism* (Princeton, NJ: Princeton University Press.

Hagedorn, J. (1998) 'Frat Boys, Bossmen, Studs and Gentlemen', in L. Bowker (ed.), *Masculinities and Violence* (London: Sage).

Hall, C. (1992) *White Male and Middle Class* (Cambridge: Polity).

Hall, S. (1978) 'Racism and Reaction', in CRE, *Five Views of Multi-Racial Britain* (London: Commission for Racial Equality).

— (1988) *Hard Road to Renewal* (London: Verso).

— (1990) 'Cultural Identity and Diaspora', in J. Rutherford (ed.), *Identity, Community, Culture, Difference* (London: Lawrence & Wishart).

— (1991) 'The Local and the Global: Globalization and Ethnicity', in A. D. King (ed.), *Culture, Globalization and the World System* (Binghamton, NY: University of New York State Press).

— (1992) 'New Ethnicities', in J. Donald and A. Rattansi (eds) *'Race', Culture and Difference* (London: Sage).

— (1993a) 'Cultural Identity and Diaspora', in P. Williams and L. Chrisman (eds), *Colonial Discourse and Post-Colonial Theory: A Reader* (New York and London: Harvester Wheatsheaf), Ch. 22.

— (1993b) 'Culture, Community, Nation', *Cultural Studies*, vol. 7, no. 3.

— (1996a) 'When was the "Post-colonial?" thinking at the Limit', in I. Chambers and L. Curti (eds), *The Post-Colonial Question* (London: Routledge).

— (1996b) 'Who Needs Identity?' in S. Hall and P. du Gay (eds), *Questions of Cultural Identity* (London: Sage).

— (1997) *'The Spectacle of the Other'*, in S. Hall (ed.), *Representation: Cultural Representations and Signifying Practices* (London: Sage).

— (1998) 'Aspiration and Attitude ... Reflections on Black Britain in the Nineties' *New Formations*, no.3, Spring.

— (1999a) 'From Scarman to Stephen Lawrence', *History Workshop Journal*, no. 48.

— (1999b) 'Whose Heritage? Unsettling the Heritage, Re-imagining the Post-Nation', *Third Text*, no. 49 (winter).

— (1999c) 'National and Cultural Identity', paper for the Runnymede Commission on the Future of Multi-Ethnic Britain, London.

— (1999d) 'Thinking the Diaspora', *small axe*, no. 6 (Kingston: University of the West Indies Press).

Hall, S., C. Critcher, T. Jefferson, J. Clarke and B. Roberts (1978) *Policing the Crisis* (London: Macmillan).

Hamilton, G. (1996) 'Overseas Chinese Capitalism', in Wei-Ming Tu (ed.), *Confucian Traditions in East Asian Modernity* (Cambridge: Harvard University Press).

Hardyment, C. (1995) *Slice of Life: The British Way of Eating Since 1945* (London: BBC Books).

Hargreaves, J. (1994) *Sporting Females: Critical Issues in the History and Sociology of Women's Sports* (London: Routledge).

Harris Hunter, B. (1993) *The People of Bermuda. Beyond the Crossroads* (Toronto: Gagne-Best).

Harris, L. A. (1996) 'Contesting Feminist Orthodoxies', *Feminist Review*, no. 54 (Autumn), pp. 3–30.

Harvey, D. (1989) *The Conditions of Postmodernity*, Oxford: Blackwell).

— (1996) *Justice, Nature and the Geography of Difference* (Oxford: Blackwell.

Held, D. (1995) *Democracy and the Global Order* (Cambridge: Polity Press.)

Held, D., A. McGrew, D. Goldblatt and J. Perraton (1999) *Global Transformations* (Cambridge: Polity).

Hesse, B. (1993) 'Black to Front and Black Again: Racialization through Contested Times and Spaces', in M. Keith and S. Pile (eds), *Place and the Politics of Identity* (London: Routledge).

— (1997) 'White Governmentality: Urbanism, Nationalism, Racism', in S. Westwood and J. Williams (eds), *Imagining Cities* (London: Routledge).

— (1999a) 'It's Your World: Discrepant M/multiculturalisms', in P. Cohen (ed.), *New Ethnicities, Old Racisms* (London: Zed Books).

— (1999b) 'Reviewing the Western Spectacle: Reflexive Globalization through the Black Diaspora', in A. Brah, M. J. Hickman and M. Mac an Ghaill (eds), *Global Futures: Migration, Environment and Globalization* (London: Macmillan).

Higgenbotham, E. (1996) 'African-American Women's History and the Metalanguage of Race', in J. Scott (ed.), *Feminism and History* (New York: Oxford University Press).

Hill Collins, P. (1991) *Black Feminist Thought* (London: Routledge).

Hill, M. (ed.) (1997) *Whiteness: A Critical Reader* (New York and London: New York University Press).

Hobsbawm, E. (1994) *Age of Extremes – The Short Twentieth Century, 1914–1991* (London: Abacus).

Hobsbawm, E. and T. Ranger (1993) *The Invention of Tradition* (Cambridge: Cambridge University Press).

Hodgson, E. (1988) *Second-Class Citizen; First-Class Men* (Toronto: University of Toronto Press).

Home Affairs Committee (1985) *Report on the Chinese in Britain* (London: House of Commons HC102).

Hooker, J. R. (1967) *Black Revolutionary – George Padmore's Path from Communism to Pan-Africanism* (London: Pall Mall Press).

hooks, b. (1982) *Ain't I a Woman? Black Women and Feminism* (London: Pluto Press).

— (1990) *Yearning: Race, Gender, and Cultural Politics* (Boston: South End Press).

— (1992) *Black Looks: Race and Representation* (London: Turnaround).

— (1995) *Outlaw Culture – Resisting Representations* (London and New York: Routledge).

— (1996) 'Neo-colonial Fantasies of Conquest: *Hoop Dreams*', in *Reel to Reel: Race, Sex, and Class at the Movies* (New York and London: Routledge).

Houlihan, B. (1997) *Sport, Policy and Politics: A Comparative Analysis* (London: Routledge).

Human Rights Watch (1997) *Racist Violence in the United Kingdom* (New York: Human Rights Watch).

Huntingdon, S. (1996) *The Clash of Civilizations and the Remaking of World Order* (New York: Simon and Schuster).

Ifekwunigwe, J. (1999) *Scattered Belongings – Cultural Paradoxes of 'Race', Nation and Gender* (London: Routledge).

Ignatieff, M. (1994) *Blood and Belonging* (London: Vintage).

— (1999) 'Multi-ethnicity and the Liberal State', paper for the Runnymede Commission on the Future of Multi-Ethnic Britain, London.

— 'The Narcissism of Minor Differences', The Pavis Lecture, Milton Keynes, Open University.

Isaac, J. C. (1998) *Democracy In Dark Times* (Ithaca, NY: Cornell University Press).

James, C. L. R. (1980) *The Black Jacobins: Toussaint L'Ouverture and the San Domingo Revolution* [1938] (London: Allison and Busby).

— (1986) 'The 1963 West Indians', [1964] in A. Grimshaw (ed.), *Cricket* (London: Allison and Busby).

— (1994) *Beyond a Boundary* [1963] (London: Serpent's Tail).

James, L. (1994) *The Rise and Fall of the British Empire* (London: Abacus).

Jameson, F. (1991) *Postmodernism, or, The Cultural Logic of Late Capitalism* (Durham, NC: Duke University Press).

Judd, D. (1996) *Empire – The British Imperial Experience from 1765 to the Present* (London: Fontana).

Keith, M. (1995) 'Making the Street Visible', *New Community*, vol. 21, no. 4.

— (1993) *Race, Riots and Polcing – Lore and Disorder in a Multi-Racist Society* (London: UCL Press).

Kincheloe, J. L. and S. R. Steinberg (1997) *Changing Multiculturalisms* (Milton Keynes) Open University Press).

Kingwell, M. (1995) 'Keeping a Straight Bat: Cricket, Civility, and Postcolonialism', in S. R. Cudjoe and W. E. Cain (eds), *C. L. R. James: His Intellectual Legacies* (Amhurst: University of Massachusetts Press).

Klor De Alva, J. (1995) 'The Postcolonization of the (Latin) American Experience: A Reconsideration of "Colonialism", "Postcolonialism" and "Mestizaje"', in G. Prakash (ed.), *After Colonialism – Imperial History and Postcolonial Displacements* (Princeton, NJ: Princeton University Press).

Koch, E. (1995) 'Bring back the Hottentot Venus', *Mail & Guardian*, 11, 25.

Kymlicka, W. (1989) *Liberalism, Community and Culture* (Oxford: Clarendon Press).

Lacan, J. (1997) *Ecrits* (London: Tavistock).

Laclau, E. (1996) *Emancipations* (London: Verso).

Laclau, E. and C. Mouffe (1985) *Hegemony and Socialist Strategy* (London: Verso).

Lane, T. (1987) *Gateway to Empire* (Liverpool: Liverpool University Press).

Law and Henfrey (1981) *A History of Race and Racism in Liverpool 1660–1950* (Liverpool: Merseyside Community Relations Council).

Lawrence, E. (1982) 'Just Plain Common Sense: the "Roots" of Racism' in CCCS Collective, *The Empire Strikes Back* (London: Hutchinson).

Lefkowitz, M. R. and G. M. Rogers (eds) (1996) *Black Athena Revisited* (Chapel Hill: University of North Carolina Press).

Lefroy, J. (1877) *Memorials of the Discovery and Early Development of the Bermudas or Somers Island, 1515–1685* (London: Longman).

Lemert, C. (ed.) (1993) *Social Theory – The Multicultural and Classic Readings* (Boulder, CO: Westview Press).

Lewellan, Avis (1988) 'Lace – Pornography for Women?', in L. Gammon and M. Marchment (eds), *The Female Gaze – Women As Viewers of Popular Culture* (London: The Women's Press), pp. 86–101.

Lewis, D. (1996) 'The Politics of Feminism in South Africa' in Daymond, M. (ed.) *South African Feminisms: Writing, Theory and Criticism, 1990–1994* (New York and London: Garland Publishing), pp. 91–104.

Lewis, G. (1968) 'The Atlantic Perimeter. Bermuda and the Bahamas', in *The Growth of the Modern West Indies* (London: MacGibbon and Kee).

— (1992) 'Preface', in M. Opitz K. Oguntoye, K. and D. Schultz (eds), *Showing Our Colours – Afro-German Women Speak Out* (London: Open Letters).

Liebow, E. (1967) *Tally's Corner* (Nee York: Little, Brown).

Loomba, A. (1998) *Colonialism/Postcolonialism* (London: Routledge).

Lorde, Audre (1984) *Sister Outsider* (San Fransciso: Crossing Press).

Macpherson, C. B. (1964) *The Theory of Possessive Individualism* (Oxford: Oxford University Press).

Macpherson, W. (1999) *The Stephen Lawrence Inquiry – Report of an Inquiry by Sir William Macpherson of Cluny* (London: Stationery Office).

McGinn, M. (1998) *Wittgenstein – Philosophical Investigations* (London: Routledge).

McIntosh, P. (1992) 'White Privilege and Male Privilege', in M. Anderson and P. Hill Collins (eds), *Race, Class and Gender: An Anthology* (California: Wadsworth).

McLaren, P. (1994a) 'Multiculturalism and the Post-modern Critique' in H. A. Giroux and P. McLaren (eds), *Between Borders* (London: Routledge).

— (1994b) 'White Terror and Oppositional Agency: Towards a Critical Multiculturalism', in D. Goldberg (ed.) *Multiculturalism* (London: Basil Blackwell).

— (1995) *Critical Pedagogy and Predatory Culture – Oppositional Politics in a Postmodern Era* (London: Routledge).

— (1997) *Revolutionary Multiculturalism – Pedagogies of Dissent for the New Millennium* (Boulder, CO: Westview Press).

Magubane, B. M. (1987) *The Ties That Bind: African-American Consciousness of Africa* (Trenton, NJ: African World Press).

Makgoba, W. (1997) *Mokoko: The Makgoba Affair* (Johannesburg: Vivlia).

Mama, A. (1995) *Beyond the Masks – Race, Gender and Subjectivity* (London: Routledge).

Mamdani, M. (1996) 'Introduction', in M. Mamdani, *Citizen and Subject* (Kampala: Fountain; Cape Town: David Philip; London: James Currey; Princeton, NJ: Princeton University Press.

Mandaville, P. C. (1998) 'Living between the Gaps: Interstitial Identities/Transnational Spaces', paper presented to Aberystwyth Postinternational Group conference, 'Linking Theory and Practice: Issues in the Politics of Identity', University of Wales, Aberystwyth, 9–11 September.

Manning, F. (1978) *Bermudian Politics in Transition* (Bermuda: Island Press).

Marcus, G. (1992) 'Past, Present and Emergent Identities: Requirements for Ethnographies of Late Twentieth-century Modernity World-wide', in S. Lash and J. Friedman (eds), *Modernity and Identity* (London: Basil Blackwell).

Massey, D. (1993) *Space, Place and Gender* (Cambridge: Polity Press).

May, S. (ed.) (1999) *Critical Multiculturalism: Re-thinking Multicultural and Anti-Racist Education* (Brighton: Falmer Press).

May, T. (ed.) (1996) *Situating Social Theory* (London: UCL Press).

Mehta, U. S. (1999) *Liberalism and Empire: A Study in Nineteenth-century British Liberal Thought* (Chicago: University of Chicago Press).

Meis, M. (1986) *Patriarchy and Accumulation on a World Scale* (London: Zed Books).

Melzer, A., J. Weinberger and M. R. Zinman (eds) (1998) *Multiculturalism and American Democracy* (University Press of Kansas).

Mercer, K. (1994) *Welcome to the Jungle: New Positions in Black Cultural Studies* (New York and London: Routledge).

Mercer, K. and I. Julien (1988) 'Race, Sexual Politics and Black Masculinity: A Dossier', in R. Chapman and J. Rutherford (eds), *Male Order: Unwrapping Masculinity* (London: Lawrence and Wishart).

Messerschmidt, J. (1998) 'Men Victimizing Men: the Case of Lynching, 1865–1900', in L. Bowker (ed.) *Masculinities and Violence* (London: Sage).

Miles, R. (1993) *Racism after Race-Relations* (London: Routledge).

Miller, C. L. (1990) *Theories of Africans: Francophone Literature and Anthropology in Africa* (Chicago: University of Chicago Press).

Mirza, H. S. (ed.) (1997) *Black British Feminism – A Reader* (London: Routledge).

Modood T., R. Berthoud et al. (eds) (1997) *Ethnic Minorities in Britain: Diversity and Disadvantage* (London: Policy Studies Institute).

Modood, T. (1992) *Not Easy Being British* (London: Trentham).

— (1997) 'Difference, Cultural Racism and Anti-Racism', in P. Werbner and T. Modood (eds), *Debating Cultural Hybridity* (London: Zed Books).

— (1998) 'Anti-Semitism, Multiculturalism and the "Recognition" of Religious Groups', *Journal of Political Philosophy*, vol. 6. no. 4.

Morrison, T. (1992) *Playing in the Darkness. Whiteness and the Literary Imagination* (Cambridge, MA: Harvard Univesity Press).

Mosse, G. (1978) *Toward the Final Solution* (London: J. M. Dent).

Mouffe, C. (1993) *The Return of the Political* (London: Verso).

Mowzer, M. (1998) *Dark Continent – Europe's Twentieth Century* (London: Allen Lane).

Mudd, P. (1991) *Portuguese Bermudians. Early History and Reference Guide, 1849 – 1949* (Kentucky: Historical Research Publishers).

Mullard, C. (1973) *Black Britain* (London: Allen and Unwin).

Murphy, A. (1995) *From the Empire to the Rialto – Racism and Reaction in Liverpool 1918–1948* (Merseyside: Liver Press).

Musson, N. (1979) *Mind the Onion Seed* (Tennessee: Parthenon Press).

Nairn, T. (1997) *The Break-up of Britain* (London: Verso).

Narayan, U. (1995) 'Eating Cultures: Incorporation, Identity and Indian Food' in *Nations and Nationalism*, vol. 1, no. 1 (March).

Newman, D. (1994) *Bermuda's Stride Toward the Twenty-first Century* (Bermuda: Bermuda Government).

Ong, A. (1999) *Flexible Citizenship – The Cultural Logics of Transnationality* (Durham, NC: Duke University Press).

Ong, A. and D. Nonini (eds) (1997) *Ungrounded Empires: The Cultural Politics of Modern Chinese Transnationalism* (New York and London: Routledge).

Ortiz, F. (1940) *Cuban Counterpoint: Tobacco and Sugar* (Durham, NC and London: Duke University Press).

Packwood, C. (1975) *Chained on the Rock: Slavery in Bermuda* (New York: Eliseo Torris).

Padmore, G. (ed) (1963) 'Colonial and Coloured Unity (Report of the 5th Pan-African Congress)', in H. Adi and M. Sherwood, *The 1945 Manchester Pan-African Congress Revisited* (London: Lawrence and Wishart).

Pajaczkowska, C. and L. Young (1992) 'Racism, Representation and Psychoanalysis', in J. Donald and A. Rattansi (eds), *'Race' Culture and Difference* (London: Sage), ch. 8.

Parekh, B. (1991) 'British Citizenship and Cultural Difference', in Geoff Andrews (ed.), *Citizenship* (London: Lawrence and Wishart).

— (1999) 'The Logic of Inter-cultural Evaluation', in J. Horton and S. Mendus (eds), *Toleration, Identity and Difference* (Basingstoke: Macmillan).

Parker, D. (1994) 'Encounters across the Counter: Young Chinese People in Britain', in *New Community*, vol. 20, no. 4 (July), pp. 621–34).

— (1995) *Through Different Eyes: The Cultural Identities of Young Chinese People in Britain* (Aldershot: Avebury).

Peristiany, J. G. (1966) 'Introduction', in J. G. Peristiany (ed.), *Honour and Shame: The Values of Mediterranean Society* (London: Weidenfeld and Nicolson).

Philip, I. (1987) *Freedom Fighters* (London: Akira Press).

Phillips, M. and T. Phillips (1998) *Windrush – The Irresistible Rise of Multi-Racial Britain* (London: HarperCollins).

Phonenix, A. (1998) '"Multiculture", "Multiracisms" and Young People: Contradictory Legacies of Windrush', *Soundings*, no. 10 (Autumn).

Polley, M. (1998) *Moving the Goalposts: A History of Sport and Society Since 1945* (London: Routledge).

Potash, C. (ed.) (1997) *Reggae, Rasta, Revolution – Jamaican music from Ska to Dub* (London: Books with Attitude).

Prakash, G. (ed.) (1995) *After Colonialism – Imperial Histories and Postcolonial Displacements* (Princeton, NJ: Princeton University Press).

Pratt, M. L. (1992) *Imperial Eyes: Travel Writing and Transculturation* (London: Routledge).

Pryce, K. (1979) *Endless Pressure* (London: Penguin Books).

Ramdin, R. (1987) *The Making of the Black Working Class in Britain* (Aldershot: Wildwood House).

Rattansi (1992) 'Changing the Subject? Racism, Culture and Education' in J. Donald and A. Rattansi (eds), *'Race', Culture and Difference* (London: Sage).

— (1999) 'Racism, "Postmodernism" and Reflexive Multiculturalism', in S. May (ed.), *Critical Multiculturalism – Rethinking Multicultural and Antiracist Education* (London: Falmer Press).

Reay, D. (1995) 'They Employ Cleaners to do That: Habitus in the Primary Classroom', *British Journal of Sociology*, vol. 16, no. 3, pp. 353–71.

Redding, G. (1990) *The Spirit of Chinese Capitalism* (Berlin: Walter de Gruyter).

Reynolds, T. (1997) '(Mis)representing the black (super) woman', in H. S. Mirza (ed), *Black British Femisinism – A Reader* (London: Routledge).

Rich, A. (1980) 'Compulsory Heterosexuality and Lesbian Existence', *Signs: Journal of Women in Culture and Society*, vol. 5, no. 4 (Chicago: University of Chicago Press).

Richardson, H. (1948) 'Review of Economic Conditions, Policy and Organisation in Bermuda', Government Paper.

Richardson, R. (1999) *Islamophobia* (London: Runnymede Trust).

Robbins, K. (1991) 'Tradition and Translation', in J. Corner and S. Harvey (eds), *Enterprise and Heritage* (London: Routledge).

Robins, S. (1997) 'Transgressing the Borderlands of Tradition and Modernity: Identity, Cultural Hybridity and Land Struggles in Namaqualand (1980–1994)', *Journal of Contemporary African Studies*, vol. 15, no. 1, pp. 23–43.

Robinson, K. (1985) *Heritage* (London: Macmillan).

Rohlehr, G.. (1988) 'Images of Men and Women in the 1930's Calypsoes: The Sociology of Food Acquisition in a Context of Survivalism', in P. Mohammed and C. Shepherd, *Gender in Caribbean Development* (Jamaica/Trinidad & Tobago/Barbados: University of the West Indies).

Roy, Oliver (1994) *The Failure of Political Islam* (London: I.B.Tauris).

Rushdie, S. (1991) *Imaginary Homelands* (London: Granta).

Ryan, Selwyn (1975) 'Politics in an Artificial Society: The Case of Bermuda', *Caribbean Studies*, vol. 15, no. 2, pp. 5-35.

Said, E. (1978) *Orientalism* (London: Penguin).

— (1993) *Culture and Imperialism* (London: Vintage).

Said, E. W. (1985) *Orientalism* (London: Routledge and Kegan Paul).

Sarap, M. (1988) *An Introductory Guide to Post-Structuralism and Post-Modernism* (Hemel Hempstead: Harvester Wheatsheaf).

Sayyid, B. (1997) *A Fundamental Fear: Eurocentrims and Emergence of Islamism* (London: Zed).

Sayyid, S. (2000) 'Bad Faith: Anti-essentialism, Universalism and Islamism', in A. Brah and A. Coombes (eds), *Hybridity and Its Discontents* (London: Routledge).

Schmitt, C. (1996) *The Concept of the Political* [1932] trans. George Schwab (Chicago: University of Chicago Press).

Scott, D. (1999) *Refashioning Futures: Critcism after Post-Coloniality* (Princeton, NJ: University of Princeton Press).

Scott, J. (1990) *Domination and the Art of Resistance* (New Haven, CT and London: Yale University Press).

Seagrave, S. (1996) *Lords of the Rim* (London: Corgi Books).

Searle, C. (1996) 'Towards a Cricket of the Future', *Race & Class*, vol. 37, no. 4, pp. 45–59.

Serequeberhan, T. (1994) *The Hermeneutics of African Philosophy* (London: Routledge).

Sewell, T. (1998) *Keep on Moving – The Windrush Legacy, the Black Experience in Britain from 1948* (London: Voice Enterprises).

Sharma, S. (1996) 'Noisy Asians or "Asian Noise"?', in S. Sharma et al., Dis-Orienting *Rhythms*.

Sharma, S., J. Hutnyk and A. Sharma (eds) (1996) *Dis-Orienting Rhythms – The Politics of the New Asian Dance Music* (London: Zed Books).

Sharp, J. (1997) 'Beyond Exposé Analysis: Hybridity, Social Memory and Identity Politics', *Journal of Contemporary African Studies*, vol. 15, no. 1, pp. 7–21.

Sheffer, G. (1986) *Modern Diasporas in International Politics* (London: Croom Helm).

Shepherd, J. (1991) *Music As Social Text* (Cambridge: Polity Press).

Sherwood, M. (1995) *Manchester and the 1945 Pan-African Congress* (London: Savannah Press).

Shohat, E. and R. Stam (1994) *Unthinking Eurocentrism – Multiculturalism and the Media* (London: Routledge).

Shukra, K. (1998) *The Changing Pattern of Black Politics in Britain* (London: Pluto Press).

Shyllon (1977) *Black People in Britain 1555–1833* (Oxford: Oxford University Press).

Simone, A. (1994) 'In the Mix: Remaking Coloured Identities', *Africa Insight*, vol. 24, no. 3, pp. 161 73.

Skelton, T. (1995) 'Boom, Bye, Bye: Jamaican Ragga and Gay Resistance', in D. Bell and G. Valentine (eds), *Mapping Desire* (London: Routledge).

Skotnes, P. (ed.) (1996) *Miscast: Negotiating the Presence of the Bushmen* (Cape Town: University of Cape Town Press).

Small, S. (1994) *Racialized Barriers* (London: Routledge).

Smith, A. D. (1991) *National Identity* (Harmondsworth: Penguin).

— (1995) *The Ethnic Origins of Nations* (Oxford: Blackwell).

Smith, J. (1976) *Slavery in Bermuda* (New York: Vantage Press).

Smith, S. (1989) *The Politics of 'Race' and Residence* (London: Polity Press).

Solomon-Godeau, A. (1995) '*Male Trouble*', in M. Berger et al. (eds), *Constructing Masculinity* (London: Routledge).

Solomos, J. and L. Back (1996) *Racism and Society* (London: Macmillan).

Solomos, J. (1993) *Race and Racism in Contemporary Britain* (2nd edn) (London: Macmillan).

Street, J. (1997) '"Across the Universe": The Limits of Global Popular Culture', in A. Scott (ed.), *The Limits of Globalization: Cases and Arguments* (London and New York: Routledge).

Sudbury, J. (1998) *'Other Kinds of Dreams': Black Women's Organizations and the Politics of Transformation* (London: Routledge).

Surin, K. (1995) 'C. L. R. James' Materialist Aesthetics of Cricket', in H. McD. H. Beckles and B. Stoddart (eds) *Liberation Cricket: West Indies Cricket Culture* (Manchester: Manchester University Press).

Taylor, C. (1994) 'The Politics of Recognition', in A. Gutman (ed.), *Multiculturalism* (Princeton, NJ: Princeton University Press).

Thompson, J. (1998) 'Community, Identity and World Citizenship', in A. Archibugi, D. Held and M. Kohler (eds), *Re-imagining Political Community* (Cambridge: Polity Press).

Thornton, J. (1998) *Africa and Africans in the Making of the Atlantic World 1400–1800* (Cambridge: Cambridge University Press).

Tiffin, H. (1995) 'Cricket, Literature and the Politics of Decolonisation: the Case of C. L. R. James', in H. McD. Beckles and B. Stoddart (eds), *Liberation Cricket: West Indies Cricket Culture* (Manchester: Manchester University Press).

Touraine, A. (1995) *Critique of Modernity* (London: Blackwell).

Ture, K. and C. V. Hamilton (1992) *Black Power – The Politics of Liberation* (New York: Vintage Books).

Van den Berghe, P. (1984) 'Ethnic Cuisine, Culture in Nature' in *Ethnic and Racial Studies*, vol. 7, pp. 387–97.

Van der Spuy, P. (1997) 'Silencing Race and Gender: The 1997 Conference on Gender and Colonialism'.

Vincent, R. (1996) *Funk – The Music, the People and the Rhythm of the One* (New York: St Martin's Press).

Volosinov/Bakhtin (1973) *Marxism and the Philosophy of Language* (London and New York: Seminar Press).

Walcott, D. (1992) *The Antilles: Fragments of Epic Memory*, Nobel Lecture (Farrar, Strauss & Giroux: New York).

Waldby, C. (1995) 'Destruction, Boundary Erotics and Refigurations of the Heterosexual Male Body', in E. Grosz and E. Probyn (eds), *Sexy Bodies – the Strange Carnalities of Feminism* (London: Routledge).

Waldron, J. (1992) 'Minority Cultures and the Cosmopolitan Alternative', in W. Kymlicka (ed.), *The Rights of Minority Cultures* (Oxford: Oxford University Press).

Wallace, M. (1979) *Black Macho and the Myth of the Superwoman* (London: Verso).

—— (1994) 'The Search for the Good-enough Mammy', in D. Goldberg (ed.), *Multiculturalism* (London: Blackwell).

Walters, R. W. (1993) *Pan Africanism in the African Diaspora – An Analysis of Modern Afrocentric Political Movements* (Detroit: Wayne State University Press).

Walvin, J. (1973) *Black and White: The Negro in English Society 1555–1945* (London: Allen Lane).

Waters, M. (1990) *Ethnic Options: Choosing Identities in America* (Berkeley, CA: University of California Press).

Watson, J. (ed.) (1977) *Between Two Cultures* (Oxford: Basil Blackwell).

Weekes, D. (1997) 'Shades of Blackness – Young Black Female Constructions of Beauty', in H. S. Mirza (ed.), *Black British Feminism – A Reader* (London: Routledge).

Werbner, P. (1997) 'The Dialectics of Cultural Hybridity', in P. Werbner and T. Modood (eds), *Debating Cultural Hybridity* (London: Zed Books).

West, C. (1990) 'The New Cultural Politics of Difference', in R. Ferguson, M. Gever, T. T. Minh-ha and C. West (eds), *Out There: Marginalization and Contemporary Cultures* (US: New Museum of Contemporary Art).

Wieviorka, M. (1995) 'Is it so Difficult to be an Anti-racist?', in P. Werbner and T. Modood (eds), *Debating Cultural Hybridity* (London: Zed Books).

Wilkinson, H. (1973) *Bermuda from Sail to Steam: The History of the Island 1784–1901* (London: Oxford University Press).

Willet, C. (ed.) (1998) *Theorizing Multiculturalism* (London: Blackwell).

Williams, E. (1944) *Capitalism and Slavery* (London: André Deutsch).

Williams, J. (1994) '"Rangers is a black club': "Race", Identity and Local Football in England', in R. Giulianotti, N. Bonney and M. Hepworth (eds) *Football, Violence and Social Identity* (London: Routledge).

Williams, P. (1995) 'Meditations on Masculinity', in M. Berger et al. (eds), *Constructing Masculinity* (London: Routledege).

Williams, R. (1977) *Marxism and Literature* (London: Oxford University Press).

Wilson, J. (1978) 'Bermuda and the Future. The Politics of Biracialism', Round Table Debates, Bermuda Archives.

Wollstonecraft, M. (1977) *The Rights of Woman* (1790) (London: Everyman).

Wong, Sau-ling Cynthia (1993) *Reading Asian American Literature: From Necessity to Extravagance* (Princeton, NJ: Princeton University Press).

Wright, R. (1993a) *Native Son* (New York: Harper Perennial).

— (1993b) *The Outsider* (New York: Harper Perennial).

— (1995) *Pagan Spain* (New York: Harper Perennial).

Wynter, S. (1981) 'In Quest of Matthew Bondman: Some cultural notes on the Jamesian Journey', *Urgent Tasks*, no. 12 (Summer), pp. 54–68.

Yamato, G. (1990) 'Something About the Subject Makes It Hard to Name', in G. Anzaldua (ed.), *Making Face, Making Soul: Creative and Critical Perspectives by Feminists of Color* (San Francisco: aunt lute books), pp. 20–24.

Young, R. (1995) *Colonial Desire: Hybridity in Theory, Culture and Race* (London: Routledge).

Yuval-Davis, N. (1997) *Gender and Nation* (London: Sage).

Index